LEVEL 1

TEACHER'S MANUAL
NTC's
Basic
JAPANESE

A COMMUNICATIVE PROGRAM IN CONTEMPORARY JAPANESE

LYNN WILLIAMS

National Textbook Company
a division of *NTC Publishing Group* • Lincolnwood, Illinois USA

Published by National Textbook Company, a division of NTC Publishing Group.
©1992 by NTC Publishing Group, 4255 West Touhy Avenue,
Lincolnwood (Chicago), Illinois 60646-1975 U.S.A.
Manufactured in the United States of America.

2 3 4 5 6 7 8 9 0 VP 9 8 7 6 5 4 3 2 1

Contents

Introduction

NTC's Basic Japanese is the result of several years of field-testing Japanese language instruction to a variety of students, and the result of the need to have a truly communicative Japanese program.

The text and teacher's manual contain all the elements necessary to teach the basic skills and stimulate interest—grammar, vocabulary, reading, listening, writing, cultural background, and ideas for ways to implement a communicative teaching approach.

In addition, the text responds directly to student needs, with lessons that explain the information given to them without assistance; a text that they can work through at their own pace; and exercises to do on their own time to prove to themselves what they know and what they are unsure about, so that they can identify their problem areas and ask for specific help on those points.

Each unit of *Basic Japanese 1* offers teachers and students a choice of activities to suit their own time, pace, and situation. Some of the activities may appear too simple, but in practice they work, and consolidate the areas they were designed to review.

The explanatory notes on grammar and usage are detailed and full. Explanations are also clear enough for the text to work as a self-study book when necessary.

This course—complete with audiocassettes and workbook—should provide you with an exciting and reliable springboard for all beginning Japanese students. There are plenty of activities and suggestions in this manual to accommodate the needs of learners at varying levels of achievement. At the conclusion of this course, students should have a firm grasp of the basic Japanese structures, a practical vocabulary base, and at least a reading knowledge of *hiragana* and *katakana*. They will also be prepared to further their studies with NTC's *Basic Japanese 2*.

Aims of the course

- To encourage genuine communication right from the start.
- To teach listening, speaking, reading, and writing within an authentic cultural context.
- To keep interest and motivation high.
- To keep the pace lively.
- To vary the pattern of lessons.
- To make Japanese lessons fun.

How to use the manual

This manual offers only one way of approaching each lesson. It offers suggestions only. It is a guide to presenting material, but should not be seen as a rigid set of lesson plans. Adapt the lessons as you see fit. However, you will probably find the organization a useful way to approach the formal part of a lesson. The topics and units of the student textbook have been further divided in this manual into teaching lessons. The lessons represent the average amount of material to be presented in a single class period. This will vary depending on your particular class makeup. Some of the lessons are presented as review or evaluation lessons, and thus do not present material from a new unit. Although it is sometimes a help to see how someone else would break up a lesson, what activities someone

---

else has thought up, you are the person who knows your class best, and who can best measure the needs of all the individuals within it.

Maybe the activities suggested will be useful as they are, maybe they will spark ideas, maybe if you disapprove or disagree it will help you to crystallize your own ideas. There are as many different ways of presenting material to a class as there are teachers. Have confidence in your own ideas and they will work well. There is no one "right" way.

Pacing

Some people may find the pace of the lessons too hectic. If so, choose from them the activities that you feel you can handle.

Several activities reinforcing the target language are much more effective than just one, in consolidating the patterns; and there is a chance that those who did not understand a concept from one activity will have picked up the idea by the end of several.

At least one open-ended activity should be included each lesson to allow better students in particular to add their individual ideas, enriching and extending the original idea. It is exciting to let them have some freedom and to see what they can make out of very simple activities.

Maximum concentration span for average adults is about twenty minutes. Ten minutes at a time, of genuine concentration, is the reality for classes of mixed ability teenagers with their minds full of exciting projects and a range of school subjects claiming their attention. Therefore if we organize lessons with short bursts of high concentration we will succeed in teaching more effectively.

Teacher's role

Keep in mind that our purpose is maximum use of the target language by the students in every lesson. The teacher is the facilitator, not the dominator.

Overview of level one

Basic Japanese 1 is intended as the first year of a three-year course, but could provide enough material for two years, depending on the class and the number of hours allocated each week.

Book 1 covers introductions, greetings, classroom instructions and objects, school life, leisure activities, daily activities, time, days, and numbers, weather, families, friends, homes, describing people and health.

(Book 2 covers descriptions of places, directions, shopping, eating and drinking, leisure activities, hobbies and travel, and more time, dates, and numbers.)

The cultural background appropriate to the topics is included integrally with the text and in reading comprehension passages and dialogues and listening comprehension passages, exercises and recordings. The writing and reading of *Kana* begins with the very first lesson, and continues throughout the course as students develop fluency.

Additional resources

This manual contains a large number of blackline masters that are to be used in conjunction with activities described in the lessons. Do not overlook these as a very useful resource. A workbook is available to give students extra practice with language structures as well as reading and writing *Kana*.

Cassette tapes are also available. They offer native-speaker listening practice, music, and activities to accompany each lesson. Directions on when to use the tapes are indicated in each lesson.

Using dictionaries

Japanese dictionaries, even those produced for young children and foreigners, are difficult to use in the early stages of learning and present practical problems for the teacher. Japanese script dictionaries are time-consuming to use and that time, from the point of view of communicative teaching, would be better spent in learning to use the defined vocabulary well—in putting into productive use the vocabulary learned.

It is good for students to look up and use words they want to use but often that leads them into grammar structures that are inappropriate at that stage of their study and they end up confused.

They often use words in the wrong context.

If students choose their own vocabulary, teachers are pressured to spend time looking up vocabulary that may be outside their own experience. While this is desirable if one has time, the reality of teaching is that there is not time to look up and learn all the words a class may choose to use.

The course has a good basic vocabulary. The average student does not have time to assimilate more and put it into effective use in the early years. The content, well learned and practiced, provides a secure base for further study.

Lesson Chart with Scope and Sequence

Topic One Lesson One (1)

Introduction of study—Expectations, routines, rules.

Introduce Japan, its language, writing systems, pronunciation.

To teach greetings appropriate to different times of day.

To set tone for the year.

Suggestions for preparation of class.

Preparation: Flashcards of greetings.

Topic One Lesson Two (10)

To learn about Japan's position in the Pacific, and the names of some of Japan's largest cities and islands.

Practice sounds of Japanese.

Writing *ni ho n*.

Establish listening skills.

Pairwork activities and accuracy of sound and spelling.

Preparation: Blank maps of Japan, Japanese position in the Pacific.

Topic One Lesson Three (18)

To teach how to introduce selves simply (meet and greet)—*desu*.

Consolidate sounds.

Conversation openers.

Reinforce listening, responding, and pairwork rules.

Preparation: Map of Japan with places from last lesson left marked. 2 puppet figures photocopied.

Topic One Lesson Four (21)

To teach *desu* and negative *dewa arimasen*.

Teach Agreeing and Disagreeing.

Introduce vocabulary by demonstration and Japanese word rather than by translation.

Sentence patterns: *Nan desu ka, ... desu ka, ... desu, ... dewa arimasen.*

Preparation: Realia for vocabulary.

Topic One Lesson Five (22)

To teach *Dare desu ka.* Answer affirmative and negative.

Finding a particular person.

Review simple introductions and greetings.

Preparation: Pictures of well-known people.

Apple and knife for prizes.

Group desks in fours if possible.

Topic One Lesson Six (24)

To boost confidence in material learned so far.

To add the ability to say 'Excuse me'.

To identify people at a distance from the speaker.

To learn to write *a, na, ta, no, in hiragana.*

Preparation: Put up pictures and labels: *Sumimasen ga, Ano hito wa, Dare desu ka.*

Topic One Lesson Seven Evaluation

To test retention and understanding.

To introduce formal listening comprehension.

To introduce roleplay in front of a small group.

Students learn basics for evaluating own progress.

Topic One Lesson Eight (31)

O namae wa nan desu ka.

To teach how to ask someone's name, how to give own name more formally.

Introduce *honorific O*, and particles *no, wa.*

Teach how to express ownership.

Review vocabulary.

Preparation: Photocopy dicomm sheets.

Topic One Lesson Nine (33)

Teach *Namae wa nan desu ka, Nihongo no namae wa nan desu ka.*

Consolidate patterns and vocab already taught.

To boost confidence and reinforce pair and group work rules.

Preparation: Animal noise sheet. Object sheets used previously. Labels of species names.

Topic One Lesson Ten (37)

To teach students how to introduce themselves formally and ask and give nationality.

Hajimemashite doozo yoroshiku.

Doko no kata desu ka.

Preparation: Pictures of people (already on wall). Nationality sheets page 47.

Large map of world.

Class list for each student.

Topic One Lesson Eleven (44)

To teach use of name cards in introductions.

To consolidate material previously learned.

To become familiar with some Japanese names.

To give more listening practice.

To learn *hiragana wa, e, shi, ma.*

Preparation: Photocopy *meishi* cards, 2 sets from page 46, 2 sets from page 47.

Topic Two Lesson Twelve (51)

To introduce the Japanese school system.

To teach how to absorb information from pictures and text.

To teach strategies for learning new words.

To explain the need for learning cultural background.

To consolidate cultural background learned previously.

Preparation: School levels labels, boxes for quiz questions. Clear old pictures from walls.

NTC's Basic Japanese Teacher's Manual

Topic Two Lesson Thirteen (54)

To teach names of common classroom objects.

To introduce *Yonde kudasai* and teach *Janai desu*.

To teach more listening skills, and practice listening and focusing skills.

Preparation: Flashcards *ka, to. se. mi. i*.

4 sets of names of common objects page 54.

2 sets of realia of common objects.

Vocab labels from previous lessons.

Topic Two Lesson Fourteen (59)

To teach *kore, sore*.

To consolidate use of *wa*.

Preparation: Samples of newspapers, magazines, comics.

Topic Two Lesson Fifteen (67)

To teach particle *o* with *kudasai*.

To teach how to ask for things with *Kore o kudasai*.

To consolidate patterns known and review vocabulary.

Preparation: Realia of vocabulary.

Photocopy homework sheets.

Topic Two Lesson Sixteen (72)

To consolidate vocabulary and work on spelling accuracy.

To check understanding of structures learned.

Preparation: Paper for testing spelling accuracy.

Reward for good students.

New pictures/realia on walls with new sentence patterns.

Topic Two Lesson Seventeen (76)

To teach 'open' and 'close' structures: *Mado o akete kudasai*.

To teach the song *Musunde hiraite*.

To focus on picking up new words from listening, and impress accuracy of listening and matching of sounds to syllables. To identify known hiragana in a passage.

Preparation: *Hiragana* song sheet. Label windows, doors, desks, etc. in Japanese. Items for demonstrations of open, close, etc.

Topic Three Lesson Eighteen (81)

To teach how to say what languages they speak, study, and practice.

Teach how to politely tell someone that they are wrong with chigaimasu.

Introduce 6 new structures.

Consolidate particles *wa* and *o*.

Preparation: Map of the world.

Labels of nationality from previous lesson.

Labels of languages.

Topic Three Lesson Nineteen (86)

To teach how to talk about common school and after-school activities.

To consolidate *wa* and *o*, and teach *ya*.

Introduce lexically only *Donna* and *Dete kudasai*.

Preparation: Pictures of musical instruments.

Examples of school subjects (textbooks, etc.).

Photocopy homework worksheets.

Topic Three Lesson Twenty (90)

To teach how to express like and dislike. To introduce particle *ga* lexically only.

Preparation: Vocabulary cards made previously.

Photocopied class lists if desired.

Two poster-sized sheets on which to collate survey information.

Objects/pictures to demonstrate like/dislike.

Topic Three Lesson Twenty-one (93)

To teach negatives with *masen*.

Preparation: Put pictures and sentence patterns (brought by students last lesson) up around walls.

Topic Four Lesson Twenty-two (101)

To teach (Chinese set) numbers to 100.

To encourage listening and imitating skills.

Preparation: Put up self-introduction on wall.

Sets of number cards.

Chart of numbers to put on wall at end of lesson.

Topic Four Lesson Twenty-three (107)

To teach giving of telephone numbers.

Preparation: Set of bingo cards.

Small prize for winners of bingo game.

The telephone numbers of 2 or 3 of the students in the class.

Topic Four Lesson Twenty-four (109)

To teach the days of the week.

Preparation: Display number charts from last lesson.

Timetable sheets.

Dicomm sheets of days and activities.

Chart of days of the week.

Topic Four Lesson Twenty-five (111)

To teach a selection of time words.

To teach the order of sentence patterns and time words.

To test vocabulary, structures, and *hiragana*.

To consolidate sentence patterns.

Preparation: Check walls.

Decide on which check exercises to use for test. Put up the days of the week chart and *kanji*.

Topic Four Lesson Twenty-six (113)

To teach how to tell the time in hours and half-hours.

Teach structure: *Ima nanji desu ka*.

Preparation: Photocopy listening, homework, and pair activity sheet of times.

Large cardboard clock with hands, or real clock.

Topic Four Lesson Twenty-seven (117)

To teach verbs for go, come, and return: *ikimasu, kimasu, kaerimasu.*

To teach use of particle ni with these.

To teach how to ask what time people do things.

To review instructions.

Preparation: Flash cards of the 3 verbs.

Cut-outs of a person and a house for demonstration.

Topic Four Lesson Twenty-eight (123)

To teach *mashoo*—let's.

Consolidate use of *ni* particle and previously learned structures.

Preparation: Write new katakana vocabulary on board.

Photocopy dicomm activity.

Topic Four Lesson Twenty-nine (126)

To teach the past tense of verbs.

Preparation: Flashcards: *kinoo, sakuban, senshuu, yoru, asa.*

Large calendar with dates for this week, last week, next week, clearly visible to students. Write *Shukudai* on wall near old work.

Topic Four Lesson Thirty (129)

To teach the past negative tense of verbs: *masen deshita.*

To consolidate vocabulary.

Preparation: Update wall displays.

Photocopy (on card) the vocabulary sets for group work. Put each set into a container for re-use later.

Topic Four Lesson Thirty-one Evaluation

To test retention of vocabulary and structures and ability to communicate and understand ideas about daily activities.

Topic Four Lesson Thirty-two Roleplays

To give students an opportunity to show their prepared roleplays to the class.

Topic Five Lesson Thirty-three (134)

To teach adjectives to describe weather and the names of seasons.

To teach the difference between adjectives and nouns.

Preparation: Teru teru *boozu* page 136.

Temperature chart, *atsui* to *samui.*

Pictures of seasons, weather etc. with appropriate labels.

Topic Five Lesson Thirty-four (141)

To consolidate last lesson.

To teach weather nouns and their usage patterns.

Preparation: Pictures of weather conditions.

Topic Five Lesson Thirty-five (143)

To teach *deshoo* with nouns and adjectives only.

To consolidate *hiragana* learned.

Preparation: Pictures of weather conditions: rain, snow, cloud.

Write up words of song in hiragana large enough for class to read, leaving space to add roomaji later.

Topic Five Lesson Thirty-six (145)

To teach *naze desu ka.*

To encourage speed learning.

To listen for specific items.

Preparation: Tape.

Topic Six Lesson Thirty-seven (150)

Giving age with *nansai.*

Festivals: *Shichigosan/Seijin no Hi.*

Hiragana: shuu, juu, issai, hassai, kyuu.

Doubling consonants and vowels.

Preparation: Birthday party atmosphere: Balloons, cake, candles, or pictures of same.

Topic Six Lesson Thirty-eight

Review of first part of *Basic Japanese.*

Preparation: Photocopy of worksheet.

Topic Six Lesson Thirty-nine (158)

Nensei/atarashii/atarashikunai.

Review particle *no,* introduce *katakana* (friends and own names).

Review previously learned structures notes: *san, chan, kun.*

Preparation: Something old and something new.

Name cards for each student in *katakana.*

Topic Six Lesson Forty

Review order of words in questions and statements. Give opportunity to use questions and answers within framework of present knowledge.

Preparation: Photocopy sheets of questions for pairs or groups, choose activities from selection given. Scissors.

Topic Six Lesson Forty-one (optional)

Sentence and question practice.

Preparation: Photocopy sheets of questions for pairs or groups. Choose activities from selection given. Scissors.

Topic Six Lesson Forty-two (163)

Teach *shoo, joo,* and *ra hiragana.*

Encourage students to read *hiragana* sentences, practice listening and giving spontaneous replies.

Consolidate use of *wa* and *no* particles.

Remind about lack of particles between nouns and *desu.* Raise consciousness of *katakana.*

Encourage different seating patterns.

Preparation: Tape. Card for taking hiragana flashcards, *katakana* name labels.

Topic Six Lesson Forty-three (167)
Teach *he, be, ri, se, ze, o, hiragana*.
Review structures and situations taught previously. More Japanese festivals. More practice in reading and listening. Encourage different seating patterns.
Preparation: Tape. Put out *katakana* name cards randomly. Photocopy list of review questions for each group of 4 (without answers). Cut one list into strips. *Hiragana* flash cards from last lesson.

Topic Six Lesson Forty-four (169)
To consolidate previously learned material.
To teach *ge, ga, ru, chi, choo, hiragana*.
To research more Japanese festivals.
Preparation: Photocopy profile cards for each group of four. *Katakana* name cards.

Topic Six Lesson Forty-five (172)
To give opportunity for listening.
Find out more about Japanese festivals.
To research material.
Preparation: Resource books and magazines about Japanese festivals. Paper for poster making. Labeled pictures for walls.

Topic Six Lesson Forty-six (177)
Teach months of the year.
Practice in reading hiragana.
Introduce song *'Sakura Sakura'*.
Introduce 'lineups'.
Preparation: Tape. *Katakana* name cards, large calendar, pictures of seasons labeled in hiragana, calendar pages to label during lesson, poster paper to make chart of class birthdays.

Topic Six Lesson Forty-seven (182)
Giving dates.
Reading practice.
Preparation: Tape. *Katakana* name cards. Large writing, list of dates 1st to 31st.

Topic Six Lesson Forty-eight (optional)
To remind of Chinese numbers.
Review giving of telephone numbers. Review telling time in hours and half hours.
To consolidate months, dates, days, and other time words.
Preparation: pack of number cards for each group. Photocopy time worksheets.

Topic Six Lesson Forty-nine (188)
To review verbs in all tenses known.
To teach particle *mo*.
Reading and listening practice.
Preparation: Tape. Enlarge New Year card for wall.

Topic Six Lesson Fifty (193)
Teach how to describe physical characteristics. Teach one use of particle ga. Introduce color adjectives and two color nouns.
Preparation: Pictures of people (preferably large, color). Wall label for stories *'hanashi'*. Labels of color adjectives and nouns. Chart of colors. Colored origami paper or similar.

Topic Six Lesson Fifty-one (196)
Reading practice.
Consolidation of structure patterns.
Give students opportunity to use reading skills and check vocabulary and structures
Preparation: Tape.

Topic Six Lesson Fifty-two
Test understanding of tenses.
Practice role play.
Encourage good listening skills.
Preparation: Photocopy of test for each student.

Topic Six Lesson Fifty-three (200)
To teach more names of parts of the body.
To give interview practice.
To describe people.
Preparation: Photocopied profiles (one card per student).
Large picture of person, parts of body labels.
Pictures of people used previously.

Topic Six Lesson Fifty-four
Practice descriptions.
Learn *jankenpon*.
Preparation: Sheets of plain paper for drawing to instruction. Paper for making drawings of strange creatures.

Topic Six Lesson Fifty-five (208-209) (review lesson)
Check students understanding and productive use of Topic 6 material.
Preparation: Read through pages 208-209
Choose activities.

Topic Seven Lesson Fifty-six (214)
Genuine conversation.
Traditional/Present-day Japanese family life.
Introducing own mother and father.
Enquiring after someone else's parents.
Preparation: Photocopy pictures of two families for each student.
Photos of families/parents to put on wall.
Labels.

Topic Seven Lesson Fifty-seven (optional)
Produce first part of class magazine.
To consolidate material known.
Preparation: Set up room for interviews with 3-4 desks at front of class.
Camera (optional) to photograph interviewees for magazine.

Topic Seven Lesson Fifty-eight (223)
Teach *kochira* and *doozo*. Teach own younger sister and own older brother.
Reading practice from *hiragana* and *roomaji*.
Consolidate own family patterns.
Role play practice.
Preparation: Tape. Tape recorder with record facility.
OR
Video camera.

Topic Seven Lesson Fifty-nine (optional)
Produce more material for class magazine.
Consolidate material learned in a different way.
Preparation: Tape.

Topic Seven Lesson Sixty (230)
Own family labels for younger brother and older sister. Review reasons for using particles *wa, o, ni, ga, to, mo*.
Practice spontaneous informal use of Japanese.
Preparation: Tape. Photocopies of pictures page 234 for each group.

Topic Seven Lesson Sixty-one (optional)
Magazine production.
Consolidation.
Preparation: Display material already produced for possible inclusion in magazine.

Topic Seven Lesson Sixty-two (237)
Asking about other people's families.
Counting people.
Preparation: Tape.
Words of song written in large lettering.
Labels for counting people, pictures of people to put on wall and label with people counter labels.

Topic Seven Lesson Sixty-three (242)
Teach qualitative nouns. Review adjectives.
Raise consciousness of accepting differences in language. Use of *aimasu* vs. *mimasu*.
Review verbs. Review *kore, sore, are, dore*.
Practice recombining elements known in different ways. Demonstrate students developing power over language.
Preparation: Tape, paste or glue.
Photocopies of handsome, beautiful, ugly.
Photocopies of short dialogues and stories.

Topic Seven Lesson Sixty-four (optional)
Free story-writing session.
Worth further on last lesson's new material.

Topic Seven Lesson Sixty-five (242)
Encourage comment on statements made.
Use of family labels.
Practice questioning.
Survey families.
Preparation: Photocopy sets of Happy Family cards for each group.

Topic Seven Lesson Sixty-six
Checks 1, 2 and 3.
Preparation: Choose activities and check exercises to do.

Topic Seven Lesson Sixty-seven (250)
Teach *mo ... mo*—both ... neither.
Preparation: Tape.

Topic Seven Lesson Sixty-eight (252)
Sentence building with *mo*. Roleplay with *mo*. Encourage students to work with different people.
Preparation: Photocopy vocabulary cards for 5 groups.
Put out vocabulary cards made earlier.
Photocopy page 253 and cut into cards.

Topic Seven Lesson Sixty-nine (255)
Occupations.
Preparation: Tape.
Photocopy family tree if chosen.
Paper for results of surveys.
Paper or card for competition.

Topic Seven Lesson Seventy (259)
Review introductions.
Preparation: Tape.

Topic Seven Lesson Seventy-one (261)
Listening comprehension. *Hiragana* reading practice. More practice in questioning and understanding from passages.
Preparation: Tape.
Choose suitable activities from list of suggestions. Decide needs.
Photocopy 3 worksheets for each student.

Topic Seven Lesson Seventy-two (game lesson)
Play games made by students.
Student-student interaction of a different sort.
Preparation: Students bring games made ready to play.

Topic Seven Lesson Seventy-three
Bridging lesson between friends and families and homes.
Describing own home.
Saying where you live.
Review adjectives and position in sentence.
Preparation: Tape. Photocopies of Japan with major cities marked.

Topic Seven Lesson Seventy-four (268)
Consolidate descriptions of friends and family and introductions.
More spontaneous roleplay.
Preparation: Tape.
Photocopy student answer sheets.

Topic Seven Lesson Seventy-five (268)
Introduction to Japanese homes.
Preparation: Pictures and information about homes.

Topic Seven Lesson Seventy-six (check lesson)
Check lesson for Topic seven.
Preparation: Choose appropriate check exercises.

Topic Eight Lesson Seventy-seven (277)
Particle de for location of activity.
Describing own home simply.
Preparation: Pictures of homes.

Topic Eight Lesson Seventy-eight (283)
Consolidate use of de—location of activity.
Listening comprehension.
Preparation: Photocopy 2 sets of worksheets for each pair—1 listening comprehension answer sheet for each student.

Topic Eight Lesson Seventy-nine (285)
Consolidate use of dc.

Topic Eight Lesson Eighty (287)
Teach arimasu.
Teach ni wa.
Preparation: Photocopy dicomm sheets.

Topic Eight Lesson Eighty-one (291)
Teach itte mairimasu, itte irasshai lexically.
Teach koko soko asoko doko.
Teach doko ni arimasu ka.
Preparation: Tape.

Topic Eight Lesson Eighty-two (optional)
Prepare advertisements of all types for magazine. Make reports on activities.
Consolidate de and arimasu.
Consolidate times, days, and dates.
Preparation: Photocopies of genuine Japanese advertisements.

Topic Eight Lesson Eighty-three (roleplay)
Roleplay practice.
Use new material in own way.
Preparation: Decide on groups to include weaker and stronger students in each group for fairness.
Photocopy roleplay structure for each group.

Topic Eight Lesson Eighty-four (roleplay)
Act out planned roleplays.
Preparation: Tape.
Organize suitable room or space for roleplays.

Topic Eight Lesson Eighty-five (298)
Daily activities.
New verbs of okimasu, nemasu, tabemasu, nomimasu etc.
Review times and days.
Consolidate de—location of activity.
Preparation: Tape. Comments on roleplays (last lesson).

Topic Eight Lesson Eighty-six (300)
Give opportunity for students to tell about own daily activities.
Self-introduction.
Response to listening.
Consolidate new verbs.
Oral assessments.
Preparation: Depends on activities chosen. Page 300.

Topic Eight Lesson Eighty-seven
Oral assessments.
Preparation of self-introductions.
Preparation: Depends on activities chosen.

Topic Eight Lesson Eighty-eight (302)
Talking about a day's activities.
To give the opportunity to use new vocabulary.
Preparation: Tape.
Tape recorder with recording facility.
Hiragana song sheets of songs known.

Topic Eight Lesson Eighty-nine (304)
Prepared talks, to encourage good listening and good pronunciation and encourage support of students for each other.
To teach de as 'means of movement'. Give practice in telling times of activities.
Preparation: Tape recorder.

Topic Eight Lesson Ninety (300-307)
Listen to more talks.
Reading practice from hiragana.
Consolidate patterns and vocabulary.
Preparation: Tape recorder.

Topic Eight Lesson Ninety-one (optional)
To express comparisons using adjectives and qualitative nouns.
To give real experience of Japan through film or native speaker contact.
Preparation: Resource magazines of Japan.
Japanese film or Japanese national.

Topic Nine Lesson Ninety-two (309)
Introduce Japanese attitudes to health.
Teach how to express pain.
Preparation: Photocopy family illustration for each student for listening activity.
Display chart of parts of body used earlier.

Topic Nine Lesson Ninety-three (317)
Describing more ailments.
Responding to specific health enquiry.
Preparation: Tape.

Topic Nine Lesson Ninety-four
Consolidate health vocabulary.
Practice roleplays.
Preparation: Photocopies of illustration doctor's waiting room for each student.

Topic Nine Lesson Ninety-five
Reading and talking practice.
Preparation: Photocopies of doctor's waiting room B.
Numbers to put by each face before judging.
Drawing pins.

Topic Nine Lesson Ninety-six (optional)
Class magazine.
Add material, put magazine together, photocopy and make available for students to read and enjoy.

Topic Nine Lesson Ninety-seven (check lesson)
Preparation: Choose appropriate activities.

Notes to teachers

Classroom routines

Establish routines from the first lesson.

- How do you want students to enter?
- How do you want them to greet you?
- How do you want them to be seated?
- Where is homework to be put for marking?
- On which days of the week will you collect books or homework?
- How much time do you expect students to spend on homework?
- How do you want students to present their work?

What organization do you need to set up for putting furniture where you want it each lesson (and returning it to its former state at the end of the lesson)?

- What control methods will you use for stopping and starting activities efficiently?
- What expectations have you of the students' behavior
  - work habits,
  - participation,
  - interaction,
  - courtesy?

Equipment required by students

Ideally:

- One lined book for notes and cultural background items.
- One large squared book for writing Japanese script.
- Two notebooks for homework so that students have one to work in while you are marking the other.
  - A small notebook for vocabulary.
  - Ruler.
  - Eraser.
  - Sharp pencils.
  - Ballpoint pens (red and black/blue) (I prefer students to work in pencil:
    a) because it's more Japanese
    b) because it's easier to correct *hiragana* and spelling mistakes neatly if pencil is used.
  The ballpoint pens are used for note taking in English and underlining.)
  A waterbased felt pen for listening games and activities.

Equipment required by teacher

- Marker pens and felt tips for wall displays.
- Drawing pins.
- Scissors.
- Colored and plain paper for mounting work.
- A long ruler.
- Eraser.

  If possible:
- A source of cardboard and paper (offcuts from factories, etc.) for making posters and flashcards.
- Gradually accumulate:
- A file of magazine pictures to use for many things.
  - colors, numbers, people, places, things, actions.
  Gradually try to build up a file of pictures that fit the vocabulary and topics of the course.

Look for line drawings from children's books and other language books to use for vocabulary brainstorming, sentence making, storymaking.

Japanese realia, such as kimono, books, etc. Try to accumulate the items you need to enliven cultural background teaching. Tickets, maps, advertisements, posters, coins, things everyday living (bathroom stools and bowls etc.) bring the textbook information alive. Visitors may be happy to help you to build up a collection.

Notes on teaching communicatively

Teaching communicatively puts the onus on the students to communicate with others by putting them in realistic situations in which for the most part an information gap has been created. The students must communicate and share information in order to complete activities.

The teacher is the facilitator and joins in activities or monitors unobtrusively by moving around the room, gently correcting or complimenting.

The activities have a clear goal. Students know what is expected of them and what they will achieve by participating. They report back to the group after activities so there is a purpose in doing the activity aside from practicing the target language during the activity. The target language is given maximum exposure through tightly guided and open ended activities.

When everyone is communicating at once, students feel relaxed.

Noise is not a problem because students are trained to work quietly so that everyone can hear their partner or group, and activities usually only last about five minutes so the class comes back to order and quiet again.

Working alone, in pairs, in small groups, half a class, or as a whole class, the students get used to working with a number of randomly selected people, not just their particular friends.

Students are given the experience of producing what they want to say in given situations. They are not constrained by set dialogues.

Dialogues are provided for models and reading practice but are only a small part of the students' daily experience of the target language.

Written work and reading skills are still an important part of the course. Students must learn to communicate in writing and need to be able to read information too. So these skills are not neglected in a good communicative approach, although they may often be less formal in nature in class time.

Strategies for class management

Basically you hope that your lessons will be sufficiently enjoyable for the class to accept your need for speedy responses and no chatter in English, but it sometimes takes a while for students to learn of your expectations.

Be well prepared so that the students feel a sense of purpose and know they will achieve something each lesson.

Praise and compliment work. At first students will perhaps watch others to see if the group intends to participate at your bidding, not wanting to be seen to enjoy activities but gradually they usually warm up.

Negativity breeds negative response so try hard to manage students by positive reinforcement.

With some groups icebreakers and initiative games in English or Japanese will help your class to settle down together. Sometimes it is necessary to break the ice with a group to establish your own. Social studies and drama teachers have books of activities that can be adapted to your purposes. These games may help your students to relax into being able to join in the language activities you want them to try. (See "Useful Resources, page xxiii.")

It is important to start the class formally, to establish that the students enter quietly and wait quietly for the teacher to greet them. They must know that once the lesson has begun they will achieve more and will be able to work through more activities if they are ready to start as soon as the teacher chooses.

Students need to be given tight timing to achieve set goals.

If they are given a specific amount of time, to prepare, for example, a roleplay or do some other activity, the fact that they will have to report back or show off their play to a group at the end of that time means that they cannot afford to mess about because they will be unable to perform later.

Every contribution is acceptable. Gradually, as students' confidence and trust grow they will contribute more. If the tasks set are very short and easily achievable, the students will lose their reluctance to participate.

If students are trained well and allowed to stop if they start to flounder, they feel relieved; but they need to know that they must try, and will be given credit for making an attempt. They won't get away with 'opting out', though a very simple attempt will be accepted if they really can't manage more.

Go around the room and monitor all students as closely as possible by looking in on them two or three times in each activity.

When activities are finished students should return quickly to their places and be ready without talking for the next activity.

List of useful classroom instructions

(The students don't need to know the grammar at this stage. They just need to get used to responding appropriately)

tatte kudasai	Please stand
suwatte kudasai	Please sit
hon o yonde kudasai	Please read your books
mite kudasai	Please watch
kokuban o mite kudasai	Please look at the board

kiite kudasai	Please listen
koko ni kite kudasai	Please come here
O namae o kaite kudasai	Please write your name
hon o akete kudasai	Please open your books
NOOTO o akete kudasai	Please open your notebooks
hon o tojite kudasai	Please close your books
osoi desu	You're late
shitsurei shimasu	Apology for being late
hayaku shite kudasai	Please do it quickly
hayaku kaite kudasai	Please write quickly
enpitsu de kaite kudasai	Please write in pencil
hanasanai de kudasai	Please don't talk
nihongo de hanashite kudasai	Please speak in Japanese
eigo de hanasanai de kudasai	Please don't speak in English
moo ichido itte kudasai	Please repeat
yukkuri hanashite kudasai	Please speak slowly
hakkiri hanashite kudasai	Please speak clearly
isshokenmeini benkyoo shite kudasai	Do your best
yoku dekimashita	Well done!
omedetoo gozaimasu	Congratulations!
O tanjoobi ...omedetoo	Happy birthday!
daijoobu desu	It's OK
daijoobu desu ka	Are you OK?
ii desu	It's good
shukudai o kudasai	Please hand in your homework
arigatoo gozaimasu	Thank you
doozo	Here you are
sore o kudasai	Please give me that
NOOTO o kudasai	Please may I have your notebooks?
isu wa tsukue no ue ni (ushiro ni) oite kudasai	Put your chairs up on the desk (behind the desk)
sore o misete kudasai	Please show me that
mado o akete kudasai	Please open the window
mado o shimete kudasai	Please close the window

List of School subjects

eigo	English
nihongo	Japanese
FURANSUgo	French
DOITSUgo	German
ITARIAgo	Italian
RATENgo	Latin
suugaku	Math
chiri (gaku)	Geography
kagaku	Chemistry

rika	Science
seibutsu	Biology
rekishi	History
bijutsu	Art
taiiku	Physical Education
SUPOOTSU	Sports
ongaku	Music
keizai	Economics
kaikei	Accounting
shakai	Social Studies-Humanities
engeki	Drama

Teaching vocabulary

The principle to be observed is to introduce vocabulary with realia, pictures, demonstration, graphs, collecting words around a topic, always trying to put the word into context with a sentence or situation—any way that encourages understanding of its meaning from the Japanese before introducing the English.

Teaching "grammar"

Grammar as such is not a fashionable word. Students who continue to academic levels in Japanese will easily add the formal labels at a later date. For most students, studying Japanese at school for only two or three years, understanding of the structure is important but very formal labels are not necessary. As they are no longer demanded in English, students find them confusing and difficult to absorb. Language teachers often find it necessary to teach the function of nouns, adjectives, adverbs etc., but it is not necessary for students at this level to understand the complications of present perfect tenses etc. The course has to present the idea of tense and gives the labels negative, past, etc., but avoids labels for other structures beyond the everyday ones of, eg: particles, nouns, adjectives, adverbs, qualitative nouns, making requests, giving instructions, etc. The Japanese verb forms are labeled *masu* form, *te* form, *tai desu* form, to avoid complicating students' lives unnecessarily.

Sufficient information is given for students to understand the structures of sentences that they are required to make in the written component of the course.

Teaching Japanese script

Japanese script may be taught directly from the chart or in small groups as teachers prefer. My reason for teaching it gradually is that students have a lot to absorb and if we are to make lessons active and make the students really feel they are communicating we should avoid bogging them down with long sessions of formal writing practice. Keen students will learn the whole *hiragana* chart quickly and enjoy using it. Others will enjoy copying words from the vocabulary lists. Both these groups may be encouraged to follow the stroke order given on the charts at the back of the book. Those who find it difficult or have too much to absorb at once if we offer all the chart at once, will achieve high standards of writing following the textbook, and will know the chart well by the end of their first year, leaving *katakana* until later and consolidation of both scripts in writing and reading to Year Three. There is really no need to rush. As students develop their need to write more they will naturally tend to learn more of their own volition. Putting samples of students' work up on the wall and making posters of information as outlined in some lessons is a great incentive to others to reach the same competency.

The linking of particles to the previous word as is standard practice in writing Japanese kana has been left until the third year to ensure that students understand the function of the particles and are totally familiar with the vocabulary before having to cope with reading and mentally separating the word from the particle in order to achieve understanding. It takes a long time for familiarity with the vocabulary and particles to be absorbed and adds an unnecessary difficulty if we join them too soon. Grading work in manageable steps until we achieve a more natural result is a building program that, from experience, works more successfully for the average student if done gradually.

Teaching cultural background

This is more interesting if it is an integral part of every lesson. Small bits of information from the teacher's reading or experience enliven lessons and awaken curiosity. There are sections in the textbook at the beginning of each topic as more solid cultural background learning, and students may be encouraged to bring newspaper articles, pictures, videos of Japan, letters from penpals or anything Japanese to show and discuss.

Sometimes it may be possible to show videos or to go to the library for a research period in which students find out about aspects of Japanese life that interest them; bringing back to the classroom something to show what they have learned, or reporting back in English verbally.

Sometimes there are film festivals that have Japanese films but check suitability first!

Ask visitors to come to talk about experiences in Japan or living in Japan.

Consider inviting Japanese students to your school and setting up sister-school relationships with Japanese schools.

Grouping students

It is important that students don't always sit with their friends for activities. Working in random groups breaks down their inhibitions much more quickly, and boosts their confidence about communicating with people they don't know so well. It often helps to make new friendships, particularly for people who don't make friends easily, and makes the class more cohesive and supportive of one another.

In the first half of the text book, this is not stressed, as students need time to get used to new ways of working, but by the second half, they should be ready, and sufficiently confident to work with randomly selected groups.

The ideas below also help to get students asking relevant questions, using Japanese communicatively for even such simple and quick tasks as forming groups.

Suggestions for making groups and pairs

- Decide on the number of groups required. Number students one to (five)—the number of groups required. Repeat those numbers around the class. Ask all "number ones" to group together, two's, etc. in different parts of the room. This helps to avoid students always choosing the same group with whom to work.
- The same idea but give *hiragana* syllable labels—*a i u e o* etc.
- Make sets of 5/6 *hiragana* cards of same syllable. Students go around the room quickly to find others with same and group together. Asking each other: ... *o motte imasu ka*. They don't need to know the grammar, merely to understand the phrase lexically. Which group first?
- Make sets of *hiragana* syllables. Five different in each set. Students have to find the other students who have the same set as theirs. Ask ... *o motte imasu ka*. Group together. Which group first? (Adjust numbers of cards to number required in each group.)
- Choose students by initial syllables of names.
- After colors have been taught, give each student a color group to find. *(Akai o motte imasu ka)* etc.

OR

- Have two piles of colored paper. Each student must pair with one who has different color.
- After physical characteristics have been taught: Call out *(otoko no ko), wa tatte kudasai. (Me ga aoi otoko no ko) wa koko ni kite kudasai. (Me ga chairo otoko no ko wa), koko ni kite kudasai*, separating boys into two groups.
  Do the same for girls, thinking up other differences to give you the number in a group that you require.
- Choose students by the number of people in their family, whether they have brothers and sisters, etc.

For pairwork

- Set out desks in pairs before lesson.
- Put out *katakana* name cards before lesson. Ask students to find and sit at desk with own name.
- Students randomly take a *katakana* name card from box on entering room. Must find and sit with the person who is holding their own name card. Ask each other, showing card: *Anata no namae desu ka*, or *Kore wa anata no namae desu ka*. Tell each other: *sore wa watashi no namae desu*.
- Sort out the name cards into groups before lesson, of students of comparable ability. Give one student from each group the job of finding out who is in their group by holding up a card and asking *Dare desu ka* until they have discovered the whole group.
- The same may be done with pairs of cards, one student finding the other.
- Stand at door while students are entering, and count off the required number for a group to sit together or pairs.
- After teaching Families, ask students to find someone else who has a little sister etc. Asking *Imootosan ga imasu ka*. Answering with own family label *Imooto ga imasu* etc.

OR

  going around telling everyone *Ani ga imasu. Anata wa?* Answering *Ani mo imasu*.
- Birthdays are another way of grouping.

Students ask *O tanjoobi wa nangatsu desu ka,* or *O tanjoobi wa ichigatsu desu ka,* etc. and group with students of same birth month. If groups are too uneven, teacher may judiciously split them.

Hiragana reading practice

For students to learn *hiragana* and *katakana* easily it needs to become relevant to their everyday lives, and not only because it will be tested! The more they use it, the more spontaneous their writing and reading of it will become. BUT it doesn't need to be always formal. Reading and Writing exercises are often accepted as part of the deal by students but not really seen as relevant to their real lives.

- It can be fun to have challenges for students, puzzles, observation "tests". If the walls are constantly being updated and students know that they should get into the habit of checking for information, it is fun to be first in the classroom to find the challenge of the day.
- New vocabulary, phrases, messages and instructions made into a game, make awareness of *hiragana* and *katakana* grow, and recognition become automatic.
- Who can find the new label and read it?
- Who knows what this says? Your instructions for the start of this lesson are on the wall/board. Who is the first to obey?

  eg: *Suwatte kudasai/Hon o akete kudasai/NOOTO o akete kudasai/Kokuban o mite kudasai/ Tatte kudasai/TEEPU o kiite kudasai/Hon o yonde kudasai.*

  - all things that they have heard now many times but may not be so quick to recognize in *hiragana*.

As their knowledge of grammar structures grows the instructions can be more complex.

- Songs are a marvelous way to get students reading *hiragana*. Write out the words of songs on large sheets to use as flash cards. Put up on wall and get students to read the lines as they sing the song. Sing several times through. Bring out in odd moments.
- Give groups a sheet each, to prepare before the class sing the song. They teach the class the song.
- Make messages for the wall in *hiragana*. Ask for first volunteer to read. Reward occasionally.
- Label everything that it is possible to label in the classroom.

  Don't leave labels up in the same place too long.

  Occasionally ask if someone has noticed a new label or message. What does it say?

  Use occasional rewards to keep students alert.
- Put up names of days, dates, numbers, counters, etc. for constant reference.
- *Katakana:* Put up names on wall under labels of commendation, people you would like to see etc.
- Put up maps of countries or label towns on a map. Give one or two each week for students to identify.

  Give students jobs to do, eg:

  Closing windows at end of lesson: *mado—KAIRI*

  Cleaning blackboard: *kokuban—HEMI*

  Putting chairs tidy at end of lesson: *isu—RISA*

  The actual job may be explained in English. Change monitors each week.
- Put up lists of older students who are willing to help younger students—a *sempai* system

- Tell students to put up their names on a list in *katakana* if they want an appointment with you.
- If you are able to see a certain number of students privately each week for a tutorial, put up the names of this week's group.

Useful resources

During the latter part of the first year it would be useful to gradually accumulate more teaching resources.
- The vertical files of your school or town library may yield good pictures of Japanese families, homes and festivals.
- Libraries, too, are often most helpful in putting together boxes of books on a subject for teachers to borrow as a set for a prescribed period of time. If this is available to you, it may be helpful if your order is placed early so that you can be sure of having books available when you need them.
- *Pacific Friend* is a magazine that is widely available on subscription and through libraries. It is very useful for background information, although care needs to be taken to check that information found relates to Japanese before using it, as a proportion of each issue is devoted to other Pacific countries. Students using the magazine for research also need to check carefully before using information.
- Newspaper offices sometimes have photo files that are useful and will get copies made or even sometimes give old photos to schools.
- Newspaper offices are also a useful source of photos of people doing activities that are marvellous for captioning for the classroom walls or for discussion.
- Old calendars are very useful when teaching dates, days, and months, and their pictures are excellent for describing places, weather, temperature, etc.
- Children's picture books often have very good illustrations of everyday life that are useful in the classroom for vocabulary games, descriptions of places, descriptions of activities, for 'what happened next?' situations, transport pictures etc. They can often be bought very cheaply at secondhand shops and Jumble sales and the appropriate pages cut out and mounted for classroom use. Sometimes friends or students in your class are happy to give them to you instead of throwing them away.
- Old magazines often have very useful illustrations of people and activities to cut out and file ready for future use under the topic headings.
- There are several very good videos that accompany other courses which are excellent for showing students natural Japanese situations and homes, eg:
  YANsun produced by NHK, the Japanese TV network, for its own language teaching program.
- A handy resource of Japanese games is *Let's Play Games in Japanese,* published by National Textbook Company.

Evaluation

Evaluation of your own lessons is important for continuing to grow professionally. Looking back over lessons and thinking through which parts were most successful and which did not work with your particular group is valuable for future planning.

Often what works well with one group is a dismal failure with another.

Our aim in evaluation is to find out how well students can communicate information, and respond to situations. Therefore the tests we set need to have definite goals in mind. What can students be expected to know thoroughly and put into spontaneous production? A test which seeks to 'trip up' students achieves little. Tests are most successful when they have realistic goals. Students productive exam or test level is always appreciably lower than their apparent classroom competence level. An exam or test that is too difficult can undo months of careful confidence building and produce a negative reaction in the class which takes a long time to overcome. Therefore tests are most successful when students know exactly what their goals are, are given time to achieve them, and have a very good chance of achieving a successful result.

It may even prove a good idea to give students a very clear outline of the situations they have learned to communicate in before the test. The aim is to find out if students are competent in those situations. If they become competent because they have reviewed thoroughly for the test, that may prove to be a very valid test of their true ability, where leaving them to face an unknown situation may mean that even good students do not achieve as well as they could. As they progress through the course they will become adept in using the material they know spontaneously in familiar and unfamiliar situations.

We are looking for a response that is as automatic as the native tongue and the ability to put sentences together by 'feel' and intuitive knowledge, not by painstaking academic dictionary hunting.

Students need to know, regularly, how they are going. They need to be able to measure their success and know they are progressing steadily. They may monitor their own progress using the check exercises or it may be done formally by the teacher using the formal check exercises for direct translation, listening comprehension, or reading practice.

The achievement based tests in each book give situations. From these it is easy to evaluate the student who can truly communicate.

The idea is to achieve a balance of different sorts of tests to give your students the widest opportunities possible for demonstrating what they know and for improving their own level of competence.

Students may be encouraged to help each other to achieve these goals. For some students the rate of progress may be slow so it helps them to feel good about the subject if the goals set for them are measured in small but recognizable steps of progress, eg: "You couldn't remember how to introduce yourself to a stranger last week. Set yourself a goal to achieve that this week."

The dismissal suggestions in the presentations are useful in finding out if students have grasped a particular structure and in specifically listening to each students' pronunciation each lesson.

Because of the nature of the course it is also possible to evaluate participation levels as you move around the class during activities; to keep unobtrusive notes on students who need help or praise etc., to feel when some students are ready for extension and to prepare more open-ended activities to challenge them to extend themselves.

Making tapes and prepared roleplays are valuable evaluation aids too.

Correcting errors

Gentle correction as activities are monitored may be made without weakening confidence.

The most important thing is to support the student and boost confidence while helping him/her to improve accuracy.

Roleplays give an opportunity for students to enjoy each other's competence without feeling afraid of being corrected in front of peers. The teacher may like to mentally note common errors to review later without reference to a particular group's performance.

Pair activities may be gently corrected without upsetting the delicate confidence level since students are usually working with people they like.

If they have been asked to work with people who are not their chosen friends they may prefer not to be corrected in front of them. Gradually, as their trust in the teacher is consolidated and their security within the group grows, they learn to cope with it knowing that no one will 'put them down'.

Written work may be marked by the teacher away from the student, by the teacher with individual students, by the students themselves, or by their friends.

Sensitivity to students' possible embarrassments pays dividends in building their trust.

Formal examinations and tests have their place too, even if only in giving students experience of formal situations and, by practice, helping them to overcome nervousness. Students need experience in exam technique—timing, selecting order of work, etc.

Facing strangers for orals is very nerve wracking but with practice students learn to take it in stride and are able to cope well. Therefore to give them this sort of experience has value.

Oral assessment

Oral assessment is often difficult. Time is the most difficult factor. How can one test all students in a class fairly, within class time?

Several methods are worth considering:

Tape assessments

Students may be asked to produce tapes for assessment two or three times a year. Depending on the cirumstances of the students, they may be asked to provide a tape on which they will record assessment work over the whole period of their school study. If that is unrealistic, one or two tapes per class may be provided by the school.

Whoever the tape belongs to, students will always state their name and class at the beginning of their work to identify themselves clearly.

A tape recorder is made available in a quiet space. Students are released from class to make their recording, needing only to push the record buttons, and to switch off the tape when they complete their portion.

For this sort of assessment it is possible to work two ways:

1 To allow the students homework time to prepare a story or to answer questions that will assuredly be asked. Allow time for the work to be corrected so that you are sure that they are not consolidating incorrect patterns, and give some help with pronunciation.

OR

2 Do not warn in advance

It is necessary to decide, too, what you want to test.

Is it pronunciation?

Is it comprehension?

Is it response?

Is it the ability to read from *hiragana* and *katakana?*

There are valid reasons for testing all of these, but not all need to be tested during the same session.

Pronunciation tests

A test of pronunciation may only need a passage for students to read from *roomaji*. Each student takes a turn to go and read to the tape. The teacher marks later.

If this is the test, students should know in advance what the criteria are going to be. You may like to consider the following:

- Attempt to sound Japanese
- Long sounds
- R sounds
- Word grouping
- Smoothness of reading
- Speed and fluency

If testing from *kana,* it is important to separate the skills involved, as they will often determine the quality of the actual reading. For such a test it is necessary to give students time to read at least three times through the passage before being asked to read it to the tape, or the academic inability to read the *kana* may defeat the intention of hearing the sound.

It may be worth considering two short passages in *kana,* one to be prepared to overcome nervousness or difficulty in reading the *kana,* and one very short unprepared one to test the ability to read *kana* aloud.

OR

to separate the tests and make reading from *kana* a reading test rather than primarily a pronunciation test.

Comprehension tests

Care must be taken here to determine whether tests are for AURAL (listening) ability or ORAL (speaking) ability.

Aural comprehension tests

Passages may be put on tape and played to students individually or as a whole class.

Comprehension may then be tested by written means:

- Multiple choice answers in English,
- Checking against pictorial information given,
- Circling correct information given in English,
- True and false written answers in English, or by oral answers in English.

Tests that demand the ability to quickly understand and match information from a tape or teacher's reading with written Japanese (even if given in *roomaji*) are asking for a great deal more than straightforward aural comprehension. These sort of tests disadvantage a good listener who does not have good reading skills.

Oral tests

ORAL tests are testing the students' ability so speak in Japanese.

It is possible to assess pronunciation as part of an oral test.

The major intention of oral assessments is to find out the students' capability in using the material learned to make spontaneous conversation.

A secondary intention is to find out if students can accurately answer questions or requests or make comments in loosely structured situations. Care should be taken in assessing the different skills being demanded if tests are demanding listening and oral expertise.

Often a student may be able to understand a question or a passage, but not be able to frame an answer or comment at that moment.

Credit has to be given for the understanding.

The ideas for oral assessments below, which have been frequently used, do not give the student much, if any, opportunity to show spontaneous use of the language learned.

1 A student offers information on a given subject that has been prepared, eg: a week before a subject is announced. Students work to refresh their memory of words and structures needed and prepare a short talk on the subject.
2 A student offers information on a subject with limited preparation. A selection of subjects are offered for the student to choose from. Work is done in class on the topics.
   The student arrives at the assessment knowing that he or she could be asked questions on any of the prepared material.
3 Students are given lists of questions from which a selection will be asked at the interview.
4 A student has no pre-knowledge of what will be asked.

This last, for beginner students, may produce anxiety that may totally negate the purpose of the exercise, as the student fails to respond, not from actual lack of knowledge, but from anxiety.

All of the above demand an inordinate amount of time to get through a whole class even if the students are responding to a tape while the teacher is working with the body of the class.

If students tape work individually, the teacher is faced with hours of listening and evaluating to do out of class.

How to be fair, to assess spontaneous contributions, to take pressure off the teacher, and off the student, is the task we need to address.

Group and pair oral assessments

Group and pair assessments make sense. They take pressure off the students by giving them some support from their peers in an unthreatening situation. The teacher is left free to listen attentively without having to think up strategies to keep the students talking, or discipline the class while trying to be fair. Students are given a much better chance to offer what they know.

The 2-4 group assessment method

The students may be given the chance to review material on various topics studied or given no warning past the fact that they will be expected to talk on topics they have learned.

Four students at a time are withdrawn from the class.

The teacher acts as a facilitator, keeping conversation going. As the teacher is known to the students, this is nonthreatening. A Japanese national or second Japanese language teacher is asked to make the actual assessment to defined criteria sitting outside the group unobtrusively.

Students give their names for the benefit of the assessor.

The teacher starts the ball rolling by chatting to the students generally. The students try to respond as they would in normal conversation. The teacher asks a question of someone in the group.

With older students they may be asked to tell the group about their hobby or their holiday. With beginners, conversation may be kept to simple sentence offerings. The teacher starts the conversation off, but the onus is on the students to keep it going - to answer and to find out something from another student or comment on what was said. The teacher intervenes if one student is too dominant, to encourage others to have their say.

The assessor listens and notes the interaction within the group, the number of contributions made, the quality, the ease or lack of ease of participants.

With beginner students it can be something as simple as asking them what they plan to do at the weekend, or what they did last night.

Five minutes of listening to such a group gives a very good indication of the oral competence of four students.

Therefore a whole class can be assessed very fairly in a lesson.

With a senior group you may allow twenty minutes or longer per group, but senior classes may be smaller.

This may be thought to be too difficult to organize, demanding as it does, a second adult.

In fact a senior student could take the place of the teacher for beginner groups, or students could be given a list of questions to ask each other while the teacher listens in. The onus then is on the students not to be content with one response to a question but to ask how others feel about it too and open up the subject with the whole group.

When they have exhausted one question they start on the next, each taking a turn to initiate the conversation

If a second helper is not available it is possible to tape the conversation and assess it later.

Pair assessments

Taking two lessons to assess a whole class:

Pair assessments may be organized by giving the whole class a task planning roleplays with each other so that there is a quiet buzz of conversation. The tasks may be related to the conversation you'd like them to have in your hearing.

Students try to find out, for example, about each other's families, questioning, listening to each other, and commenting.

The teacher listens in and adds the odd comment to keep the conversation going if necessary, to make sure that students aren't disadvantaged by having a less able partner.

The teacher moves around the room giving each pair about five minutes.

Group assessments

Taking one lesson to assess a whole class:

Give the students a task, eg:

Give them a list of fifteen items and ask them to decide in their group what they would take if they were (for example)

- stranded on a desert island,
- going for a camping trip,
- preparing for a birthday party. They give reasons for taking or not taking something.

The groups will start discussing in Japanese. The teacher moves around each group, asking briefly how they have got on with the previous topic. The teacher needs to know only what they decided to take and why, then gives a new topic for discussion to each group and listens to about five minutes of their discussion.

PICTURES on topics studied may be used, with or without preparation. Preparation usually gives better results. Brainstorm the words that might be applicable in talking about a picture and the sentence patterns that could be used, a few days before the assessment time.

Oral assessments using pictures

As for group assessments, pictures on topics studied may be used with or without preparation.

Students come to talk to the teacher and after a few comments and questions to settle the student down, teacher and student start talking about what they can see in the picture, both giving information, both asking questions, leading out of the picture to areas of imagination - suggest what the people will do tomorrow, what did the tourist do yesterday?, etc. This can also be done in pairs or groups.

Evaluation suggestions

Question blocks

- for students to ask each other,
- for oral tests,
- for written answers,
- for quizzes,
- for matching,
- for surveys (each student has one or two questions to answer by going around the class and then reports responses to the group).

Students should, however, realize that conversations also start from comments as well as from questions, so it's important to practice them as well.

The selection of questions given is very limited. You and your students will be able to make far more comprehensive lists and may like to do so in group, pair or individual competition, eventually making a composite list of all the questions thought up under various topic headings.

Each group of questions may be expanded to allow students to ask more and to add comments.

Questions have been grouped as perhaps following on from one another.

Suggested use

1 A block of questions is given to a group of three or four students.

    One student asks the question. They all answer and comment, eg: I did that too, or: I didn't go because it was cold etc. to try to make a genuine conversation out of the material they are working on. The teacher may decide to give each group a different block of questions or each group a copy of the same.

    Groups work on the possibilities to extend and enrich and the teacher moves around the class to monitor and make notes on oral competency.

    In some situations it may prove worthwhile to ask students to record briefly answers given, eg: How many think it will be cold tomorrow?

2 Pairwork.

General questions

O namae wa nan desu ka.
Nansai desu ka.
Doko no kata desu ka.
Doko ni sunde imasu ka.
Anata no gakkoo wa doko desu ka.
Anata no uchi wa doko desu ka.
O tanjoobi wa itsu desu ka.
Tanjoobi wa nangatsu desu ka.
Tanjoobi wa nangatsu nannichi desu ka.
Gakko de nani o benkyoo shimasu ka.
Anata no benkyoo wa nani ga suki desu ka.
Anata no benkyoo wa nani ga kirai desu ka.

Dates and weather

Kyoo wa nannichi desu ka.
Kyoo wa nanyoobi desu ka.
Kyoo wa atsui deshoo ka.
Kyoo wa samui deshoo ka.
Ashita wa ame deshoo ka.
Ashita wa atsui deshoo ka.

    Suggest things to do because of the weather or tell about things you did or didn't do because of the weather.

Activities out of school this week

Konshuu nani o shimasu ka.
Doko ni ikimasu ka.
Dare to ikimasu ka.
... yoobi wa nani o shimasu/shimashita ka.
Nanji ni ikimasu ka.
Nanji ni kaerimasu ka.
Shukudai ga arimasu ka.
Donna shukudai ga arimasu ka.
Anata no heya wa gocha gocha desu ka.
Heya no sooji o shimasu ka.
Kazoku wa kuruma ga arimasu ka.
Kuruma o sooji shimasu ka.

Yesterday and last week

Kinoo no rokuji ni nani o shimashita ka.
Doyoobi ni nani o shimashita ka.
Nichiyoobi ni nani o shimashita ka.
Senshuu no (kinyoobi) ni doko ni ikimashita ka.
Kinoo wa TEREBI o mimashita ka.
Kinoo wa doko ni ikimashita ka.
(Senshuu) eiga ni ikimashita ka.
(Kinoo) PUURU ni ikimashita ka.
(Senshuu) toshokan ni ikimashita ka.
SUPOOTSU o shimasu ka. Donna SUPOOTSU o shimasu ka.
Itsu SUPOOTSU o shimasu ka.
Doko de SUPOOTSU o shimasu ka.
(Kinoo) no GEEMU ga suki deshita ka.
Tomodachi ni aimashita ka.
Nanji ni aimashita ka.
Doko de aimashita ka.
Tomodachi wa dare desu ka.

Home

Uchi wa hiroi desu ka semai desu ka.
Doko desu ka.
(Describe home)
Daidokoro wa hiroi desu ka semai desu ka.
Ima wa?
Shinshitsu wa?
Niwa wa?

Family

Oniisan ga imasu ka. (etc.)
Nansai desu ka.
Se ga takai desu ka se ga hikui desu ka.
Kami no ke ga nagai desu ka mijikai desu ka.
Me ga aoi desu ka chairo desu ka midori iro desu ka.
Shigoto o shimasu ka.
Doko de shigoto o shimasu ka.
Benkyoo shimasu ka.
Doko de benkyoo shimasu ka.
(Okaasan) wa nani ga suki desu ka,
(Okaasan) wa nani ga kirai desu ka.
Ask the same for other members of the family:
Imootosan ga imasu ka. (Remember, 'own family' labels in reply.)
Otoosan ga imasu ka.
Oniisan ga imasu ka.
Oneesan ga imasu ka.
(Okaasan) wa nanji ni okimasu ka.
(Okaasan) wa nanji ni nemasu ka.
SUPOOTSU o shimasu ka.
Donna SUPOOTSU o shimasu ka.

Friends: ask same questions as above.

Animals

Doobutsu ga suki desu ka.
Donna doobutsu ga suki desu ka. PETTO o katte imasu ka.
Anata no PETTO wa donna doobutsu desu ka.
Nani iro desu ka.
Namae wa nan desu ka.
Ii (inu) desu ka joozu desu ka.

Health

O Genki desu ka.
Chotto guai ga warui desu ka.
Atama ga itai desu ka.

Continue with things you will or will not do because of health.

Classroom

Kyootshitsu ni wa nani ga arimasu ka.
Kyooshitsu ni wa dare ga imasu ka.
Kyooshitsu ni wa nannin imasu ka.
Watashi no hon o mimashita ka.
Shukudai o yomimashita ka.

Politeness pairs

Questions	Answers
O namae wa nan desu ka.	*Watashi no namae wa ... desu.*
O namae wa nan to iimasu ka.	*Watashi wa ... to iimasu.*
Oikutsu desu ka.	*... sai desu.*
Nansai desu ka.	*... sai desu.*
Doko no kata desu ka.	*... jin desu.*
Nanijin desu ka.	*... jin desu.*
Ano hito wa dare desu ka.	*... san desu.*
Ano hito wa donata desu ka.	*... san desu.*

Matching activities

Students enjoy making matching activities.

Each student makes a set of sentences in a notebook and gets them checked for accuracy by the teacher.

The sentences are then separated and rewritten on paper into two halves. The second half is jumbled in order.

The completed puzzle is given to a friend who makes sure that you can't get two possible answers for one sentence. If so, discard and replace.

The neatly written, completed *roomaji* or *hiragana* puzzles are given to the class to try.

Match the pairs

Phrases: Provide the automatic response.

Photocopy class sets, and cut into strips.

Uses

May be used for pairwork, first pair to sort wins.

Group competitions: Fastest team wins.

Individual work: works better at own pace or the most able students have too much of an advantage.

Individual work within groups of similar ability works well.

One student reads one half of a sentence, and the group races to find the other half before companions. Winner keeps that strip and reads next half from sheet.

Students are given one half of the pair each and go around room to find the owner of the other half. They ask: kami o yonde kudasai.

If wrong, say sumimasen ga.. chigaimasu. If correct, race to front of room to be first. Line up in order of finishing and watch the rest complete the task.

1 Cut up responses in strips to rearrange for matching.

2 Cut all up into strips. Students find the matching pair.

Matching pairs

Ogenki desu ka	*Okage sama de genki desu*
Tadaima	*Okaeri nasai*
Doko ni	*ikimasu ka*
Yoji ni	*uchi ni kaerimasu*
Okaasan wa	*se ga hikui desu*
Imooto no me ga	*aoi desu*
Uchi wa	*ookii desu*
Watashi no tomodachi wa	*Hiroshikun desu*
Ashi ga	*nagai desu*
Doko ni	*sunde imasu ka*
Atsui desu kara	*PUURU ni ikimasu*
Ashita ame	*deshoo*
Kinoo	*kaze deshita*
Neko dewa	*arimasen*
Anata no inu	*desu ka*
O tanjoobi wa	*itsu desu ka*
Tanjoobi wa	*gogatsu itsuka desu*
Ima nanji	*desu ka*
Yoji	*han desu*
Sanji ni BENsan	*ni aimashoo ka*

Match the pairs for Topics 8 and 9

Eiga wa	*omoshiroi desu*
Itte mairimasu	*Itte irasshai*
Nodo ga kawakimashita	*Onaka ga sukimashita*
Atama ga itai desu kara	*Gakkoo ni ikimasen*
Suzushii	*desu ne*
Sore wa	*ikemasen ne*
Ii	*otenki desu ne*
Atama ga	*ii desu*
Doo	*shimashita ka*

Watashi wa	juuyonsai desu
Otanjoobi	omedetoo gozaimasu
Yoi	otoshi o
Konshuu watashi no	tanjoobi desu
Ano hito wa	AMERIKAjin desu ka
Nihongo o	benkyoo shimasu
Me wa	aokunai desu
Ani no kami no	ke ga nagai desu
Kyoo	gakkoo wa sukijanai desu
soro soro	shitsurei shimasu
iie, ashi wa	itakunai desu
DOA o	shimete kudasai
Mado o	akete kudasai
koko ni	kite kudasai
kiite	kudasai
hon o mite	yonde kudasai

Missing particles

1 Use as they are, for writing or oral puzzle.
2 Cut up and use in strips for a quiz.
3 Use cut up for matching with answers.
4 Use for checking understanding.
5 Use for students to test each other.
6 Give correct complete sentences to one half of the class. The others have the one with the missing particles. Find each other and match, asking *Anata no kami wa nan desu ka*. The one with missing particles must fill in the gaps. Other student checks against correct answer. Redistribute and play again so that all students have a turn filling in the particles.

Find the particle, set 1

1 *Hon wa doko ... arimasu ka.*
2 *Inu ... doko ni imasu ka.*
3 *Hana ... kirei desu.*
4 *Imooto ... imasu.*
5 *Okaasan ... se ga takai desu.*
6 *Otoosan wa kuruma ... suki desu.*
7 *Watashi wa shukudai ... kirai desu.*
8 *KIMU san ... OOSUTORARIAjin desu.*
9 *Kore wa anata ... hon desu ka.*
10 *Sore ... kudasai.*
11 *Kyoo hon ... yomimashita.*
12 *Ashita eiga ... ikimashoo.*
13 *Dare ... enpitsu deshoo ka.*
14 *Watashi ... seito desu.*
15 *Kore ... watashi no NOOTO desu.*

16 *Sumimasen ... ima nanji desu ka.*
17 *Inu ga suki desu ...*
18 *REE san ... BESU san wa watashi no tomodachi desu.*
19 *REE san wa me ... chairo desu.*
20 *Fudebako ni wa PEN ... enpitsu ga arimasu.*

Find the particle, set 1 answers

1 *Hon wa doko ni arimasu ka.*
2 *Inu wa doko ni imasu ka.*
3 *Hana wa(ga) kirei desu.*
4 *Imooto ga imasu.*
5 *Okaasan wa se ga takai desu.*
6 *Otoosan wa kuruma ga suki desu.*
7 *Watashi wa shukudai ga kirai desu.*
8 *KIMUsan wa OOSUTORARIAjin desu.*
9 *Kore wa anata no hon desu ka.*
10 *Sore o kudasai.*
11 *Kyoo hon o yomimashita.*
12 *Ashita eiga ni ikimashoo.*
13 *Dare no enpitsu deshoo ka.*
14 *Watashi wa seito desu.*
15 *Kore wa watashi no NOOTO desu.*
16 *Sumimasen ga ima nanji desu ka.*
17 *Inu ga suki desu ka.*
18 *REE san to BESU san wa watashi no tomodachi desu.*
19 *REE san wa me ga chairo desu.*
20 *Fudebako ni wa PEN ya (to) enpitsu ga arimasu.*

Find the particle, set 2

1 *Kyoo ... watashi ... tanjoobi desu.*
2 *Anata ... inu desu ka.*
3 *Kinoo gakkoo ... ikimasen deshita.*
4 *Ashita eiga ... ikimasu ...*
5 *Kyoo watashi ... tomodachi ... JIMU san ... uchi ... kimasu.*
6 *Oniisan ... imasu ...*
7 *Ane ... juurokusai desu.*
8 *Watashi ... Nihonjin ... tomodachi ... namae ... Yukiko desu.*
9 *Watashi ... kaban ... ... hon ... zasshi ... arimasu.*
10 *Watashi ... heya ... ... REKOODO ... arimasu.*
11 *Kyooshitsu ... ... nani ... arimasu ...*
12 *Kyooshitsu ... ... dare ... imasu ...*
13 *Kore ... anata ... PEN desu ...*
14 *Sore ... kudasai.*
15 *Mado ... akete kudasai.*
16 *Koko ... kite kudasai.*

17 *Kokuban ... mite kudasai.*
18 *BOBU san ... kooen ... TENISU ... shimashoo.*
19 *Anata ... heya ... yonde kudasai.*
20 *Daidokoro ... ryoori ... shimasu.*

Find the particle, set 2 answers

1 *Kyoo watashi no tanjoobi desu.*
2 *Anata no inu desu ka.*
3 *Kinoo gakkoo ni ikimasen deshita.*
4 *Ashita eiga ni ikimasu.*
5 *Kyoo watashi no tomodachi no JIMUsan wa uchi ni kimasu.*
6 *Oniisan ga imasu ka.*
7 *Ane wa juurokusai desu.*
8 *Watashi no Nihonjin no tomodachi no namae wa Yukiko desu.*
9 *Watashi no kaban ni wa hon to (ya) zasshi ga arimasu.*
10 *Watashi no heya ni wa REDKOODO ga arimasu.*
11 *Kyooshitsu ni wa nani ga arimasu ka.*
12 *Kyooshitsu ni wa dare ga imasu ka.*
13 *Kore wa anata no PEN desu ka.*
14 *Sore o kudasai.*
15 *Mado o akete kudasai.*
16 *Koko ni kite kudasai.*
17 *Kokuban o mite kudasai.*
18 *BOBUsan to kooen de TENISU o shimashoo.*
19 *Anata no heya de yonde kudasai.*
20 *Daidokoro de ryoori o shimasu.*

Fill in the missing words

This sort of activity is a good one for students to make, in order to test others. Students write a short passage, and leave out (for example) five words. Teacher marks passage before words are extracted. Student rewriters passage, omitting words, and gives to partner to do, keeping original in notebook from which to give partner answers. The set made may be kept for spare time games.

Watashi no namae wa HEREN desu. AMERIKAjin desu.
SHIKAGO ni sunde imasu. Watashi no uchi wa chiisai desu.
Kazoku wa yonin desu. Okaasan to ani to otooto to watashi desu.
Watashi wa juusansai desu. Ani wa juurokusai desu. Otooto wa juuissai desu.
Inu no namae wa ROBAA desu. ROBAA wa chairo desu. Mimi ga kuroi desu.
Kinoo kazoku to umi no kooen ni ikimashita. Umi ga suki desu.
Ii otenski deshita.
Kyoo Nichiyoobi desu. Shukudai o shimasu. Ashita mata gakkoo ni ikimasu.
Ashita wa nihongo to rekishi to suugaku to eigo o shimasu.
Nihongo to rekishi to eigo ga suki desu. Suugaku wa sukijanai desu. I chiji han ni SUPOOTSU desu.
SUPOOTSU ga suki desu.

Words to choose from: Spaces are deliberately small to avoid recognition of words by length.

Suggested use: Students rewrite passage in full in notebooks or write the missing words in notebooks.

If the photocopied sheets are covered with plastic they last well.

(Four of these words will not be used.)

chairo	watashi	mimi	umi	sukijanai	kooen	namae
wa	HEREN	ani	jin	sunde	ROBAA	sai
nihongo	desu	samui	suki	ii	kaerimasu	kyoo
shukudai	gakkoo	hon	ichijihan	chiisai	yonin	zasshi
sensei						

Watashi no ... wa ... desu. AMERIKA ... desu.
SHIKAGO ni ... imasu. Watashi no uchi wa ... desu.
Kazoku wa ... desu. Okaasan to ... to otoooto to ... desu.
Watashi wa juusan ... desu. ... wa juurokusai desu. Otoото ...
juuissai desu. Inu no namae wa ... desu. ROBAA wa ... desu.
... ga kuroi desu.
Kinoo kazoku to ... no ... ni ikimashita. Umi ga ... desu.
... otenki deshita.
... nichiyoobi desu. ... o shimasu. Ashita mata ... ni ikimasu.
Ashita wa ... to rekishi to suugaku to eigo o shimasu.
Nihongo to eigo to rekishi ga suki ... Suugaku wa ... desu.
... ni SUPOOTSU desu. SUPOOTSU ga suki desu.

Extra activities

Communicative games

Photocopy *Nan desu ka* sheet onto thin card and cut up.

1 Use for 'Snap' type game where students call out the name of the pair in Japanese and win if correct.
2 Use for 'pairs' game (Pelmanism). Place cards face down on desk. Turn over two cards, saying the name in Japanese as they are turned up. Student who turns up two the same keeps the pair and tries again. If a pair is not found, the cards are turned back over and the other student takes a turn. (Useful not only for vocabulary, but also for memory training)
3 Spread out cards face upwards on desks (groups of four or five to each set). Teacher calls out names in Japanese. First group to find the names holds them up and win.
4 Guessing. One student chooses a card from those on the desk and secretly writes down the card chosen. Others must guess which card was chosen asking *'kami' desu ka,* etc. (Answer *Hai, soo desu,* or lie *soo dewa arimasen*).
5 Student or teacher calls out initial syllable of each word. Students race to find the appropriate card(s). The student who ends up with the most cards wins.
6 Call out the last syllable of each word. Students race to find the appropriate card(s). The student who ends up with the most cards wins.

7 Looking for sets. Each student in a group chooses and secretly writes down five words to look for. Share out a set of the cards. Each student must ask *Sumimasen ga (kami) o motte imasu ka* (Don't worry about teaching the grammar of the phrase, just tell the students that they are asking 'have you got ...?') and they take turns asking each other for the cards (they may ask any member of the group). They must give up the requested card if they have it, handing it over with doozo, and the recipient must reply with arigatoo. The first one to get their full set is the winner.

Use the same cards for a similar game after teaching kore o kudasai, then students must ask *(kami) o motte imasu ka,* and if the answer is *hai,* say *sore o kudasai.* Student who hands over the card says *doozo.*

After Topic Five the same cards may be used for a guessing game:

8 Whole class, groups or pairs. All cards are put on the desk face upwards. Students close their eyes *(Me ga tojite kudasai).* One card is removed. Students guess *(kami) deshita ka.* Answer either *hai soo desu,* or *iie soo dewa arimasen deshita/(kami) dewa arimasen deshita.* Student who guesses correctly takes the next turn.

Photocopy animal sheets and people sheets onto thin card and cut up.

1 Place cards face down on desk in two piles. Turn up two cards, one from each pile, and make a sentence including both items of information, eg: *(INU) wa (JON) san no desu,* or *(JON) san no (INU) desu.*

2 Students place cards as for 1, above. Other members of the group ask nan desu ka. Answer *(INU) desu.* Group ask *dare no desu ka.* Answer *(JON) san no desu.* Student One may then ask *nan desu ka,* and *dare no desu ka* to elicit the information from the group. Next student takes a turn.

3 Put out all cards face upwards, and while students close their eyes *(me ga tojite kudasai)* take away one card. Students guess which one is missing. Winner takes the next turn to select a card.

Photocopy people's heads sheet onto thin card, and cut up.

1 Pair activity. Place cards face downwards on desk. Students pick up a card each and introduce those two people to each other.

2 Each student decides a nationality for the people on their cards secretly, and they then ask each other nationality with *(OOSUTORARIA) jin desu,* etc. until they have guessed all correctly.

3 Later use the same cards for picking up and making stories about the people's life and daily activities.

4 'Who is missing' as in activity 3 (animal sheets) above. Different questions may be asked to elicit information. *Dare desu ka, Doko no kata desu ka, (OOSUTORARIA) jin desu ka.*

Photocopy *Meishi*/Name cards onto thin card and cut up for group activities.

1 Put out five *meishi* and five picture cards for each group to see. Teacher or student calls out name and nationality and an object belonging to that person. Students try to be the first to find that pair of cards.

2 Spread out *meishi* face upwards on the desk. One student calls out a nationality, and the others have to find the appropriate meishi and then give information (name, etc.) to win the card. The student with the most cards at the end wins.

3 Give the name first, students respond by grabbing the card quickly and giving nationality, OR in the case of the Japanese cards, the name of their home city.

4 Listen for initial syllable of Japanese name. First student to pick up the card wins, or has to spell the name to win the card without looking at the *meishi* again.

5 Match up the males and females by giving each student a *meishi* with Japanese name. They go around the room asking the name of the person, and if they are the same sex as their person, the students go on together to ask someone else. All the females line up on one side of the room, all the males on the other.

6 Make two sets of Japanese *meishi* cards. Give them out randomly around the class. Students go around the class asking *O namae wa ... desu ka,* until all have found their 'twin'. (The Answer must be a complete sentence, *watashi no namae wa ... desu.* Stand in pairs and wait quietly until all have found their 'twin'. Then introduce themselves to the rest of the class.

7 Cut name cards into strips downwards, and give one student in each group the list of five names. The other students have a name card each. Students with the whole list must find all the others in their group by going around asking *(Lim Choong) desu ka, O namae wa nan desu ka,* etc.

Lesson Plans for Basic Japanese Level 1

TOPIC ONE

Lesson One (Introduction, page 1)
Assuming 45-minute lessons

Aims and objectives

- To introduce the study of Japanese, your expectations of the class, routines and rules.
- To introduce Japan, its language, its writing systems and pronunciation.
- To teach students greetings appropriate to different times of day and homecoming.
- To make students feel satisfied that Japanese is going to be fun to learn but that it requires input from them too.

Preparation

Before class prepare the environment. If possible, even if you are sharing wall space with another subject, put up Japanese signs and pictures from magazines or travel agents around the room. Try to have some items of Japanese realia and/or library books about Japan/folk stories/factual magazines, etc., to stimulate students' interest in "things Japanese".

Big posters of the greetings, put up on the walls, will reinforce your first lesson. *Hiragana* charts or the greetings written in *hiragana* as well as *roomaji* will give the room a very Japanese appearance and establish it as the Japanese language area.

Make sure the room is arranged and tidy—obviously ready for action in whatever groupings allow the activities to take place unhampered by the need for movement of desks during the lesson.

Decide (alongside your school's policy) how you would like students to enter.

Once the students are inside they need to feel that this class will be something special, something that you have taken trouble over, and worthy of their input and attention.

Maybe you will be able to model a *kimono* or *yukata* or have an *ikebana* flower arrangement on your table or some other Japanese object to stimulate their interest.
If possible arrange to play some Japanese music while students are entering the room. (TAPE)

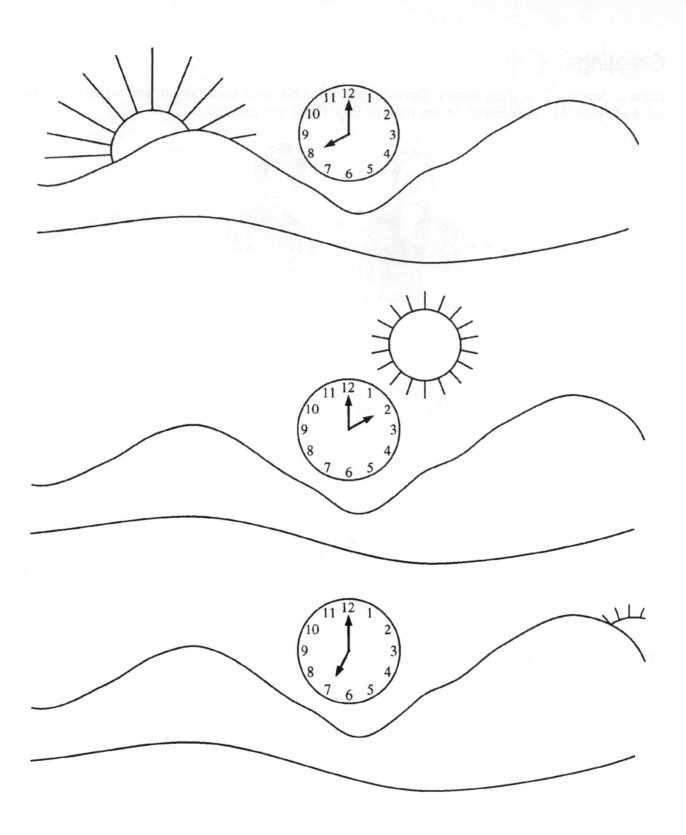

Greetings

Draw 2 people. Give them names. Draw a speech bubble over each person, and write inside (in *roomaji*) greetings appropriate to the time of day. Color the picture.

For many of your students this will be their first contact with anything Japanese so it is important that things like Japanese-style courtesy, the lesson itself and attention to detail, excite their interest and respect.

The lessons have been deliberately written to give you time to establish your routines, your rules, your control before allowing the students too much freedom, while building their confidence to be able to participate fully in what you ask them to do.

The lessons move at a lively pace for two reasons: to keep the feeling of active Japanese, and to get the students used to responding and changing activities quickly. The quicker their response the more practice they get and the more fun the learning becomes. They feel confident that they can do what is asked of them. They know that they are making progress.

You may feel slightly apprehensive about meeting your first class; they will have the same feeling unless you have had previous contact. It is important that all of you feel at ease but that you, as the teacher, have control of the situation.

If possible arrange that students have the writing materials and notebooks they need before coming to their first lesson so that you can devote your time to getting the course started in the way it will continue—thoroughly prepared, varied and fun.

If students carry bags with them around the school you may prefer to have them leave bags in a defined area to leave more freedom of movement within the class for roleplays and other activities.

Introduction (10 minutes)

TAPE Music.

When all have arrived leave the music playing for a moment or two and wait until all are listening. Show that you are listening too. Turn off the tape.

Signal that students should stand with a hand movement, while saying *tatte kudasai*.

Main theme

1 When all are standing watching, bow and greet them according to the time of day. Introduce yourself *(BURAUN) desu*. Signal them to sit down while saying *suwatte kudasai*.

2 Invite them to give you some feedback on the Japanese pictures and objects in the room if you have them. Find out what they already know about Japan and Japanese people and what their expectations are in choosing to learn Japanese. Tell them a little about the Japanese things in the room. See what they noticed was different when you greeted them and introduced yourself: (bowing; comment on different hand gesture used by Japanese to say 'I' (pointing to nose not to chest). Comment on the fact that many things are different about learning Japanese and that each day they will find out more about a country, people and customs very different from their own.

3 Explain the rules of the class by telling the students about the 122 million people living in Japan and the need for consideration and courtesy if the society is to function. Explain that no one in Japan puts others down and that the first rule for Japanese classes is that everyone helps everyone else as much as they can and never under any circumstances puts any one else down.

Something similar to the following may help you to set the tone of your class:

Participating is essential. Don't worry if you feel a bit shy, most people do, but you will not be put in embarrassing situations. You will be appreciated for what you offer and no one will put you down because they know that they want others to appreciate their contribution in their turn. Communicating only works if people are willing to work cooperatively, share information, listen attentively to each other and get into the spirit of the moment to help everyone to enjoy and to learn.

You will be given the opportunity to practice and to show off what you have learned. Gradually your confidence will build so that you will be able to volunteer yourself for roleplays and activities. Until that time comes remember that as long as you support the others who are more easily outgoing, you too are playing your part. For your own sake try to participate a little more each lesson because that way you too will gain confidence.

Sometimes you will be asked to work alone, at other times in pairs or in small groups. It is your responsibility to join in such activities to the best of your ability so that you don't end up feeling bad because you think you have let others down. Your Japanese lessons will be active and fun if you finish tasks and activities sensibly and quickly and then wait politely for others to finish. If everyone is quiet and ready for the next part of the lesson you actually get more time to do active things.

Sometimes you will be asked to move around the class to fulfill tasks. This gives you a chance to stretch your legs, but the purpose is a set activity. When you finish the task, return to your place and watch and listen until everyone has finished. It is not a time for chatter in English with your neighbor!

Any questions?

Now—Let's learn some Japanese!

(5 minutes)

4 Signal class to stand, with hand movement and *tatte kudasai*. Explain that Japanese people bow when they meet and that that is what you did at the beginning of this lesson.

Ask them to listen carefully to the greeting again and to be ready to see if they can greet you afterwards in the same way. Point out that men bow with hands at sides and women arms down hands in front. Demonstrate, then ask class to stand *tatte kudasai*. Receive their greeting and their *ojigi*.

(If you are using *konnichiwa* make sure that students right from the beginning pronounce the two *n*'s in the middle—*kon-nichiwa* not *konichiwa*.)

Signal to sit down with hand movement and *suwatte kudasai*.

Point out if you wish, or leave as tacitly understood, depending on the sort of class you have, that in this simple way several things have been established:

a) A formal beginning to each lesson ensures that students are watching and listening and aware that this is the start of the lesson. Time to switch into 'Japanese mode'!

b) Japanese will be used as often as possible in instructions and that they will be able to understand—they've just proved it.

c) That in learning a language they need to watch, listen, imitate and remember.

d) That they will all be required to join in during Japanese lessons and have proved that they are able to do so already.

(5 minutes)

5 Teach greetings for different times of day using the textbook.

a) Put a time line on the board to make it easier for students to link the appropriate greeting to the appropriate time of day. Ask students to answer together to avoid any being anxious.

b) What would I say at: 9am, 8pm, midday, etc.?

(15 minutes)

c) Write up on the board the *hiragana* for each greeting and explain that there are three different scripts, this one being *hiragana*.

d) Write the word *hiragana* in *roomaji* and *hiragana* showing the syllabification. Discuss the sample of script on page 4 pointing out that words have been separated to help foreigners and that in the initial stages of learning Japanese they will only have to cope with this separated script.

e) Look at the sample of fully joined script and discuss.

6 Use photocopy of song to help students to understand the syllabification and the way *roomaji* matches *hiragana*.

TAPE

7 Sing the first verse of the song. Repeat two or three times until students can sing it easily.

TAPE

8 Show students the *hiragana* chart and go through the syllable sounds with the students repeating the sounds.

9 Play a game asking 'Who can find . . . '—looking for the *hiragana* syllables that you call out from the chart. (Try six or seven until you're sure students have got the idea of the sound being a syllable not just a letter.) Compliment with phrase *yoku dekimashita*.

10 Can the students find the syllables from the song sheet on the *hiragana* chart on page 6? Point out that gradually shapes become recognizable just as our alphabet became recognizable when they learned to read English and now it's no problem. One day Japanese will become that easy. The way to make it easy is to keep practicing every day, not to leave it for a grand effort before a test!

Point out that students are free to learn the whole chart if they want to get ahead but that they can take it gently through the course with the textbook if that seems too daunting.

(10 minutes)

11 Look at the *katakana* chart on page 7 and pick out syllables for own first names. Copy them onto the cover of notebooks carefully. Explain that the sounds are the same as *hiragana* even though the shapes differ and that they will learn *katakana* after they have mastered *hiragana*.

12 Tell students about the *kanji* and show them step by step how to write the *kanji* 'Nihongo' on the cover of their Japanese notebook.

Homework

Students may read over the information to page 9, draw beautiful title pages for this year's work, enter the greetings into their notebooks accurately, and learn them for next lesson.

Compliment them on the way they responded today. Reassure them that they will all be able to manage and that the course will take them step by step through what they have to know. Their only responsibility is to make sure that they keep up with learning vocabulary and go over what has been done in class after every lesson so they don't fall behind. Suggest that when they go home they use *tadaima* to tell their family they are home and *o yasumi nasai* before they go to bed.

Dismissal: With *tatte kudasai—sayonara* and a bow, eliciting *sayonara* from students as they file past.

Lesson Two (Japan: the country, page 10)

Aims and objectives

- To learn about Japan's position in the Pacific.
- To learn names of some of Japan's largest cities and islands.
- To practice the sounds of Japanese.
- To learn to write *ni ho n* in *hiragana*.

Today's work will help to establish listening to and repetition of sounds, pairwork activities and accuracy.

Preparation

Blank maps of Japan.
Blank maps of Japan's position in the Pacific.
Something new in the classroom (see Introduction).
TAPE Music.

Introduction

TAPE.
Japanese music for entry. What is different about the room since last lesson? (Have a different picture up or the *hiragana* versions of the greetings to get students aware that the wall space is part of their learning area too and should be checked every day for new information.)

TAPE
(5 minutes)
Greet. Sing song learned last lesson to reinforce sounds and syllables. Teach another verse.

(5 minutes)
Any questions from students about last lesson?

100kms

Japan's position in the Pacific

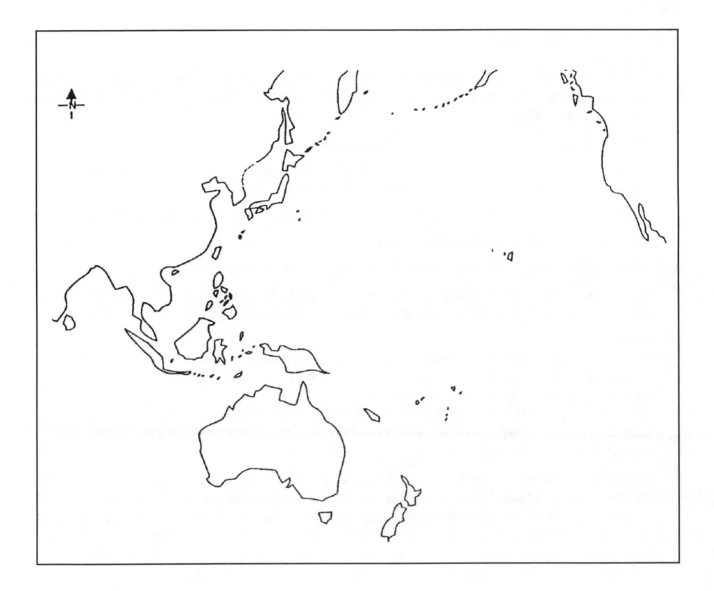

Check learning of greetings and homework. Show good examples.

Tell them that today you will play a guessing game first. Turn to page 10 in books. Give out blank maps of Japan.
Benkyoo shimashoo!

Main theme

(Listening and recognition exercises)

(10 minutes)

1 Find the name of the place I call out by looking at the map in your textbook on page 10. Write the name in pencil on your blank map in the correct position. Work quickly and be ready for the next name called.

Teacher: I'm thinking of a place that begins with *sa*.

(Students quickly find Sapporo on map in textbook, check its position and enter it on blank map. Go on quickly to make them concentrate and work fast but not so fast that they give up!)

to *(Tookyoo)*, hi *(Hiroshima)*, ki *(Kyooto)*, naga *(Nagasaki)*, oo *(Oosaka)*, na *(Nara)*

I'm thinking of an island that begins with:

shi *(Shikoku)*, kyuu *(Kyuushuu)*, hon *(Honshuu)*, ho *(Hokkaidoo)*

Check and compliment. (Get students to read out the place names to you. Help with pronunciation where necessary. For example, in *Sapporo* note the double *p* needs time for each letter.

(5 minutes)

2 Give out maps of Japan's position in the Pacific saying *doozo* as you hand each paper over. Now let's try countries:
I'm thinking of a country that begins with:
RO *(ROSHIA)*, KANA *(KANADA)*, OO *(OOSUTORARIA)*, chuu *(Chuugoku)*, ka *(Kankoku)*, A *(AMERIKA)*, NYUUGI *(NYUUGINIA)*, TO *(TONGA)*, FI *(FIJIi)*, NYU *(NYUUJIIRANDO)*, SA *(SAMOA)*, IN *(INDONESHIA)*.

Check and comment on the closeness and yet difference in the *katakana* names. Point out the countries written in *katakana* and explain that in their course *katakana* words are always written in capital letters to help them to know which syllabary to use when writing them. Explain why Korea and China are in *hiragana* (early contact with Japan—other countries only at most 400 years and *foreign* to Japanese thinking, therefore not appropriate to write in *hiragana*) Remind students of the need for accuracy in spelling Japanese words.

(5 minutes)

3 Play guessing game asking: What do we call... e.g.: *FIRIPPIN*?
Go over pronunciation of all the names encountered. Compliment with *yoku dekimashita*.

(5 minutes)

4 Pairwork: Student One writes name of place secretly.
Student Two tries to guess name written by giving initial syllable, e.g.: *sa* or whole place name. May have 5 guesses. If not successful first student has a second go.

If successful writes a word for Student One.
Allow three turns to see who is the winner out of three.

(5 minutes)

5 TAPE. Look again at the *hiragana* chart. Listen to sounds and read through sounds together to reinforce short sounds of vowels: *i* as in pig, not *i* as in mine, etc.

(5 minutes)

6 Writing practice *ni ho n* from book pages 14-15.

7 Conclude with quick check on information gathered this lesson (Activities page 12 as time permits).

Homework

Each student to find as much information about Japan as possible from pages 12–13 and list in notebooks neatly. Enter new words in vocabulary notebook. Learn words in vocabulary list on page 16, List One. Stick maps completed in class neatly into book.

Lesson Three (Unit 1, page 18)

Aims and objectives

- To teach the students how to introduce themselves simply.

- To consolidate sound patterns and recognition of syllables.

- To teach the students some conversation openers.
  Students will reinforce listening and responding and pair work rules.

Preparation

New item in classroom or something missing.
Map of Japan with places introduced last lesson, boldly labeled in *hiragana* and *roomaji*.
Two puppet figures photocopied for roleplay.
TAPE Music

Introduction

(Your entry pattern will by now be well established. Today a dismissal strategy may be introduced.)

Main theme

(2-3 minutes)

1 Introduce as much vocabulary as possible by demonstration with students watching intently.

Encourage to watch by miming and saying *mite kudasai, kiite kudasai*. Don't explain these phrases, just allow them to gradually be absorbed and added to the students' list of instructions.

2 Introduce self again showing word *desu* on the board with the *u* crossed through to show that it isn't pronounced.

a) Go around the class introducing yourself to two or three students,

e.g.: BURAUN desu. Sensei desu.

b) Ask some students names as you go round class with name + *san* + *desu ka* and hoping to elicit a nod at least!
Tell other students names of students from above activity with . . . *san desu.*

c) Elicit the pattern from the students for asking names and giving names.

d) Draw 2 stick people on the board and a time, (name them with . . . *san*) and review the greetings by asking what students think they are saying to each other. Draw several examples eliciting information from the class.

(10 minutes)

3 Explain that person one is meeting 2 after a long time and act out what he is saying. Get students to suggest what he would be likely to say in that situation. Write the phrase *Ohisashiburi desu ne* on the board and practice the pronunciation together. Find out what students would be likely to say in English as the next part of the conversation and lead students to 'How are you?' if it doesn't immediately come.
Act out the greeting *Ohisashiburi desu ne* and add on *Ogenki desu ka*. Elicit the phrase from the students. How many can say it correctly from just one hearing? Compliment with *Yoku dekimashita.*

(5-7 minutes)

4 TAPE. Open text books and study the dialogue together. Listen to tape or model the reading to demonstrate sounds and explain the honorific *O*. Get students to practice the conversation (page 18) in pairs. Move around room to gently correct pronunciation errors.

5 Have a quick quiz to see who can remember the phrases without looking at the book.
Comment on use of *Ogenki desu ka* only being used if you know someone has been ill or after a long gap in contact—not used like 'How are you?' in English.

(10 minutes) page 19

6 Teach new phrase by eliciting from students the usual reply in English. ('Thank you for asking, I'm fine') *Okage sama de genki desu.*
Write on board and then in pairs practice again.
(Firmly establish pairwork rules. Work sensibly together to give each other maximum communication possibility but stop after once through/twice through etc. as requested by teacher, and wait and listen until all have finished.
Point out that there are two separate situations in greeting people—people you know and strangers. If your students are shy, give them cutouts of people to 'puppet play' the conversations. This takes the pressure out of the situation for the students and they can focus on the puppet instead of on their own embarrassment. Others may be happy to get up and act out the scenes and show them off to others in another part of the room. This will help to introduce the idea of moving from a seat and returning, without disruption to others, after completing a task.)

7 Do exercise on page 20 orally with partner. Check through with whole class.

(5 minutes)

8 Check on last lesson's homework. Ask for homework information from last lesson. Students tick off on own notes information given. If they have more they may offer it and see who has the longest list of relevant information.

(3-4 minutes)

9 Could anyone get up and meet someone, speaking in Japanese, without looking at books? If someone volunteers, let him/her act out a meeting in front of the class to consolidate lesson and get others listening. Say *mite kudasai, kiite kudasai* to get class ready to watch.

Homework

Exercise on page 20 as a written exercise.
New phrases to learn and record in notebooks. Read over textbook to page 20.

Dismissal: Dismiss students by calling out *hiragana* syllables. If their name begins with the syllable called they may leave, saying *sayonara* as they go.

Lesson Four (page 21)

Aims and Objectives

- To teach verb *desu* and negative *dewa arimasen.*
- To teach sentence patterns: *nan desu ka, ... desu ka, ... desu, ... dewa arimasen.*
- Agreeing and disagreeing.
- To introduce vocabulary by demonstration and Japanese word rather than by translation.

Preparation

Something different in classroom. As many as possible of the following realia: Flowers on desk, book, pencil, umbrella, apple, bag, toy car, cat, dog, and picture of a mountain. (Or draw items on board quickly without labels.) (Hide realia in bag or cupboard.)
Tape Music
Large writing: verse three of song for end of lesson and *ni ho n* written in *hiragana.*

Introduction

TAPE
(2-3 minutes)
Greet and use instructions in Japanese already learned.
When students are seated put up the date and say it aloud as you go without translating. (Year, month, date, day)
TAPE Sing song ending with *benkyoo shimashoo.*

Main theme

(5-7 minutes)

1 Bring objects out of a bag or from hidden store as if you are a conjuror. Ask yourself in a puzzled way as you feel the object before bringing it out *nan desu ka*. Give the answer with a flourish. Ask students *nan desu ka* and elicit the response (remembered from your introduction of the word).

(5-7 minutes)

2 After all the new vocabulary has been mentioned draw it on the board and without explaining say, e.g.: *neko desu. Nan desu ka.* Elicit response. The stranger your drawing, the funnier students will find it and the easier it will be for them to remember.

Write the words up on the board in *roomaji* and *hiragana* or *katakana*. (Students are not expected to read the Japanese script but many may like to try to copy it later, and it's part of the recognition and assimilation of *kana* training.)

(5 minutes)

3 Negatives: Show flower and say *neko dewa arimasen, hon dewa arimasen,* etc. while shaking your head. Light up your voice and your affirmative reaction when you ask them *nan desu ka* and get their answer.

Ask them, holding up, e.g.: an umbrella, *hana desu ka* and elicit *hana dewa arimasen, kasa desu.*

(5 minutes)

4 Clean board. Open books at page 21 and cover the vocabulary list with a note book. Explain *desu* and *dewa arimasen* giving examples in English for negatives as some students may not be sure what is meant by the term.

In pairs looking at illustrations, students ask each other *Nan desu ka, Inu desu ka,* etc. keeping a score of the ones they know and the ones they don't.

(5 minutes)

5 Activity 1, page 22.

In pairs Student One asks about seven items and Student Two asks eight looking at the vocabulary list if necessary to be sure that they can match all the pictures with the correct word.

(5-10 minutes)

6 In pairs do Activity 2. Remind about rules for pairwork. Encourage to do it without looking up any words. Volunteers may like to act it out for the class.

(10 minutes)

7 Check on last lesson homework by having a mini quiz. Each student thinks of a question to ask the class about something contained in the homework set, e.g.: Vocabulary items or cultural/factual information. If they ask a question already asked they are 'out' and come to the front. Remind of *ni ho n hiragana.*

(5 minutes)

8 TAPE

Sing song adding on last verse with *asobimashoo.*

---

nan desu ka

A   B   C   D   E

F   G   H   I   J

K   L   M   N   O

Dare desu ka

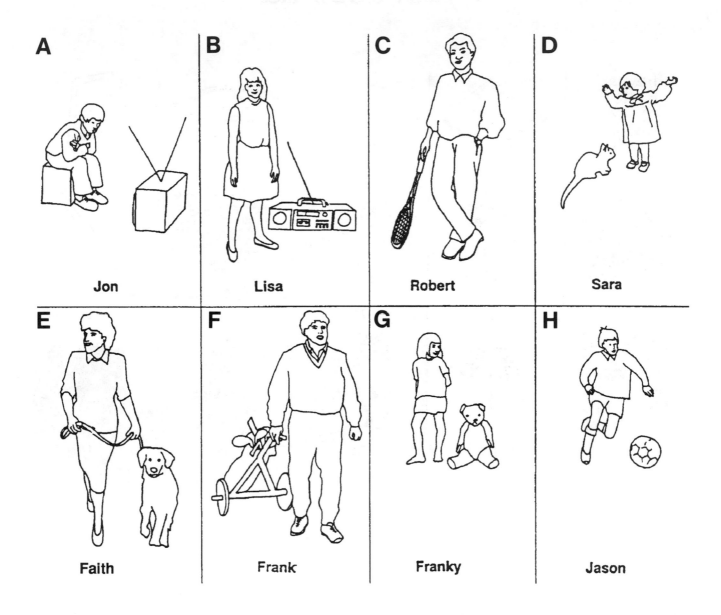

A Jon

B Lisa

C Robert

D Sara

E Faith

F Frank

G Franky

H Jason

Homework

Find magazine photos of famous people (local or international). Cut out and bring to school for next lesson. Write (in *roomaji*) a conversation similar to the one practiced in class. Read over textbook up to page 22.

Dismissal: Around class with students giving their name and *desu* as they file out.

Lesson Five (page 22)

Aims and objectives

- To teach *dare desu ka*.
- To answer in the affirmative and the negative.
- To be able to find a particular person.
- Review simple introductions and greetings.

Preparation

TAPE Music

Pictures of famous/well known people.

Put up one or two pictures of well known people on the wall or board with a big question mark beside them. Have bold labels ready with the target question *dare desu ka* and names followed by *san* and *desu*.

Take in an apple and a knife if possible. Hide away.

Blank strips of paper to write names + *san* + *desu* on.

Photocopy *Nan desu ka* sheet (covered with plastic they last a long time and save future photocopy costs).

Blank cards and one with *Jiroo* written on it for activity page 23.

Group desks in fours if possible.

Introduction

TAPE Music. Greetings and instructions as usual. Write up date.

Main theme

(5 minutes)

1 Show students pictures on wall or board and ask *dare desu ka* (Name of student in class) *desu ka*. Students should pick up the meaning and answer Mary *san dewa arimasen* with a bit of prompting! Ask again (several names) and then elicit the correct answer. Get students to ask you the question as you point to the pictures and answer them.

Demonstrate *hai* and *iie*. Practice pronunciation of *i i e*.

(5 minutes)

2 Activity. Pairwork
Use *nan desu ka* sheet to practice words learned previously

(10 minutes)

3 Written test on vocabulary introduced: *hana, ringo, hon, inu, neko, enpitsu, kasa, uchi. Ohayoo gozaimasu, konnichi wa, konban wa, O yasumi nasai, tadaima, san, sensei, kaban, kuruma, nihon, nihongo, ki, yama, nan desu ka, desu, dewa arimasen.*
Quickly check 2 marks possible—one for word and one for spelling accuracy. Score out of 50. Ask winner to answer SKILL(!) question to get the prize. Show class apple. Ask: *nan desu ka, (ringo desu).* Reward with apple or cut apple in portions if more than one winner. Hand over and compliment with *yoku dekimashita.* If some have scored poorly remind that keeping vocabulary learning up to date is essential for feeling good about the subject. Remind them to spend time getting it all up to date before next lesson.

(10 minutes)

4 Point out that with things we ask—*nan desu ka* and with people—*dare desu ka.* Quickly ask questions about known objects pointing to pictures in book or students in the class to establish.

5 Ask for pictures collected as homework from last lesson to be put on desks. Class is already sitting in groups of approximately four. Ask them to show their pictures to each other saying *dare desu ka,* answering *hai* or *iie* and telling correct name if it's not guessed. As they finish, they write labels for each picture . . . *san desu,* and keep for later to put on wall.

6 Groups challenge each other to identify the collected pictures of their group taking it in turns to ask *dare desu ka.* Give in finished pictures and labels and also unlabeled pictures.

(5 minutes)

7 Pairwork. Study dialogue page 23 in book. Check that understanding is clear. Move around class listening to reading—correcting pronunciation, answering questions.

8 Look for *Jiroo.* Activity 2, page 23.

Homework

Draw pictures of 10 or more items from the vocabulary lists of all the lessons so far and write a sentence under each saying . . . *desu,* . . . *dewa arimasen.*
Draw a person and write underneath: *dare desu ka ... san desu.* Encourage to write in pencil and to copy the *hiragana* if they wish from the textbook. Read over textbook to page 23.

Dismissal: Each student gives the name of an object in Japanese as they file out in order, must not be the same as the person in front. + *Sayonara.*

Lesson Six (page 24)

Aims and objectives

- To boost confidence in using the material learned so far.
- To add the ability to say *excuse me*.
- To identify people at a distance from the speaker.
- To learn to write *a na ta* and *no* in *hiragana*.

Preparation

Put up on wall the pictures of people with labels prepared by students last lesson and unlabeled pictures with *dare desu ka* label.
Textbooks.
TAPE

Introduction

TAPE Music. Greet as usual, put up today's date while students listen.
Ask three or four students to come to the front of the class and stand in a group using *(JON)san, koko ni kite kudasai* and Japanese hand movement—hand held in front of right shoulder, move fingers up and down, palm still. This is the Japanese hand movement for 'come here' and will amuse the students as it's so much like waving goodbye to most of them. Choose students who have appeared reasonably confident in previous lessons. Ask class to *mite kudasai, kiite kudasai* miming actions.

Main theme

(5 minutes)

1 Go up to one of the selected students and say *sumimasen ga (JON) san desu ka*. Student should be able to answer *hai*.Tell class *(JON) san desu, (JON) san, koko ni kite kudasai*, and take him/her to the other side of the class. When there, ask him/her *sumimasen ga ano hito wa dare desu ka*, pointing with whole hand to the other two people. He/she may be able to reply, if he/she doesn't immediately, prompt him with *ano hito wa (AN) san desu ka* etc.
Say *arigatoo gozaimasu* to the three and ask them to *suwatte kudasai*.

(2-3 minutes)

2 Go round class asking *Sumimasen ga ano hito wa dare desu ka* of people at a distance from both of you and getting the reply from several students (and using pictures on wall as well). *Ano hito wa (Natalie) desu.*

(2-3 minutes)

3 Pairwork. Write the pattern on the board (Question and Answer) and ask them to practice with each other finding out the names of five people or five unlabeled pictures each and pointing with whole hand to identify the person they mean.

(5 minutes)
4 TAPE. Listen to dialogue, page 24 (or teacher models) and practice pronunciation with tape.

(2-3 minutes)
5 Check that everyone understands. Open textbooks. Pairwork
Get students to read the same dialogue in pairs.

(2-3 minutes)
6 TAPE Listen to the next dialogues and see how much is understood without any review.

(5 minutes)
7 Reading Practice 1. Students practice in pairs (Encourage students to stand up and act it out—everyone doing the practice at the same time but as soon as they finish going to sit down. Move around room listening and picking up common mispronunciations.)

(5 minutes)
8 When all are sitting down again go over the poorly pronounced words briefly.

9 TAPE. Listen and then practice all together number 2.

(5 minutes)
10 Cover the English translation and get the students to do the 'Check your understanding' either as a written or oral exercise.

(2-3 minutes)
11 TAPE. Put on the tape and listen to the conversation on the tape. How many understand everything?

12 Writing practice. Review *ni ho n* then go over *a na ta no,* page 27.

13 Check last lesson's homework has been done. Pick out one or two good examples to show the class and compliment.

Homework

Second activity page 26 as a written exercise. Learn new vocabulary and go over previous vocabulary for test next lesson. Learn new *hiragana.* Start to prepare a conversation with a friend to do in front of a small group next lesson.

Exercise (page 28)

Answers

a: 2	f: 1
b: 5	g: 4
c: 1, 2, 3	h: 2, 4
d: 2, 3	i: 2
e: 2, 4	j: 1, 2, 3

Lesson Seven (an evaluation lesson)

Aims and objectives

- To test the students' retention and understanding of material learned.
- To introduce to formal listening comprehension.
- To introduce role playing in front of a small group of students.
- Students learn to evaluate own progress.

Preparation

TAPE
Vocabulary lists page 29
Write on board before tape listening comprehension (page 25)
- What time of day did the people meet?
- Did they meet yesterday?
- Are the people feeling ill or well?
- Name the people involved in the conversation?

Introduction

TAPE Music. Greet, put date on board. Quickly check last lesson's homework

Evaluation

(20-25 minutes)

1 Put up *TESUTO*.
Ask students to open notebooks, copy the date, and write *TESUTO*.
TAPE. Ask students to listen to the tape and find the answers to the questions on the board (the tape gives conversation from page 25).
Self check answers from page 25 as they listen again to the tape. Total marks?

2 Students test each other on vocabulary from page 29.

(15 minutes)

3 Students have five minutes ONLY to prepare conversation with a friend (begun yesterday) (page 27). They should be ready to show it to a small group without recourse to books in five minutes. Move round and note pairs as they work. As three or four groups will be working at once they should not be too shy as they are not having everyone's attention upon them. If they are, allow them to sit down to talk to each other. Patience pays dividends.
They are not being 'marked', but it will give you the opportunity to see the level of participation and general pronunciation and fluency.

4 Invite one pair to volunteer to act out their play for the whole class. Tell class you will ask questions afterwards so *yoku kiite kudasai* Listen well! (Strategies for ensuring that students genuinely listen to each other and don't switch off are very important.) Ask class questions

afterwards in English (or some Japanese if the particular conversation allows for it) to establish level of understanding and compliment this group particularly and class in general for the way they have worked if appropriate.

Homework

Look for pictures of animals from magazines and newspapers, cut out and bring next lesson. No other homework today unless score on test was below 50%, in which case words and structures must be learned.

Dismissal: Read the *hiragana* as they file past. Hold up the syllables they should know: *ni ho n* asking each student one or two randomly.

Topic One Vocabulary Cards

genki desu	san	hon	ringo	ushi
doomo arigatoo gozaimasu	Okage sama de	hana	neko	usagi
dewa arimasen	Ogenki desu ka	enpitsu	kuruma	uma
desu	Ohisashiburi desu ne	denwa	ki	O namae wa nan desu ka
dare	nan desu ka	sumimasen ga	kasa	Watashi no namae wa Jo desu
ano	minasan	sensei	kaban	yama
anata	ka	seito	inu	uchi

hako	iie	KANADA	ORANDA	watashi
enpitsu	hai	ja mata	OOSUTORARIA	wa
e	FURANSU	ITARIA	hito	sayoonara
chizu	FIJII	INDO	jin	sayonara
BOORUPEN	DOITSU	IGIRISU	nin	SAMOA
juku	AMERIKA	HONKON	nanijin desa ka	ROSHIA
kootoogakkoo	isu	hajimemashite doozo yoroshiku	namae	PEN

tsukue	arigatoo gozaimasu	sore	kore o kudasai	chuugakkoo
PEN	jin	shinbun	doozo	shoogakkoo
NOOTO	NYUU JIIRANDO	manga	yonde kudasai	yoochien
kyooshitsu	namae	kore	kiite kudasai	kaite kudasai
kokuban	no	doko no kata desu ka	mite kudasai	zasshi
kami	watashi	dare	suwatte kudasai	dore
kaban	janai desu	ano	tatte kudasai	are

IGIRISU	KANADA	hitsuji	usagi	uma	KOARA	buta
Konnichi wa	Ohayoo gozaimasu	HONKON jin desu	NYUU JIIRANDOjin desu	FURANSUjin	DOITSUjin	AMERIKAjin
Nihonjin	Nihongo	Nihon	sensei	Tadaima	O yasumi nasai	Komban wa
Shikoku	Honshuu	Hokkaidoo	hiragana	katakana	kanji	Ojigi
TONGA	NYUU GINIA	TAIWAN	INDONESHIA	Chuugoku	Kankoku	Kyuushuu

Lesson Eight (Unit 2, page 31)

Aims and objectives

- To teach how to ask someone's name, how to give own name more formally.
- To introduce honorific *O*, particle *no* and particle *wa*.
- To teach how to express ownership.
- To review vocabulary learned previously.

Structure patterns

(A) wa . . . san desu.
O namae wa nan desu ka.
Watashi no namae wa . . . desu.
(A) san no namae wa . . . desu.
Watashi no inu desu.
Anata no inu desu ka.
Inu no namae wa . . . desu.
Watashi no desu.
Anata no desu.

Preparation

TAPE Music.
Photocopy dicomm sheets of people.
Photocopy object sheets.
Photocopy dicomm ownership sheets.
Have a name label with own name threaded on necklace string to wear.

Introduction

Music, Greet.

Main theme

(5 minutes)

1 Give out object sheets and ask class to name each one in chorus as you ask *(A) wa nan desu ka,* answering *(A) wa (inu) desu,* etc. to boost confidence and remind of vocabulary and pronunciation.
Ask if anyone can guess what *A wa* means. If so compliment and give your explanation that *A wa* means *talking about A,* in other words *A* is the topic of the conversation. Quickly take papers back in.

(2-3 minutes)

2 *Mite, kiite kudasai.* Hold label up and tell class, pointing to name—*namae desu, namae wa . . . desu.* Put on label and tell them *watashi no namae wa ... desu,* pointing to self with label.
Go around the class saying to several students as you stand by their desk *(Ohayoo gozaimasu) watashi no namae wa . . . . desu,* pointing to the label you are wearing.

Dare no desu ka

Find out who the following items belong to by asking other people in your group.

Question: *(Neko) wa dare no desu ka.*

Answer: *(Neko) wa (Ann) san no desu.*

pencil	Sue	dog	Natasha
			Sue
sunflower		cat	Nick
			Richard
telephone	Nick	umbrella	Chris
			Natasha
briefcase		apple	Chris
book	Richard	house	Jason

Dare no desu ka

Find out who the following items belong to by asking other people in your group.

Question: *(Neko) wa dare no desu ka.*

Answer: *(Neko) wa (Ann) san no desu.*

		Sue
Natasha	Chris	Nick
		Richard
		Natasha
Jason	Sue	
		Chris
	Jason	
		Jason

Dare no desu ka

Find out who the following items belong to by asking other people in your group.

Question: *(Neko) wa dare no desu ka.*

Answer: *(Neko) wa (Ann) san no desu.*

Dare no desu ka

Find out who the following items belong to by asking other people in your group.

Question: *(Neko) wa dare no desu ka.*

Answer: *(Neko) wa (Ann) san no desu.*

にあおう
ni a o u
Cat

ぶんぶん
bu n bu n
Bee

ぐえぐえ
gu e gu e
Frog

ひ ひ
hi hi
Horse

ぶ ぶ
bu bu
Pig

Ano hito no namae wa nan desu ka

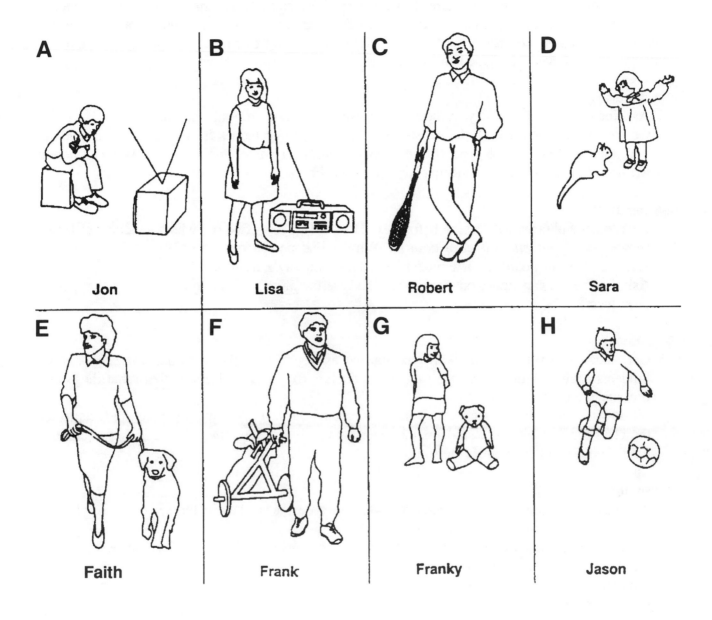

A	B	C	D
Jon	Lisa	Robert	Sara

E	F	G	H
Faith	Frank	Franky	Jason

(5 minutes)

Ask if anyone can say the phrase you have been using. What do they think it means? Why did you put *wa* after *namae*? What is different about the sentence from its English equivalent? (Word order). Comment on the fact that Japanese sentences always tell you what they are talking about before giving more information. How do they think *watashi no namae wa . . . desu* would be spelled?

Write it up on the board as they offer words one by one. Show them the *hiragana* beneath. Which of the *hiragana* syllables do they already know? Look carefully at *namae*. Go over pronunciation carefully to produce all syllables *na ma e*. Teach the students the rhythm of the phrase by pausing slightly after *watashi no namae wa* — (*. . . desu*) and telling them that the phrase is spoken as if all the words have been glued together.

(2-3 minutes)

3 Ask for volunteers to tell you their names using this more formal pattern.
   Go round class and ask *O namae wa nan desu ka* eliciting names from three or four students you think will be able to cope with the reply *watashi no namae wa . . . desu*. Write *O namae wa nan desu ka* on board and explain the honorific *O*.

(2-3 minutes)

4 Link today's phrases with lesson before test. How did students find out who someone was lesson before last? (*Ano hito wa dare desu ka,* Who is that person over there?)
   Write phrase on board as a reminder. Ask how you say *Excuse me . . . .*
   Ask if someone can figure out how to say 'Excuse me please..what is the NAME of that person over there?'

(5 minutes)

5 Get students to walk round room greeting and asking five people *O namae wa nan desu ka.* Students answer with full pattern *watashi no namae wa . . . desu.* Remind them that they don't use *san* after their own name.
   Sit down in silence as soon as they have completed the task. Ask two or three students to tell the class the names of the students they met with *Ano hito no namae wa . . . . desu* (pointing with whole hand to identify person)

(5 minutes)

6 Ask students if anyone has worked out what purpose the *no* has in the sentence. Explain its use.
   page 32 (belonging to): Do some examples together using realia if possible on desks,
   e.g.: *Kaban wa anata no desu ka.*
   Enpitsu wa watashi no desu.
   Watashi no hon desu.
   Enpitsu wa dare no desu ka.

(5 minutes)

7 Pairwork. Give out dicomm. Explain that the information missing on their sheet may be found by asking their partner to supply it. Explain the need to hide papers efficiently from partners. Write lightly in pencil so that sheets may be used again for other purposes. Explain that talking

about picture (A's) name they'll be asking *A san no namae wa nan desu ka* and the answer will be *A san no namae wa . . . desu.* Check by comparing sheets. Gently erase answers. Write patterns on the board in *roomaji*. Give in cleaned dicomm sheets. Ask if anyone can work out how you would ask the name of a cat (*neko no namae wa nan desu ka*). Compliment or teach necessary phrase.

8 Choose an activity from page 32,

    OR

Give out second dicomm which gives objects and owners. Remind of rules for dicomms.

Q: *(Hon) wa dare no desu ka* A: *JONsan no hon desu.*

(Students will use the sheets to write full sentences for homework with the collated information)

9 Do exercise together page 33.

Homework

Write sentences in Japanese *roomaji* (or copying words in *hiragana* from text) from the dicomm or 10 sentences similar to the ones practiced above. Read text book over up to page 33.

Dismissal: each person gives his/her name with *watashi no namae wa . . . desu* and *sayonara.* They may like to add *arigatoo gozaimasu* if they have enjoyed the lesson.

Lesson Nine (page 33)

Aims and objectives

- To teach how to ask for names of animals and objects in Japanese.
- To consolidate patterns and vocabulary already taught.
- To boost confidence and reinforce pair and group work rules.

Preparation

TAPE.

Desks in groups of four if possible.

Animal noise sheet to cut up and stick on pictures of animals as lesson progresses.

Pictures of animals collected from students last lesson.

Put up a few pictures on the wall with label *Nihongo no namae wa nan desu ka* and some with *Namae wa nan desu ka* alongside your pictures of people from the other day.

Have labels of species name prepared for other animals in your collection—one for each kind of animal.

Object sheets used previously.

Introduction

TAPE. Animal noises in Japanese.

Greet.

Listen again to tape and point to animal pictures on wall if appropriate as noises are made.

Main theme

(5-7 minutes)

1 Introduce (tape) listening comprehension. TAPE or teacher: Listen to (tape) conversation (it is read twice). After it has been read twice you will be asked to answer five questions. So *Yoku kiite kudasai.*

Ken and Mariko met outside the park as Mariko was walking towards a waiting friend.

Mariko	*Kensan, konnichi wa. Ohisashiburi desu ne! Ogenki desu ka.*
Ken	*Okage sama de genki desu. Anata wa?*
Mariko	*Genki desu. Arigatoo gozaimasu.*
Ken	*Anata no inu desu ka.*
Mariko	*Hai. Watashi no desu.*
Ken	*Inu no namae wa nan desu ka.*
Mariko	*Kipi desu.*
Ken	*Soo desu ka . . . Sumimasen ga, ano hito wa dare desu ka.*
Mariko	*Haruko san desu.*
Ken	*Arigatoo gozaimasu.*

Students listen. No books open. Students open note books and write in date as you put it up on the board (reading it aloud as you do it). Students number 1-5 down page. Students quickly write answers during second reading. Give a moment or two after (tape) reading stops for students to check work. Quickly write on board during first reading:

a) What three things did Ken want to know?
   (If Mariko was well, The name of her dog, The name of a person he saw waiting a little way away)

b) What was the name of Mariko's dog?
   (Kipi)

c) What was the name of Mariko's waiting friend?
   (Haruko)

(10 minutes)

2 Show the pictures of animals to the class and give the Japanese name (If you have no pictures use the textbook). Get students to repeat. Make a game of it, testing their memories on three at a time and getting them to give the name and the noise Japanese–style. Gradually stick up on the wall the labels made in your preparation to one example of each animal for reference. Explain that some are written in *katakana* because they were not known to the Japanese long ago.

Names

JON san no neko — FLUFFY

PETER san no inu

MIRIAM san no usagi

KIT san no KANGARUU — JUMP

SCOTT san no uma — CANDY

ELIZA san no sakana

MARK san no hitsuji

AMY san no usagi — BOB

KELLY san no inu — SKIP

ROB san no uma

TERI san no hitsuji

COL san no neko — PICKY

JON san no neko

PETER san no inu · REX

MIRIAM san no usagi · TWITCH

KIT san no KANGARUU

SCOTT san no uma

ELIZA san no sakana · BLIP

MARK san no hitsuji · BAA

AMY san no usagi

KELLY san no inu

ROB san no uma · TROT

TERI san no hitsuji · CURLY

COL san no neko

Names

Fill in your own suggestions for names and then ask each other in Japanese what names were given.

JON san no neko

MIRIAM san no usagi

SCOTT san no uma

MARK san no hitsuji

KELLY san no inu

TERI san no hitsuji

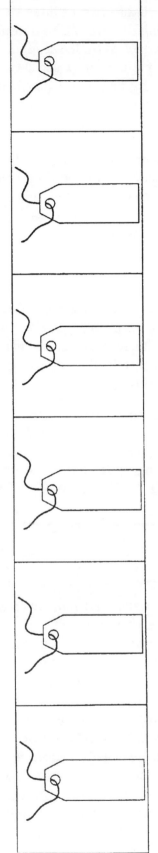

---

3 Give out pictures to original owners saying (*inu wa dare no desu ka*). After demonstrating two or three choose two or three students to join you going round the room holding up the pictures and asking . . . *wa dare no desu ka* OR *anata no (neko) desu ka*, eliciting replies (*Watashi no desu/Watashi no (neko) desu*) until all pictures have been returned to owners. Students who forgot to bring pictures may use those in the textbook. Handing over pictures say *doozo*, and elicit *arigatoo*, or they don't get their picture back!

Ask students to write a suitable given name for each animal on the back of the picture.

(3 minutes)

4 Show them your pictures and tell them the names . . . *uma no namae wa . . . desu*. Explain that in asking a question the honorific *O* is not used for animals or objects except in very very polite language for a few items. Ask students to tell you how they would say 'Japanese name' (*nihongo no namae*) and teach phrase *nihongo no namae wa nan desu ka*, reminding them about the functions of *no* and *wa*.

(4-5 minutes)

5 Pairwork. (While students are working, pin up animal noises sheet where students can see it easily.) Students show their pictures to each other in turn and tell what animal it is with *nihongo no namae wa (uma) desu* etc. After that information, the partner asks the given name of the animal with *uma no namae wa nan desu ka*. Answer *uma no namae wa . . . desu*. The same student then tells the name of one of his/her animals and Student One asks the given name etc.

OR

Dicomm sheets for students who can cope with an extension:
Question: *(JON) san no neko no namae wa nan desu ka*.
Answer: *(JON) san no neko no namae wa . . . desu*.
Explain that it is possible to have two *no* in one sentence and that you are saying 'the name belonging to the cat belonging to Jon'.

(10 minutes)

6 Group work (two options depending on the sort of class you have). Move around room listening and gently correcting structures and pronunciation as you go, during the next activity.

Groups of four or five put all their pictures face up into the center of the group. Students need to watch, listen and remember very carefully as the information they gain will be needed in a later stage of the activity.

Each in turn picks up a picture and asks *uma wa dare no desu ka*.
Owner answers *watashi no desu*.
Variation: Questioner asks *anata no uma desu ka*, showing a picture to a particular student who can reply *watashi no dewa arimasen or Hai watashi no desu*.

All pictures are then put back in the center of the group and students try to remember to whom each picture belongs. If they can say *Mary san no desu* or *Mary san no uma desu*, or even claim back their own with *watashi no desu*. If no one else has claimed it before and it is correct they win the picture temporarily. To collect it they must make the Japanese noise for that animal. The winner is the one who collects most.

Pictures then collected back to be put on the wall with labels, or to be stuck into students' books with sentences underneath.

OR

Students read the dialogue on page 34 in threes and try to learn it by heart.

(10 minutes)

7 Make sentences together as shown on page 36 using the object sheets for refreshment of vocabulary, making up names of owners of objects as you go, e.g.: *Mary san no uma desu* or *uma wa Mary san no desu.* Collect object sheets.

Homework

Make ten sentences similar to examples on page 36 OR Activity 1 and 3 on page 36. Students review names of countries from the map on page 11. Review *hiragana* syllables learned so far—*ni ho n a na ta no.* Learn new vocabulary from page 33. Read textbook up to Page 35.

Dismissal: Play tape of animal noises. If students give correct Japanese name of animal they may go!

Lesson Ten (Unit 3, page 37)

Aims and objectives

- To teach students how to introduce themselves to strangers formally.

- To teach students how to ask for and give nationality.

Preparation

TAPE.
Pictures of people already on wall.
Nationality sheets (cut one up for own use).
Blue tack or tape to stick nationalities to large map.
Large map of world (or point to map page 11).
Class list for each student.

Introduction

(2-3 minutes)
TAPE
Greet.
Ask students how many have had to introduce themselves to strangers at some time. Discuss briefly the differing levels of formality. Remind that they know two ways of introducing themselves . . . . *desu,* and *watashi no namae wa . . . desu.*

Main theme

(5-7 minutes)

1 a) Listen to Tape of dialogue.

   b) Open books and read along with the tape. Practice the new phrases. Quickly read through information in textbook pages 37–38.

(10 minutes)

2 Pairwork. Do Activity 1.

(5 minutes)

3 In pairs do 'Check your understanding' page 39.

(3-5 minutes)

4 Ask students 'AMERICA' *wa nihongo no namae wa nan desu ka,* etc. Have a quick fun quiz on how many countries they can remember. Japanese to English/English to Japanese.

(5 minutes)

Pointing to countries on the map, ask students to supply the names. As they give them, put up the picture of a person from the nationality sheet saying: *Doko no kata desu ka . . .* and supplying the answer *AMERIKAjin desu* etc. while sticking the label on the appropriate country.
Go through the countries corresponding to your labels. Ask students what they think you mean by *doko no kata desu ka* and *(AMERIKA)jin desu.*

If necessary explain. Teach *doko no kata* as 'a person belonging to where', and explain that sometimes it's not possible to translate literally from one language to another, that some phrases just have to be understood. Teach *doko no kata desu ka/nanijin desu ka.*

5 Pairwork. One student opens textbook at page 1, the other at pages 39-40. Do the first three activities on pages 40-41. Suggest meeting three different people and then sitting down.

OR

Do activity 4 writing a conversation.

OR

Students take out notebooks and write date as you put it on the board and title *Doko no kata desu ka.* They then go around the room and do a survey on the nationalities within the class, writing information against class list as they go, in pencil (If preferred, they can ask for family nationality rather than the students' nationality to get a bit of variety). This survey can then be stuck or transferred into books in sentence form: *(Kim) san wa AMERIKAjin desu* etc. or a poster made with the information gathered. (It's important that students see an end product/a purpose in what they are asked to do.)

OR

Group work, page 42.

6 Tape. Students read silently as tape plays (sentences on page 43) and try to understand. Each student then matches the sentences.

Homework

Read over textbook to page 43. Do exercise on pages 43–44.
Dismissal: Each student gives own nationality or family nationality and leaves.

Names and Nationalities (A)

I have to meet two visitors at school today, but I've forgotten their names.
Please help me to work out who they are!
Find out the nationality, then answer the question (ask in any order to fill your blanks)
Question: (Sue) *san wa doko no kata desu ka*
Answer: (Sue) *san wa (. . .) jin desu*
My visitor is Chinese.

KANADA Sue	Frances	OOSUTORARIA Michelle
AMERIKA Jill	Berwick	MEKISHIKO Paul
Maria	PANAMA Delcia	Robert
Richard	Pamela	ITARIA Julio

Names and Nationalities (B)

I have to meet two visitors at school today, but I've forgotten their names.
Please help me to work out who they are!
Find out the nationality, then answer the question (ask in any order to fill your blanks)
Question: (Sue) *san wa doko no kata desu ka*
Answer: (Sue) *san wa (. . .) jin desu*
My visitor is German.

Sue	HONKON Frances	Michelle
Jill	IGIRISU Berwick	Paul
DOITSU Maria	Delcia	FURANSU Robert
NYUU JIIRANDO Richard	INDO Pamela	Julio

Lesson Eleven (page 44)

Aims and objectives

- To introduce the use of name cards in introductions.
- To consolidate material learned previously.
- To build confidence in participating.
- To become familiar with some Japanese names.
- To have more listening practice.
- To learn *hiragana wa shi e ma.*

Preparation

TAPE.
Photocopy on thin card 2 sets or as required page 46.
Photocopy on thin card 2 sets page 47.
Make sure all *hiragana* syllables students have learned are displayed on the wall.
Change around or relabel some of the existing wall decoration to vary the environment.

Introduction

TAPE. Greet and put up date.

Main Theme

(5 minutes)

1 Talk about the derivation of Japanese names page 44.
TAPE. Students listen as the name cards are read through on the tape or as teacher reads them out in random order, and look at textbook page 46 and 47 to identify—pointing quickly with finger to each one called.
Remind of phrase *hajimemashite doozo yoroshiku,* to use when meeting someone for the first time.

(5 minutes)

2 Pile of name cards is put face down in the middle of each group. Each student picks up a card and introduces self with *hajimemashite doozo yoroshiku* and giving the name on the card. (Students must stand to do this so they can bow properly.)

(2-3 minutes)

3 Each student now has a name card to use. Show students how to exchange cards—handing card with right hand (explain that Japanese people are trained from babyhood to be right-handed), bowing, and receiving with two hands, looking carefully and seriously at the card, checking pronunciation of the name and company and then putting it securely away in a wallet to show that you are treating it with respect. The way the card is treated will symbolize the way you are likely to treat the relationship. If people are careless with the card they are unlikely to be offered a continuation of contact. (Very important for business people to know.)

(5-7 minutes)

4 TAPE. Students listen to tape and put up hands or stand as their Japanese name is given.

5 Each student then goes around class and by asking *O namae wa nan desu ka,* finds the person/people of the same name and groups together with them at front of class. Which is first group to find each other? Depending on size of class they may only be looking for one person or may have 3-4 to find.

OR

Sit in circle or take turns round class to ask names. Activity 2 page 4. Group together when partners found.

(5 minutes)

6 Give out nationality cards Activity 3 page 45. Put them out face up on the table in the middle of each group.

(5 minutes)

7 Writing practice

8 Round up time. Brainstorm information,

OR

Have a vocabulary game. Activities page 49,

OR

Make up a quiz in small groups to test the rest of the class.

Homework

Each student makes up ten questions to ask class, page 49, writes them on paper and cuts them into separate strips. Checked, accurate answers should be written in different color pen on the back of each question.

Read over textbook to page 47.

Learn the new *hiragana* and write the list of *hiragana* words known in *hiragana* books.

TOPIC TWO
Lesson Twelve (In the classroom, page 51)

Aims and Objectives
- To introduce the Japanese school system.
- To teach how to absorb information from pictures and text.
- To teach some strategies for learning new words.
- To explain the need for learning cultural background.
- To consolidate cultural background learned previously.

Preparation
TAPE.

Clear previously used pictures and labels from the walls and keep for future use in a file for Topic One.

Labels of school levels in *roomaji* and *hiragana* put up as a time line (*juku* could be put up alongside a drawn clock to show that it is after school).

3-4 boxes or containers to put quiz questions in.

Introduction
TAPE: A school song.

Greet.

Explain that the quiz for which they have prepared questions will take place in the second half of the lesson. In notebooks write date and 'The Japanese school system'.

Main theme

(5 minutes)

1 Students study pictures on walls and in books. Have students list all the items of information they can find without reading the text. Who can make the longest list in two minutes? (Uniforms, caps, school bags, black hair, teacher's attitude, out-of-school trips, kindergarten, primary school, school photos, classroom desks, art room, etc.) Brainstorm the information onto the board.

(5 minutes)

2 Ask the students: 'Who can work out what *yoochien* probably means? *Shoogakkoo? Chuugakkoo? KootoogakkooI? Juku?*

Can they think of some way to lock that information into their brains?

Talk about associations or mnemonics for helping to remember difficult words (e.g.: *shoo—gakkoo* is where the teacher SHOWS the way into learning. At junior high, students CHEW up the information without any cares. The COATS of high school students are really different from own uniforms etc!). Enter in books as a time line from youngest to oldest. List *juku* separately with a clock or something else that defines time for *juku* activity.

(3-4 minutes)

3 Optional—Show the *kanji* for *gakkoo* on page 52 for interest.

Remind about *kanji* background. Write *shoo, chuu,* and *koo* on the board and ask for first student to be able to identify which *kanji* relates to which school level? 'Read' the *kanji*.

(5 minutes)

4 The Japanese Education System. What appears to be different from the U.S. system? What is similar?

Students read the text and see how many similarities and how many differences they can list in their own notebooks from the text page 51–52.

(10-15 minutes)

Have a student read out his/her list. Other students say if they have the same.

Ask for other items from other students. If they are considered relevant, students add them to own lists. Can anyone add information from own pre-knowledge?

Discuss:

Which item did students find most interesting about the information they just collected? Why? Encourage to find more information from encyclopedias and library books for homework.

Collecting and retaining information is a big part of learning a language. If this half of the lesson seemed like social studies, students must realize that they will never understand the language properly if they don't find out about the culture as well. The cultural background is fascinating, and will help to keep them motivated when sometimes they find learning structures and vocabulary difficult. In the end all the tiny items of information will fit together like a jigsaw puzzle and help their understanding of how and why the language is as it is.

Whether they are learning Japanese to make their brains more flexible, for eventual tourism or business, or just as another interesting examination subject, the cultural background is valuable. Nothing learned or experienced is ever wasted! Every item of information, every experience, is picked up and stored by the brain, brought out and applied to help people to cope in situations often undreamed of at the time the information was gathered.

(5 minutes)

5 The Quiz! Divide class into 6 or 8 teams. Seat two teams opposite each other. Put the questions (written and cut into strips for homework) into 3 or 4 boxes randomly. Each student in turn pulls out a question for opposing team to answer and records marks. Correct answer should be on the back so don't reveal to opposing team!

Work quickly to maximize number of questions for each student and give the game a feeling of challenge.

Homework

Read over again pages 51–52.

From encyclopedias and library find out more information about the Japanese education system. Try to find at least five more items of information each. Write up on paper to be displayed on wall alongside pictures up already.

Dismissal: The winning team leaves first etc.

Nationalities worksheet

Take turns asking for the missing information, and fill it in on this sheet.
Ask: *Ano hito no namae wa nan desu ka. Doko no kata desu ka.*
Answer: *Ano hito wa namae wa .... desu. ....jin desu.*

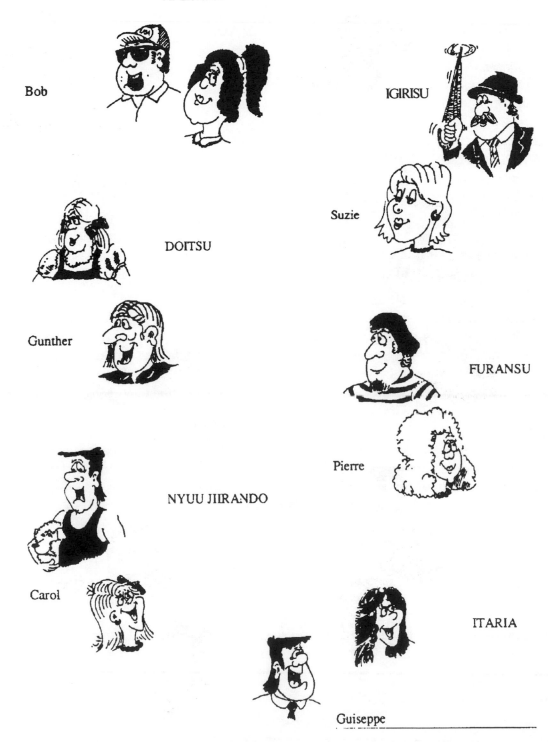

AMERIKA

Bob

IGIRISU

Suzie

DOITSU

Gunther

FURANSU

Pierre

NYUU JIIRANDO

Carol

ITARIA

Guiseppe

Nationalities worksheet

Take turns asking for the missing information, and fill it in on this sheet.
Ask: *Ano hito no namae wa nan desu ka. Doko no kata desu ka.*
Answer: *Ano hito wa namae wa .... desu. ....jin desu.*

AMERIKA

Sue

IGIRISU

Nick

DOITSU

Natasha

FURANSU

Pierre

Richard NYUU JIIRANDO

Carol

ITARIA

Lesson Thirteen (Unit 1, page 54)

Aims and Objectives

- To teach the names of common classroom objects.
- To introduce *yonde kudasai.*
- To teach *janai desu.*
- To teach more vocabulary learning strategies.
- To practice listening and focusing skills.

Preparation

Desks in pairs.
Four sets of the names of common objects written in *kana* and *roomaji* (flashcard size) page 54
Paper, ballpoint pen, box, pencil, bag, map, chair, picture, desks, blackboard, notebook. (Add if you wish *monosashi, keshigomu, gomibako* (ruler, eraser, garbage can).
And 2 sets of the above realia available for use during the lesson except, of course, the blackboard.
Labels of vocabulary from previous lessons.
Hiragana flashcards of *ka to mi se i.*

Introduction

(5-10 minutes)
Tape.
Greet using all instructions learned so far.
Put up date as usual. Quickly check on last lesson's homework. If anyone found more information ask them to tell class briefly. Put the work up on the wall for everyone to read in spare moments.

Main Theme

(5 minutes)

1 Suggest that students *yoku mite, yoku kiite kudasai,* and try to remember the names of the things you show them. Without speaking hold up an object. Have the students ask *sumimasen ga ... nihongo no namae wa nan desu ka* in chorus. Hold up the label and ask class to *yonde kudasai.* Prompt class to read the label. If necessary correct pronunciation. Repeat while associating with real item. Go through all today's vocabulary.

2 Quickly remind of word and object by showing all again.

3 Make sure that two sets of the item realia are available except for blackboard.
Spread out two sets of labels face down on each of two desks at opposite sides of the room (i.e.: 2 sets per team).
Divide class into two teams. Students must come to the front of the room, pick up a label, read it out aloud to their team, and put it on the appropriate object anywhere in their half of the room. Hurry back to place. Next student may only get up and go when previous student has sat down. If the student can't remember the word, others in the team may mime the item but may not speak.

Topic Two

When a team has found homes for all their items they sit up straight and totally silent. Teacher checks that all labels are correctly placed and proclaims the winners!

(5 minutes)

4 Students take out notebooks, enter date and title *Kyooshitsu*.
Dictate spelling of words in syllables e.g.: *ka mi (kami)*. In pencil students write word, do a quick sketch of the item beside it. Take out textbook and check work against the list on page 54.
One mark for correct spelling one for correct picture.

(2-3 minutes)

5 Teach *janai desu* as a less formal alternative for *dewa arimasen*, page 54.

(5 minutes)

6 Students do one or two activities on page 55 in pairs.
Encourage to role play a situation similar to the one given on page 55 between Mark and Jiroo.

(5-7 minutes)

7 TAPE. Close books and listen to a conversation on the tape. Open books and identify which one was read. Can anyone offer an English version? Close books.
Listen to tape again, and again identify the dialogue heard.
OR
Activities on page 56.

(10 minutes)

8 Writing practice. Teach *ka to mi se i*.

Homework

Write an English equivalent for one or two of the dialogues. Correct and if necessary redraw items from new vocabulary. Practice the *hiragana* learned today.

Dismissal: Each one reads a *hiragana* syllable and may then leave.

Lesson Fourteen (Units 2 and 3, page 59)

Aims and objectives

• To teach *kore* and *sore*.

• To consolidate use of *wa*.

Preparation

If possible have samples of Japanese newspapers, magazines and comics in the room.
If you have no Japanese ones put up or have out on show local newspapers labeled *Shinbun,*
magazines and comics labeled appropriately.

Introduction

TAPE.

Greet.

Look at the illustrations of magazines pages 59–60, saying *kore wa manga desu, kore wa shinbun desu,* etc. Talk about the enormous variety available in Japan, the reading of comic books, books and newspapers on and waiting for commuter transport, the use of English on covers being 'trendy,' the fact that even adults read a lot of comics in Japan, the size of commuter—reading comics and books being tailored to fit people's pockets easily when traveling and people folding newspapers so they don't invade anyone else's space. Definite 'Japanese' cute drawing styles.

1 Illustrations on pages 59–64. Elicit differences between illustrations and format and students' local reading material.
Try to identify any *hiragana* syllables known.
Point out the cost and convert into local currency, page 60–63, and *kanji: en.* Compare prices with what students pay.
What age groups do students think they would appeal to?

2 Look at newspaper and discuss: Find date—what is different from own newspapers way of presenting date? (Year, month, date, day)
Teach students how to identify the date—refer to magazines, too. Can anyone identify the *kanji* for person? How do people read the paper? What would be difficult? What do students think main story might be about? How would students feel if that was their home? People the world over feel the same about disasters and all enjoy relaxation and entertainment. There are many things that we all have in common even though language, writing and culture may be very different.
What news and information can students derive from the samples without being able to read them? (In learning Japanese there will always be the need to put two and two together and so many times when students won't know the precise meaning of all the words in a conversation, but they can pick up a general idea. They need to learn to look, listen, watch body language, be aware of the context, i.e.: to learn to pick up clues from everything available, to help them to understand not only the words being used but the subtle inferences that are not stated—reading between the lines or knowing the culture so well that they understand the situations being discussed. Reading around the subject from magazines and books about Japan will really prove worthwhile, as is going to see Japanese films when films suitable for their age group are being shown or watching TV and video films with Japanese background. So much information may be collected and stored from even the most lighthearted film. For example just seeing that newspaper would mean that it would be possible in Japan to make a comment like 'how dreadful' as part of a 'passing the time of day' type conversation.)

Students should be asked to note the different styles of writing Japanese script.
Explain that eventually it's only the same as reading different people's handwriting in English even though at first it looks very confusing.

Main theme

(15 minutes)

1 Teach *kore wa nan desu ka. sore wa ... desu.*

Use with all the vocabulary known so far—look around room and find all that the students can be expected to know. Return to previous vocabulary pictures in text and around room.

Demonstrate *kore wa* holding something close to you and pointing out an object closer to students with *sore wa.*

Ask students if anyone can work out the difference. Demonstrate again and have students who get the message to demonstrate for students who don't pick it up so quickly until all understand.

Point out that *kore* and *sore* mean this thing HERE, that thing THERE. Some students may find it a help if you tell them that the *re* on the end of heRE and theRE may be a reminder in their minds that *koRE* and *soRE* are talking about things in a particular place.

Do some of the activities on pages 62–64.

(5-10 minutes)

2 Remind of instructions on page 65 and have a quick game of Simon Says (*Jiroo San Says!*) before the end of the lesson. Look at the photo on page 66. Can any student identify a *hiragana* syllable? (*no*).

Homework

Write all the instructions learned so far into notebooks.

Ask students to make a notebook sized poster to show *kore wa ...*, *sore wa ...* e.g.: Two sketches of people, one pointing to things close to himself saying *kore wa,* another picture of two people with one person pointing to objects beside the second person saying *sore wa ...* to demonstrate clearly the difference between the two, using any vocabulary learned so far, to put up on the wall. Read over textbook pages 59 to 65.

Dismissal: Ask students to tell you a sentence using *kore wa ... desu* as they leave the room, showing you the object that they are talking about. Remind that they may be able to say 'this is MY ...' as well as the simpler sentence.

Lesson Fifteen (Unit 4, page 67)

Aims and objectives

- To teach particle *o*.
- To teach how to ask for things and actions with *kore o kudasai .... o kudasai* etc.
- To consolidate patterns already learned and review vocabulary.

Preparation

TAPE.

Realia of vocabulary items to hand from one to another during lesson (some may be borrowed from students during lesson).

Put up all the instruction phrases the students should know, on the wall in *roomaji* and in *hiragana*.

Pin up some of the students posters of *kore* and *sore*.

Homework worksheets photocopied.

Introduction

TAPE.

Greet, put up date as usual.

Main theme

(5 minutes)

1 Use instruction phrases known to have a quick game before they sit down. Call out instruction, last one to obey is out and sits down. The last one standing is the winner. Ask students what they have been doing (Obeying instructions. They have been asked to do something at your request.)

(5 minutes)

2 Move around room borrowing items and amassing them on the front desk until all students are intrigued by what is going on.
Then go through all the items saying *kore wa nan desu ka,* and eliciting response *sore wa .... desu.*

(5 minutes)

3 Return items to owners by asking *dare no desu ka, ... san no desu ka, Hon wa dare no desu ka,* eliciting *watashi no desu, watashi no hon desu,* etc. from students. If you try to return an item to the wrong owner the class should say *... san no (hon) dewa arimasen* or *watashi no dewa arimasen.*

(5 minutes)

4 Talk about the fact that all the items you have been talking about are OBJECTS/THINGS and that really you shouldn't have taken them without asking their owners or you could have been mistaken for a thief! From now on you are going to ask properly when you want to use items from students' desks!
Show the students particle *o hiragana* and write *o* beside it. Draw a few items on the board with e.g.: a book followed by *o* and a dotted line. Point out that each item has been put first followed by the reminder that it is an OBJECT or THING.
Kore o ...
(Hon) o ...
Ask students to give you names of some more objects or let them quickly draw on the board items from previous vocabulary lists. Class call out together *nihongo no namae wa nan desu ka.* Student artist replies *nihongo no namae wa .... desu.*

(5 minutes)

5 Go around class asking for several items drawn on the board with *sumimasen ga ... Kore o kudasai. (PEN) o kudasai,* putting out hand to receive item from student. After several examples ask the class if they can guess the missing word in the sentences on the board. See if the person who offers the answer can make an attempt supplying the syllables needed to write the *ku da sa i.* Write it in in both examples.
Explain the sentence pattern and the fact that *kudasai* means 'please give me,' not just 'please', so it's not possible to say *hai kudasai* as we say 'yes please'. Link with game at beginning of lesson when *kudasai* was used to request an ACTION. Explain that the request now is for an OBJECT. Point out the difference—That *kudasai* in the game was meaning 'please DO this for me', now you are using the same word to mean 'Please GIVE me ...'.
In English we say:
1) 'Please sit down', for example to get someone to perform an action.
2) 'Please may I have a ...', if we want someone to give us something.
When we use pattern 2, we put 'a' in the sentence or 'an' to let people know we want an object or thing.
It's similar in Japanese but the word order is different—when we want an object we must use *o* after the word and then *kudasai.*
Explain *doozo*—here you are ....

Nihongo no namae wa nan desu ka

Ask questions to fill in the missing words. Give answers to your partners.
Question: *A wa .... nihongo no namae wa nan desu ka.*
Answer: *Nihongo no namae wa .... desu.*

A	B	C	D	E
F	G	H	I	J
K	L	M	N	O
P	Q	R	S	T
U	V	W	X	Y
Z				

Nihongo no namae wa nan desu ka

Ask questions to fill in the missing words. Give answers to your partners.
Question: *A wan .... hihongo no namae wa nan desu ka.*
Answer: *Nihongo no namae wa .... desu.*

(10 minutes)

   6 Do the activities on page 68.

(10-15 minutes)

   7 Writing practice *so re ko te ha* and activities.

Homework

Review all *hiragana* syllables learned so far. Find and write at least ten words from the vocabulary list that can be written using *hiragana* they know. Read over the text book to page 71 inclusive. Fill in the answers on the homework work sheet.

Dismissal: Stand at front with homework worksheets. Show sheets and tell them *shukudai desu.* Students ask for a sheet saying *shukudai o kudasai.* You answer *doozo* and hand it out as student passes.

Lesson Sixteen (Units 5 & 6, pages 72)

Aims and objectives

- To consolidate vocabulary and work on spelling accuracy.
- To check understanding of structures learned.

Preparation

TAPE.
Paper for testing spelling accuracy.
Reward for good students.
Put up on the wall the new patterns with pictures or realia if possible, e.g.: *shinbun o kudasai* etc. or cartoon sketches of people saying *kore o kudasai/sore o kudasai/are o kudasai* (see sketch).

Introduction

(5 minutes)

Check last lesson's homework and find out which student managed to find the most words to write in *hiragana.* Check the best list over with the class, writing the words up on the board in *hiragana* and getting the class to read them as you do so. Have a mini—competition to see who can read the *hiragana* words out from the board after all have been written up.

(3-4 minutes)

   1 Discuss *are* and *dore* read over for homework and make sure students understand *are o kudasai* and *dore desu ka,* as discussed on page 71.

(1-2 minutes)

Give out paper. Ask two or three students *O namae wa nan desu ka*. Ask students to write their names at the head of the paper by demonstration and *O namae o kaite kudasai*. Remind that their name is a thing so you said *O namae o ... kaite kudasai*. Ask who can work out what you want them to do. The students obey the instruction.

(10 minutes)

2 Pair work. Each student thinks of ten words to ask his/her partner (must check that spelling is correct before asking the partner to spell them). Ask class to work out how they would say 'Please write ...' (page 73). Test each other and mark.

(5 minutes)

3 The sheets are then handed in for the teacher to see and possibly record for spelling accuracy.

(5 minutes)

4 Compliment the good students and remind of the difference it will make to all of them to be able to spell words accurately because of changing *roomaji* words into *hiragana* later.

(5 minutes)

5 Together do the 'Check your understanding' on page 73, then ask students to test their friends.

(10 minutes)

6 In pairs work together to do the exercise on page 74 orally then write down answers in notebooks.

(4-5 minutes)

7 Mark and record own marks.

Homework

Read textbook over to Page 75 inclusive. Make up ten sentences of their own and write them neatly using any Japanese patterns they know.

Dismissal: By *hiragana* syllable of name.

Lesson Seventeen (Unit 7, page 76)

Aims and Objectives

- To teach 'Open the window', 'Close the door', 'Open your books', etc., structure: *mado o akete kudasai*.

- To teach the song *musunde hiraite*.

- To focus on picking up new words from listening.

- To impress accuracy of listening and matching of sounds to syllables.

- To identify previously learned *hiragana* syllables in a passage.

Preparation

Song Sheet in *hiragana*.

Use book to check students offers of words from the song and for writing up the *roomaji*.

Label windows, doors, bookcases, desks, tables, etc. in Japanese.

Box, bag, notebook, for demonstration of 'open' and 'close'.

Photocopy on card the vocabulary sheets (following Lesson 31 of this guide), or photocopy the vocabulary lists from the book, pages 78-79 (two sets for every 4 students).

Introduction

TAPE. Listen to new song *Musunde hiraite*.

Ask students if the music sounds like Western music. If not, what is different?

Comment on the different expectation we have of songs—coming down at the end whereas this song stays up in a way that may sound unfinished to us. Comment on the fact that many such aesthetic differences exist between Japanese people and ourselves, and it is good for us to learn to appreciate the differences.

(5-7 minutes)

1 Listen to song again. Demonstrate along with the tape.
   Clench your hands, open your hands, clap your hands twice, clench your hands.
   Open them again, clap your hands.
   Put your hands up, clench your hands, open your hands, clap your hands.
   Verse two is the same except you put your hands down.

Ask students if they can guess from your demonstration what the song is saying.

Explain that as in any language there will be different words available to express yourself, e.g.: in Japanese there are several words that have a similar meaning *to open* just as there are in English: 'unfold' and 'undo' can sometimes mean *open*—we use them in different contexts. Students are offered a limited set to learn, to make it easier for them in the early stages but this is why, when they talk to Japanese people, it is not always immediately obvious to the Japanese person what they are trying to say. People who are not used to learning foreign languages often don't understand that there are limits to the words students can be expected to know! In this lesson they will be offered two words for 'open' but they are not expected to know how to use the word for 'open your hands' except in singing the song.

Sing the first verse through two or three times and then see if any students can offer words (correctly spelled). Write them up on the board in *roomaji* as they are offered.

(5 minutes)

Students may copy them into their notebooks.

Which of the words could they write in *hiragana* with the syllables they know?

Show the *hiragana* version and see if students can identify any of the words.

Sing the song again together.

2 Teach by demonstration *mado o akete kudasai, DOA o shimete kudasai, kaban o akete kudasai* etc. Bring out a closed box. Hold it out to a student saying *hako o akete kudasai*. Say *arigatoo*, pass it to another student, and say *hako o shimete kudasai*, motioning the required action. Do it several times until sure that the class have taken in the message. Go around the room telling the students *mado desu* and pointing out label etc.

Then return to front and give students instructions to open windows, close doors, open bags, stand, sit, listen, etc. as a game.

Ask one or two students to volunteer to obey your instructions or those given by selected students while class look, listen and judge if they are obeying accurately.

In pairs students order each other around, three different activities each, then sit down and wait for all to finish.

Explain that even though windows and doors are not things you pick up they are still objects and must be followed by particle *o*.

(20 minutes)

3 Choose activities from page 77
   Collect in homework

Homework

Learn the words of the song. Write up notes on ... *o akete kudasai* etc.

Dismissal: While class sings song, signal to individual students to leave. When song is finished the remainder leave.

Shukudai (homework worksheet)

Fill in the blanks with appropriate words or particles.

o _____ kudasai.

_____ _____ kudasai.

PEN _____ _____ kudasai.

enpitsu _____ kudasai.

Write ten more sentences of your own with the same pattern as above.

1. _____

2. _____

3. _____

4. _____

5. _____

6. _____

7. _____

8. _____

9. _____

10. _____

TOPIC THREE
Lesson Eighteen (School life and Unit 1, page 81)

Aims and objectives

- To teach students how to say what languages they speak, study and practice.

- To teach how to tell someone politely they are wrong, with chigaimasu.

- Introduce new structures: *shimasu,*

  compound verb *benkyoo shimasu,*

  renshuu shimasu,

  hanashimasu,

  go for language,

  soo desu ka/soo desu.

- To make use of particles *wa + o.*

Preparation

TAPE.
Labels of languages.
Map of the world.
Previously made labels of nationality.

Introduction

TAPE.
Greet. Write date.

Main theme

(5 minutes)

1 Tell class that they are *dookyuusei*—classmates: *minasan wa dookyuusei desu.*
  Put up on board a simple time line of school classes by year, and show that the students in one year are *dookyuusei, senpai* are students in the year above, and the *senpai* call their juniors in the year lower, *koohai.* Talk about the *senpai-koohai* system briefly (page 82) and stress its importance not just at school, but through life for Japanese people. Have your students anything similar? Discuss briefly advantages etc.

(10 minutes)

2 Tell students that today's lesson will teach them how to say what languages people speak, study and practice.
  Put up the map of the world. Elicit from students the names of countries in the world without referring to books. Elicit the name of the nationality for the countries. Remind that when students write the names of countries they are mostly written in *katakana* but the *jin* of nationality is

---

always written in *hiragana*. Tell the students *nihonjin wa nihongo o hanashimasu, DOITSUjin wa DOITSUgo o hanashimasu, FURANSUjin wa FURANSUgo o hanashimasu.*

Put on tape and ask students to listen ('Good morning' in Japanese, German, French. Then tell them *Ohayoo gozaimasu wa nihongo desu, Bonjour wa FURANSUgo desu, Guten morgen wa DOITSUgo desu.* It continues, e.g.: *FURANSUjin wa FURANSUgo o hanashimasu,* etc.

Ask students if they can say 'Good morning' in any language?. Which language is it? How do they think they could say what language it is in Japanese? Elicit the need to put 'go' on the end of the country name to tell language. Elicit the word for 'speak.' Explain that it is a verb, an action word, and that in Japanese the verb always goes at the end of a sentence (except when the question marker *ka* is at the end).

(10 minutes)

3 Study pages 84–85. Pay particular attention to *eigo for IGIRISUjin/AMERIKAjin.* Explain that compound words are words that have been combined to give a new meaning like 'play' + 'ground' = 'playground', 'show' + 'ground' = 'showground.' Elicit a few more examples to consolidate understanding of the term. Explain that Japanese is more explicit in its definitions than English in these areas—we just stay 'study', but the Japanese put in the action as well, 'do study'. As they continue their studies they will come upon this idea of giving all the actions in many situations. Listen to the tape of the dialogue. Elicit from students what they have understood. Reading practice: Read dialogue together taking particular care with double sounds.

4 Compose together several sentences using today's patterns. Write into notebooks as examples.

5 Choose an activity from page 85.

Homework

Read over textbook pages 77–85 inclusive to review vocabulary learned and today's structures, and to find out a little more about Japanese school life. Learn new vocabulary. Make a note of words they are still unsure of. Write down five questions relating to these pages, to ask another student at the beginning of next lesson.

Dismissal: *Nanigo o hanashimasu ka/Nanijin desu ka* or *Doko no kata desu ka/Onamae wa nan desu ka* as students file by.

Lesson Nineteen (Units 2 & 3, page 86)

Aims and objectives

• To teach how to say a few of the things students may do in school and in their free time.

• To consolidate *wa* and *o,* and teach *ya.*

• Introduce lexically only *donna (hon desu ka)* and *dete kudasai.*

Preparation

TAPE
Pictures or realia of musical instruments.
Textbooks or examples of science, geography, history, social studies, maths and music.

Homework worksheets photocopy (Fill in the names of subjects and instruments).
Check walls. Do they need to have new material/pictures/students' work?

Introduction

(5 minutes)

TAPE. Greet, put up date, ask students to ask their five questions of another student and get the answers. Pick out one or two to read out their questions. Student picked then chooses people to try to answer.

(5 minutes)

Play tape—sounds of musical instruments followed by statement *GITAA desu* etc. The tape leaves blanks for students to fill in name of instrument in Japanese.

Main theme

1 Bring out samples of textbooks and show them to class with *nihongo no hon desu, suugaku no hon desu*. Elicit answers from students in response to *donna hon desu ka: suugaku no hon desu*.

Check that students' understanding of the new vocabulary is well established before they write it in their notebooks.

(10 minutes)

2 Elicit from students how they would say:
   a) Study Japanese
   b) Practice the guitar
(Use of instruments has only been offered as 'practice piano/guitar' etc. because of the complication of having different verbs for different instruments at this stage.)
Build up a good selection of sentences together on the board. Ask students to write down five sentences that relate to their own lives.

(10 minutes)

3 Choose activities from page 86–87.

(10 minutes)

4 Continue to Unit 3 (Sports Activities) if time permits.

Homework

Write the conversation practiced in class in notebook. Learn new vocabulary by drawing pictures and labeling in Japanese. If Unit 3 not covered in class, do it for homework,

OR

activities from page 89.
Find pictures from magazines of classroom activities/sports/other activities/pop groups/things people do in their free time. Cut out and bring to school for next lesson. Everyone to try to find at least one.

Dismissal: Ask students a subject they may study or a game they play, e.g.: *ongaku o benkyoo shimasu ka*. Those who do, leave (*dete kudasai*). Continue with different subjects until all have gone.

SATSUMA BIWA

ODAIKO

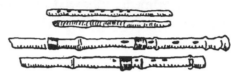

SHINOBUE·NOHKAU·SHAKUHACHI

SHIMEDAIKO

KOTO

KOTSUZUMI

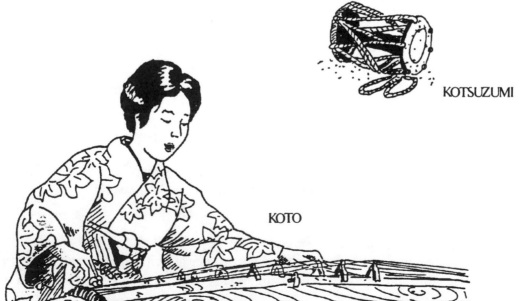

KOTO

People and activities

Ben.
Guitar.
Japanese.

Ken.
Violin.
French.

Jon
Math
French

Sue.
Guitar.
English.

Miriam .
Koto.
History.

Peter
Piano.
English

Kiyo.
Dancing.
German.

Candy
Drum.
Tennis.

Make two sentences for each person. Say what each student practices, and what each person studies.
Say what thing you study, and what thing you practice.
Give the name of your best friend, and say what he/she studies and practices.

People and activities

AMY san

Guitar.
Japanese.

ROB san

Piano.
English
Tennis.

ELIZA san

Guitar.
English.
History.

PETER san

Math
French
German

KIT san

Violin.
French.

Make two sentences for each person. Say what each student practices, and what each person studies.
Say what thing you study, and what thing you practice.
Give the name of your best friend, and say what he/she studies and practices.

Lesson Twenty (Unit 4, page 90)

Aims and objectives

- To teach how to express like and dislike.
- To introduce particle *ga* lexically only.

Preparation

Vocabulary cards made previously.
Paper to make posters.
Photocopied class lists if desired.
Two poster-sized sheets on which to collate survey information, headed ... *ga suki desu, ... ga kirai desu.*
Flowers, a photo of your pet, or of a sport—something to demonstrate 'like' and 'dislike'.
Photocopy of listening activity.

Introduction

(5 minutes)
TAPE
Collect in pictures from students and give thanks. Encourage students to use *doozo* as they hand them over. Greet. Put up date.
Ask class for as much of the information as possible—they will be used to the pattern every day so if you stand poised they will most likely guess what you want!
Nangatsu desu ka (Allow them to answer in English if they can't really be expected to have picked up the month yet. Give the Japanese).
Nannichi desu ka (They can reply in English and you give the Japanese).
Nanyoobi desu ka.

Main theme

(10 minutes)
1 Look at collection of pictures and use to demonstrate: Show class an activity/object and show your enthusiasm for it as you say, e.g.: *FUTTOBOORU ga suki desu.*
   Show a second and show your dislike, e.g.: *SAKKAA ga kirai desu.*
   Look at date and tell them whether you like (Wednesday) or not. Make sure they understand and then have students give you the spelling of *suki desu* and *kirai desu.*
   Ask them to interview you with *TENISU ga suki desu ka, hana ga kirai desu ka,* etc. Everybody tries to think of something to ask you, and as you answer you write up the items under the headings *suki desu* or *kirai desu* on the board.

(10-15 minutes)
2 Give the students a class list each and get them to go around the class doing a survey on class preferences. Give each student a topic, e.g.: *TENISU ga suki desu ka.*

Students reply either *Hai TENISU ga suki desu,* or *Iie TENISU ga kirai desu,* or *TENISU ga suki janai desu.*

(*Ga suki janai* has been offered but it is recognized that later when students learn to use *wa* with negatives they will use *wa.* At this stage, from experience, it can prove confusing to the average student to be asked to use *wa* with negatives and does not seem to cause a problem to change later. Our aim is to build confidence step by step and to keep to very simple patterns until the idea of using particles and different word order from English has been thoroughly established.)

As this is their first experience with *ga* it is offered only for them to get used to the pattern and the sound and will be reintroduced with more structural emphasis later.

Report back to class giving numbers in English because they haven't yet the means to give numbers in Japanese, e.g.: *TENISU ga suki desu*—10 people.

As they report back have two students making posters of the information gathered under *suki desu* and *kirai desu* on the posters prepared before the class.

(3-4 minutes)

3 Pairwork. Ask students to interview each other and find out as much as they can about each other's likes and dislikes as possible, taking one minute each interview time.
Nani ga suki desu ka. Nani ga kirai desu ka.
They need to listen very attentively and to take in the answers. Ask them to report back to the class what they found out. *PAMU san wa ... ga suki desu* etc.
Explain that they don't need to repeat the person's name after each item any more than they would in English. They can use *ya* to give the lists.
If the student being reported on hears misinformation he/she calls out *sumimasen ga chigaimasu.*

(5 minutes)

4 Listening activity. Tell students to mark person, likes, dislikes, or mildly dislikes as instructed on photocopied sheet.

NIKI san wa TENISU ga suki desu.
TOMU san wa inu ga kirai desu.
Junji san wa neko ga suki janai desu.
MARIA san wa hon ga suki desu.
RISA san wa hana ga suki desu.
BEN san wa shinbun ga suki janai desu.
Yukiko san wa sakkaa ga suki desu.
Masao san wa sakkaa ga suki janai desu.
REE san wa zasshi ga kirai desu.
HENRI san wa gakkoo ga suki desu.

Homework

Read over pages 83–92.
Write a self-introduction to put on the wall giving name and subjects studied, sports played, likes and dislikes, etc.

Listening

Draw a line to connect each person with an object or activity.
Place a cross in the box describing their feeling.

	likes	doesn't really like	dislikes	
Rae →				•
Henry →				•
Ben →				•
Tom →				•
Junji →				•
Yukiko →				•
Maria →				•
Niki →				•
Masao →				•
Lisa →				•

- Magazines
- Cats
- Soccer
- Tennis
- Flowers
- Dogs
- Books
- Rugby
- School
- Newspapers

Lesson Twenty-one (Unit 5, page 93)

Aims and objectives

• To teach negatives with *masen*.

Preparation

TAPE.
Sentence patterns and pictures for the walls of activities (pictures brought by students last lesson)

Introduction

Collect homework self-introductions to put on wall.
Listen to tape and see how much is understood. Did anyone spot a new word? Can they tell you what it was?
Listen again. Who has spotted new words?

Main theme

(10-15 minutes)

1 Write up the words and demonstrate reading and listening. Elicit meaning of the new words from students. Demonstrate won't read/won't listen.
Open books and listen to the tape again while reading the text, page 94. Can students work out which words gave negative responses? Elicit *shimasen*.
Write up *shi - masen*.
Comment on the structure: *shi* being the stem that contains the meaning of the actual word—'do,' and *masen* being the negative ending which 'attaches' in much the same way that different nozzles attach to vacuum cleaners. Students will learn to 'attach' lots of different endings to get the verb to express different tenses or needs. Gradually through the next few years of their study they will accumulate a lot of different endings until they can express all that they want in Japanese. Using the analogy of the vacuum cleaner you may like to explain that the extra 'tools' all add extension of usage. They have now learned two ways to add to a stem *masu* meaning WILL do something or HABITUALLY do something and WON'T/DON'T do something.
(*o* not *wa* has been used with the negatives at this point for the same reasons as given before: we are consolidating *o* particle and aiming to avoid confusion. The assumption therefore in these sentences is that we are commenting on the fact that someone does not do something rather than using it in the contrastive sense meaning I don't play TENNIS but I do play something else.)

(5 minutes)

2 Pairwork: Practice reading the dialogue on page 94.

(5 minutes)

3 Go through the examples on page 95 and discuss the order of sentences in Japanese and the use of the particles, use of *san,* use of 'go.'
Elicit the negatives of each sentence from the students. Use pictures on walls to make sentences.

(10 minutes)

   4 Do the writing practice page 97.

(10 minutes)

   5 Choose activities from page 97.

Homework

Read over pages 94–97.

Make ten sentences in Japanese about own interests. Write any words that can be written in *hiragana* with syllables learned this far, in *hiragana,* or copy *hiragana* and *katakana* from textbook and write them totally in Japanese script.

Practice the new and previously learned *hiragana*.

Encourage to study vocabulary every day.

Dismissal: Students say what they plan to do next after leaving this class and say goodbye.

TOPIC FOUR

Lesson Twenty-two (Introduction and Unit 1, page 101)

Aims and objectives

- To teach (Chinese set) numbers to one hundred.
- To encourage listening and imitating skills.

Preparation

Put up self-introductions on wall for other students to read under title *konshuu/senshuu no shukudai*.
Sets of number cards (photocopy sets onto card or use children's game cards like 'Folly').
Make a chart of numbers to put on the wall at end of lesson.
Remember to collect in homework for marking.

Introduction

(5 minutes)
TAPE
Point out homework on wall and encourage to read in spare time.
Point out the label and its meaning.

Main theme

(5 minutes)
1 Write up on the board a list of numbers 1–10.
Listen to tape and point to each number as it is read on the tape.
Listen to rhythm chant of numbers and encourage class to join in.
Point to numbers on board and elicit numbers from class in Japanese. Go as fast as you can to make it a real race.

(5 minutes)
2 Talk about consciousness of numbers in Japan, pages 101–102, before students open own books or read the information together.

(10 minutes)
3 TAPE. Ask students to listen as tape counts from 1 to 19 in Japanese. Get students to work out the pattern for numbers above 10.
Listen again to find the system for numbers above 19. Tape counts to 100.
Students follow in books and use page 103 as an aid in keeping up with the tape counting to 100.
Look at books and read through the numbers on page 103.
Use number square to read numbers around class or in small groups. The number square allows you to count down, across, or diagonally to really stretch students' agility.

(20 minutes)

    4 Choose activities from pages 104-106

    OR

    Have a team game of *hiragana* and numbers learned this far. Divide class into about 6 teams.
    Call out hiragana syllable or number. Students race to put the syllable or number on the board
    before opposing team, or to write the answers on a sheet of paper:

    ni ho n a na ta no wa e shi ma so re ko te ha ka to mi se i ku sa he nu

    25 syllables plus 25 numbers.

    If all students in a team have worked individually, count up the collective total score of each
    team's correct answers. If you have had a more physical game of people rushing out to the front
    count the teams' scores in Japanese to finish the game.

    Some classes may find it too threatening to have to take a turn to go out and write the syllable
    on the board with the chance of *letting their team down*. Choose the way that will not set back
    the confidence of your particular class. Keeping the confidence level high is very important.

Homework

Take in last homework for marking.

Produce an attractive counting chart or maths puzzle for Japanese numbers to put up on the wall.
Use only the actual numbers and the *ichi ni san* set of numbers, brightly colored and artistically
presented to avoid the problem of specific counters for specific items. Suggest different sets of
numbers for each student to make so that you get a good selection of different numbers to put on
the wall.

Dismissal: Count up to one hundred slowly with your eyes closed or back to the class. Students
must leave the room without being heard. If you hear them they have to sit down and start again.

Lesson Twenty-three (Unit 2, page 107)

Aims and objectives

- To teach giving of telephone numbers.

Preparation

Set of bingo cards for playing bingo in Japanese.
Small 'prize' for winners of game.
The telephone numbers of two or three students in the class.

Introduction

TAPE.
Greet and collect homework.

Number square for bingo

00	01	02	03	04	05	06	07	08	09
10	11	12	13	14	15	16	17	18	19
20	21	22	23	24	25	26	27	28	29
30	31	32	33	34	35	36	37	38	39
40	41	42	43	44	45	46	47	48	49
50	51	52	53	54	55	56	57	58	59
60	61	62	63	64	65	66	67	68	69
70	71	72	73	74	75	76	77	78	79
80	81	82	83	84	85	86	87	88	89
90	91	92	93	94	95	96	97	98	99

Bingo cards sheet #1

75		83		41		33			
			13				06		70
	20				39			03	

				33		48		75	
	70		19		58		40		
56		61							79

		10					36		03
53	08			41		80			
			31		78			27	

75		50			20			03	
			38	15			24		
	80					88			47

	49		63		01		88		
		58						11	30
93				43		52			

		47			06		25	
	24					82		77
31		84	37			59		

07					91		64	
		80		85		26		08
	59		73				44	

		58		17			22	
30			76		72			10
	69					92	100	

86			07			83		60
		49			96		38	
	28			64			33	

		30	55		49		38	
01				57		68		
	59						92	

95		32				19		82	
	86				25				11
			21	54			85		

	96		90				47		
27				40		81		64	
		91			17				82

	42			87					11
58		89			34		32		
			79			82		18	

		21	04		86		95		
	72			77				51	
27						52			97

	55			75					19
			04			37	22		
28		99			29			65	

Bingo cards sheet #4

			13	07		04		40
	92			25		48		
86		77					33	

	36			73	98			
		49			15		60	90
58			04				51	

46					20			59
		84	16			18	31	
	41			97			13	

43				45		41		
		36			09			54
	10		89			77	26	

71			10		75			
		54			59		34	
	84			65			07	58

Main theme

(15 minutes)

1 Give out bingo cards and remind of rules.

Students call out *owarimashita* when all numbers/or a line (depending on your choice) are covered—a line speeds the game up and keeps students alert!

Students who claim to have finished read out their covered numbers in Japanese to check against the master.

First correct receives 'prize'.

(5 minutes)

2 Having reviewed numbers write a telephone number on the board and ask students to guess what sort of number it is. Ask *anata no denwa bangoo desu ka, JON san no denwa bangoo desu ka* etc. until you find the owner.

Ask specific (confident) students to give you their telephone numbers. Ask class to quickly write down the numbers given. Who listened and remembered correctly?

(5-7 minutes)

3 Listen to dialogue on page 107.

Ask students to listen to the conversation and to write down the telephone number given. Listen again. Check.

Open books and see if they were correct.

(5 minutes)

4 Teach *doo itashimashite*—just as a phrase.
Denwa bangoo, anata no denwa bangoo wa nan desu ka, etc.

(5 minutes)

5 Give each student a portion of the class's names. Ask them to find those students, greet them appropriately, ask for, and note down the phone numbers and sit down quickly.

6 Choose an activity from page 108.

Homework

Learn new vocabulary and do a check on all vocabulary learned this far.

Stress importance of keeping up with vocabulary learning and that you will not give warning of tests.

Lesson Twenty-four (Unit 3, page 109)

Aims and objectives

• To teach the days of the week.

Preparation

Display number charts collected last lesson under the title *Konshuu no Shukudai*.
Timetable sheets.
Dicomm sheets of days and activities.
Chart of days of the week.

Introduction

(5 minutes)
Greet.
Put up date.
Students will be used to hearing you give the name every day as you write up the date.
Some may know the names of the days on which they have Japanese. Elicit these. Write them up on a time line on the board. Fill in the rest of the days with the *kanji* for interest as page 109.

Main theme

(5 minutes)
1 TAPE. Listen to tape of dialogue and activity.

(10 minutes)
2 Activity 1: A program for Kenji.
In small groups decide in Japanese on the subjects Kenji will do each day. Try not to use any English. Teacher goes round monitoring activity maintaining the use of Japanese. Students need *Kenji san wa nani o shimasu ka,* written on board for reference.
Some may say *suugaku* others *iie chigaimasu, taiiku,* etc. May need to vote on how many agree with each suggestion. All they need to say is *suugaku desu ka* and students say *hai* or *iie* in response until all the decisions are made.

(5-7 minutes)
3 Leader of each group reads out *getsuyoobi wa* and lists the subjects of that day, *kayoobi wa* ... etc. (It's important to make time for reporting back to give some purpose to the activity).

(5 minutes)
4 Dicomm activity in pairs. Find out from each other what people do on various days. Check answers with partner.

(15 minutes)
5 Choose activity from page 110.

Homework

Take sheets filled in for Kenji during group activity and write a sentence about each day, according to group decisions. Pattern *Kenji san wa getsuyoobi BASUKETTOBOORU o shimasu* OR *Kenji san wa getsuyoobi BASUKETTOBOORU o shimasen.*

Dismissal: Students tell teacher as they leave one thing they will do on the next day.

Jikanhyoo

	getsuyoobi	kayoobi	suiyoobi	mokuyoobi	kinoobi
ichijikanme					
nijikanme					
sanjikanme					
yojikanme					
gojikanme					
rokujikanme					

Days of the week activity sheet (A)

Fill in the blanks by asking your partner in Japanese for the information on his/her sheet. Ask *(Day of the week) nani o shimasu ka.*

A   **B**

Getsuyoobi
Hon o yomimasu

Kayoobi
SUPOOTSU o shimasen

Suiyoobi
Nihongo o benkyoo shimasen

Mokuyoobi
RAJIO o kikimasu

Kinyoobi
DOITSUgo o hanashimasu

Doyoobi
Ongaku o renshuu shimasu

Nichiyoobi
REKOODO o kikimasu

Days of the week activity sheet (B)

Fill in the blanks by asking your partner in Japanese for the information on his/her sheet.
Ask *(Day of the week) nani o shimasu ka.*

A	**B**
_____	
_____	Getsuyoobi
_____	GITAA o renshuu shimasen
_____	Kayoobi
_____	Zasshi o yomimasu
_____	
_____	Suiyoobi
_____	FURANSUgo o renshuu shimasu
_____	
_____	Mokuyoobi
_____	BASUKETTOBOOTU o shimasu
_____	
_____	Kinyoobi
_____	MAORIgo o benkyoo shimasu
_____	
_____	Doyoobi
_____	TENISU o shimasu
_____	
_____	Nichiyoobi
_____	BEISUbooru o shimasu
_____	

Lesson Twenty-five (Unit 4, page 111)

Aims and objectives

- To teach a selection of time words.
- To teach the order of sentence patterns with time words.
- To test vocabulary, structures and *hiragana*.
- To consolidate sentence patterns.

Preparation

TAPE.

Check walls.

Decide which of the check exercises you will use for a mini–test during the second half of the lesson.

Put up days of the week chart and *kanji*.

Introduction

TAPE.

Look at a large calendar.

Show *kyoo* and *ashita, konshuu* and *raishuu, mainichi* by demonstration.

Main theme

(4 minutes)

1 Build up a time line on the board to teach the time words on page 111.
    Kyoo - Ashita,
    Konshuu - Raishuu,
    Itsu show with a question mark.
    Itsumo show by writing *itsumo itsumoitsumoitsumo* continuously along the bottom of the board.
    Leave information on board.
    Check that students have understood the meaning.

(5 minutes)

2 Listen to the tape or read the dialogue on page 111.
    Read the dialogue in pairs.
    Quickly go through the meaning of the dialogue together or in pairs.

(10 minutes)

3 Do the exercises to refresh students' memory of patterns and vocabulary but don't give warning of test.

Dismissal: Handing in books for marking. *Kore wa watashi no NOOTO desu.*

Lesson Twenty-six (Unit 5, page 113)

Aims and objectives

- To teach how to tell the time in hours and half hours
- Teach structure: *Ima nanji desu ka.*

Preparation

TAPE.
Photocopy listening, homework and pair activity sheet of times.
Large cardboard clock with hands or real clock.

Introduction

(5 minutes)
Offer time for individual problem sorting while students are working today.

Main theme

(10 minutes)
1 Teach time using the large clock. Make special reference to *yoji* and *kuji*.
   Listen to tape.
   Open books. Read conversation in pairs.

(10 minutes)
2 Choose activities from pages 114–116. While students are busy with the activities, ask students who want to ask questions to come to see you.

(10 minutes)
3 Listening activity with times.

(5 minutes)
4 Conclude class with a game together of *Ima nanji desu ka* ... Activity 1.

Homework

Check exercises page 116.

Answers

1. It's half past two.
2. 31
3. What time is it (now)?
4. 100
5. 45
6. 389 511
7. Is it half past six?
8. 74
9. It's four o'clock (now).
10. Five plus six equals eleven.

Dismissal: *Ima nanji desu ka* to nearest half hour

A. Listen and fill in the times you hear.

Tell your partner the times you heard, and compare with each other, before you hear the correct answers.

Who was correct?

B. Work in pairs to tell each other the times shown on the clocks below.

C. Write the times shown on the clocks above into your notebooks in Japanese.

Lesson Twenty-seven (Unit 6, page 117)

Aims and objectives

- To teach verb *ikimasu*—go. *kimasu*—come, and *kaerimasu*—return.
- To teach use of particle *ni* with these.
- To teach how to ask what time people do things.
- To review instructions.

Preparation

Three flash cards *ikimasu, kimasu, kaerimasu.*
Picture of a house with a flash card *watashi no uchi* or use a dolls' house.
Cut out of a person.

Introduction

Greet.

Main theme

(10 minutes)

1 Ask a student to stand with ... *san, tatte kudasai. Koko ni kite kudasai.*
Take student to the door and call back to class *ikimasu.* Show class card.
Elicit from class what they think you are doing. 'Go'.
Turn back to class, show *kimasu* and start walking towards them. Ask class the word for that action in English, 'Come'. Explain *ikimasu* and *kimasu.* Ask what verb students would use in English for what they do after school and activities are over for the day. Elicit 'return home'. Show the verb *kaerimasu.*
Explain the use of the three verbs. Explain that in Japanese 'go' is used in some situations where in English we would use 'come'.
Students don't need to become totally at ease with this at this stage. Later it will fall into place. For now just present it as yet another interesting item of information.
Elicit their negatives.
How would students say I will go/come return home?
How would students say that someone else does those three actions?
How would they say that a dog or cat does those actions?
Teach use of *ni* particle with these three verbs and together work out sentences that students could say using the new information.

(10 minutes)

2 Use cut out figures. Show the house picture. Tell the class it's ... *san's* house.
Tell the class you like ... *san's* house. Ask if they like ... *san's* house.
Put up the house where everyone can see it. Introduce ... *san* then put him behind the house.
Show the cut out figure emerging from the house, saying *(KENsan wa) ikimasu.*
Show him meeting a friend, and indicate a place, asking *gakkoo ni ikimasu ka.*

She says 'Yes'. He asks *TENISU o shimasu ka*. She answers *hai TENISU o shimasu,* and they trot off into the middle distance.

Game over, he asks *watashi no uchi ni kimasu ka*. She answers *hai ikimasu,* and they move towards the house. He says *uchi ni kaerimasu.*

Ask class what he is doing—elicit 'Returning home'.

Put up the three cards and show *ikimasu*—go, *kimasu*—come. Remind students of the beckoning movement of the hand they learned before. Elicit the meaning of each.

Explain that they have in fact been using one of the verb forms of *kimasu* with *kite kudasai,* the *ki* bit being the stem meaning come.

Ask therefore if they can work out how to say 'I will see/watch/look'.

They know *mite kudasai*—what will the stem be? Elicit *mimasu.*

(10 minutes)

3 Draw a sketch map on the board and show the *eki* with a train alongside, *mise, gakkoo, uchi,* and *ie*. Find out from students what they think the sketches represent and label appropriately. *Chizu o mite kudasai.* Remind of *o* particle, look at the map—an object.

Eki desu, mise desu, gakkoo desu.

Draw a big signpost at the side of the map (Remind of word *chizu*).

On the signpost write *gakkoo ni* pointing to the school, and signs pointing to the station and shops with *eki ni* and *mise ni* on them.

Take the cut-out person and use him to demonstrate the sentence *hachiji desu. Gakkoo ni ikimasu.*

Then continue by joining the two sentences: *hachiji ni gakkoo ni ikimasu.*

Take the person again and demonstrate activities that he could undertake, e.g.:

Hachiji ni gakkoo ni ikimasu.

Hachijihan ni eki ni ikimasu.

Yoji ni mise ni ikimasu.

Yoji ni uchi ni kaerimasu as he 'walks' home.

Show students that it is possible to have two *ni* in a sentence.

Get students to offer similar sentences.

In pairs students work out ten sentences using the new material with any appropriate vocabulary previously learned.

Compliment.

(5 minutes)

4 TAPE. Listen to dialogue on page 117.

Open books. Read in pairs. Work out the meaning together.

(15-20 minutes)

5 Work through pages 118 and 119 together.

Stress when talking about times, that where ON or AT are used in English, *ni* is used in Japanese. Where English does not use ON or AT, don't use particle *ni* in Japanese. General time words don't have the particle. Habitual actions same as English—(Mondays) I go to school—no particle after the time word, but ON Mondays I go to school, *Getsuyoobi ni gakkoo ni ikimasen.*

Remind that the other use of *ni* is TO a place and that in English we say we'll go TO school or TO the park, we'll return TO school or return TO our house/return home (meaning TO our house). Remind that the particle is used in negatives too, e.g.: Mondays I don't go to the park, *getsuyoobi kooen ni ikimasen*, etc.

Check up on how students got on with check exercises last homework. Comment on *jikan ga arimasu ka. Jikan ga arimasen* as useful phrases to learn.

Homework

Do the writing practice on page 121.
Review all *hiragana* learned so far.
Read over textbook pages 103–120 and learn new vocabulary.

Dismissal: As students leave tell teacher somewhere they plan to go at a particular time (lessons, home, tennis, etc.). Try not to repeat what person before them has said.

Lesson Twenty-eight (Unit 7, page 123)

Aims and objectives

• To teach *mashoo*—let's.

• To consolidate use of *ni* particle and previously learned structures.

Preparation

Write new *katakana* vocabulary on board.
Photocopy dicomm activity.

Introduction

(10 minutes)
TAPE.
Greet. Put up date.
Guess the word. Introduce the new *katakana* words explaining that *katakana* words, as they have already learned, often sound similar to English. Try local names, remind of names of countries previously learned and names of nationalities and languages.
Ask for inspired guesses for meanings of new vocabulary.
Students open textbook and find the new vocabulary. Ask students to think of ways to remember the new vocabulary. What associations can they make? Encourage the students to start taking more responsibility for finding ways of learning vocabulary. Point out some of the ways that you have used to help them to remember words in the course so far—usually linking with real objects as often as possible and learning the Japanese word and its meaning in context wherever possible before seeing an English translation.

Main theme

(5-7 minutes)
1 Listen to tape of dialogue while reading silently from page 123. Listen to new material on tape. Answer the questions on paper during the pauses on the tape.

(5 minutes)

  2 Teach *mashoo* ending.

    Remind of last lesson's learning of *ikimasu* etc.

    Elicit what English phrase students would use if wanting someone to look at a book with them or go somewhere with them: Let's ...

    Write up the *mashoo* ending and show that it means 'Let's'.

    Ask students to supply the stems of all the verbs they know to put in front of *mashoo*. Write them up on the board in *roomaji* and *hiragana*.

(5 minutes)

  3 Dicomm activity: Find out what time activities will occur, who will go where, etc.

(3 minutes)

  4 Read over notes on page 124.

(10 minutes)

  5 Pairwork. Role play a conversation in which students meet, greet, talk about daily activities on particular days and suggest they go somewhere at a particular time on a particular day or this week or next week.

(5 minutes)

  6 Choose activities from pages 124–125.

Homework

Read over pages 117–124.
Learn new vocabulary.
Practice *hiragana*.

Dismissal: Students leave in pairs, one suggesting to the other an activity to do tomorrow and asking you *anata wa* to include you as they pass.

Lesson Twenty-nine (Unit 8, page 126)

Aims and objectives

- To teach the past tense of verbs.

Preparation

Past tense words *kinoo, sakuban, senshuu,* + *yoru* and *asa,* write on flash cards.
Large calendar with dates for this week, last week, and next week clearly visible to students.
Put on wall the word *Shukudai,* by the side of some of the work students have done for homework.

People, Times, and Activities

Note to teacher: Cut up one photocopy of sheets A and B and give each student one strip of information, e.g.: *(Sue) san wa (FUTTOBOORU) ga suki desu,* or *niji ni (FUTTOBOORU) o shimasu.* Each student will also receive sheet C, on which to record answers and to find out who are the two people who have an activity at the same time.

People, Times, and Activities, Sheet A

(Sue) san wa TENISU o shimasu

(Rachel) san wa BASUKETTOBOORU o shimasu

(Richard) san wa GITAA or renshuu shimasu

(Patti) san we PIANO o renshuu shimasu

Sumiko san wa ikebana ga suki desu

Shige san wa juudoo a shimasu

Mariko san wa shodoo ga suki desu

Masao san wa kendoo a shimasu

Tsutomu san wa karate ga suki desu

(Glen) san wa DOITSU go o benkyoo shimasu

(Donna) san wa FURANSU go o benkyoo shimasu

(Ken) san wa SUPEINgo o benkyoo shimasu

(Maria) san wa BAIORIN o renshuu shimasu

(Sam) san wa rikishi o benkyoo shimasu

Kimi san wa REKOODO o kikimasu

People, Times, and Activities, Sheet B

Nijihan ni TENISU o shimasu

Kujihan ni BASUKETTOBOORU o shimasu

Sanjihan ni GITAA o renshuu shimasu

Goji ni PIANO o renshuu shimasu

Sanji ni ikebana o shimasu

Shichiji ni BAIORIN o renshuu shimasu

Yojihan ni juudoo o renshuu shimasu

Hachiji ni REKOODO o kikimasu

Gojihan ni kendoo o shimasu

Shichiji ni shodoo o shimasu

Shichijihan ni karate o shimasu

Juuichiji ni DOITSU go o benkyoo shimasu

Kujihan ni FURANSU go o benkyoo shimasu

Nijihan ni SUPEINgo o benkyoo shimasu

Juuichijihan ni rekishi o benkyoo shimasu

DON'T SHOW YOUR INFORMATION TO ANYONE ELSE!
WHO IS THE FIRST TO FIND ALL THE INFORMATION?

People, Times, and Activities, Sheet C

Record the information that you need to find on this sheet.
To find out if someone has the topic you are looking for, ask *(TENISU) wa?*

If they have it, they will say '*hai*, if they haven't, *iie.*
If you want to know the time it will be played, ask *Nanji ni (TENISU) o shimasu ka*
To find out who does the activity, ask *dare ga (TENISU) o shimasu ka*
To answer, give the information on your strip of paper.

All these activities will take place at school.
Find out who the two people are who have activities at the same time.

Activity	Time	Person
TENISU		
BASUKETTOBOORU		
GITAA		
PIANO		
Ikebana		
Juudoo		
Shodoo		
Kendoo		
Karate		
DOITSUgo		
FURANSUgo		
SUPEINgo		
BAIORIN		
Rekishi		
REKOODO		

Introduction

(15 minutes)

New vocabulary:

Write date on board. Ask students day. Show calendar date and day for today.

Write up *kyoo wa (mokuyoobi) desu.* Show yesterday and ask *kinoo wa nanyoobi deshita ka.* Write up date for yesterday.

Ask *ashita wa nanyoobi desu ka.*

Draw time line of dates back to last (Thursday) on the board. Show calendar of past week.

Work back through the days to *kore wa senshuu no mokuyoobi desu.*

Elicit days from students with pattern *nanyoobi deshita ka.* Answer: *Senshuu no ... deshita.*

Using calendar again, go through last week's days with the pattern *kore wa senshuu no ... desu.* Work through *kore wa konshuu no getsuyoobi* etc. with the calendar until students are strong in using the pattern.

Draw a clock on the board and by eight o'clock in the morning write *asa.* By six o'clock in the evening write *yoru.* Ask students to guess what *PAATII* might mean. *TEREBI* (Draw a quick sketch), *DANSU.*

Offer three or four sentences about your life *watashi wa asa gakkoo ni ikimasu, yoru uchi ni kaerimasu, Yoru TEREBI o mimasu.* Elicit meaning in English. Explain that *yoru* and *asa* incorporate the idea of 'in the' so you don't need *ni* after them.

Go over all the new words again.

Ask for last lesson's homework *shukudai o kudasai*

See who can remember from the labels on the wall what they have to do. First one correct receives a small reward.

Review. Go through sports that students know in Japanese, and then ask who knows the most popular sport in Japan. Give the name *yakyuu*—baseball, and talk about its introduction from America and its rapid growth in popularity. Now the whole country gets *yakyuu* fever at times of national and local championship matches.

Main theme

(10 minutes)

1 Explain that when students need to talk about actions that happened in the past they will have to use a past tense in Japanese just as they have to do in English. Give some examples in English. Remind that they have learned before that in Japanese the stem stays the same and the ending is changed.

(10 minutes)

2 TAPE.

Ask them to listen to the tape and try to find out what the new ending will be for the past tense. Compliment those who have taken it in. Go over one or two verbs eliciting from students what is meant, e.g.: *Kinoo hon o yomimashita.* Listen again and understand what is being said. Find out how much was understood by asking questions in Japanese:

Kaeru san wa kinoo nani o shimashita ka.

Sumiko san wa kinoo nani o shimashita ka.

(10 minutes)

3 Turn to pages 126–127. Go through notes composing sentences together. Hold up flashcards and get students to volunteer sentences with each word.

4 Divide into small groups. Do a survey around the class on what students did last night. Each group member takes a turn to ask another member *sakuban nani o shimashita ka*. All group note the answers given by each person. Each student tries to give three true activities.
Each group then makes a list of all the activities of their own group by collating all the information. A leader reports to the class and a composite list of last night's activities is made on a poster.

Homework

Choose an activity from page 128.

Dismissal: While saying goodbye tell the teacher one thing done yesterday.

Lesson Thirty (Unit 9, page 129)

Aims and objectives

- To teach the past negative tense of verbs—*masen deshita*.
- To consolidate vocabulary.

Preparation

Update wall displays.
Photocopy onto thin card the sets of vocabulary for group work. Put each set into a container so they can be used again whenever you wish.

Introduction

TAPE.
Greet. Put up date.

Main theme

(10 minutes)

1 Talk to class about all the things they can now say in Japanese. They have learned how to greet people, introduce themselves to strangers, say what they like and dislike, give and understand instructions, talk about things in the classroom, say what they do at school and out of school, tell the time, count in Japanese, give and ask for telephone numbers, and say when they do, don't do and did things in their daily activities. An incredible amount for the time they have been studying—and they can write a lot of *hiragana* too! Today they will extend what they can say and practice sentence patterns to make sure that they really have got the order and the understanding correct before moving on to a new topic.

Elicit from them and write on the board all the verbs they know. Elicit the stem, *masu* form, *masen* form, and *mashita* form, and remind of the meaning of each.

Make sentences with each verb and each verb form known, commenting on the use of the particles and the sentence order.

(10 minutes)

2 Small groups. Give each group a set of cards. Students try to make sentences as fast as they can and put out in order on desks. When they only have odd words left, out of which it is impossible to make a sentence, they call out *owarimashita*.

They then take it in turns to read the sentences to the class. If any sentences are incorrect they put the words back and the game keeps going.

(5 minutes)

3 Explain that they now have a lot of possibilities for things they can say but one more structure would probably be helpful. Can anyone guess what it might be? They have some ways to say is like, dislike, please, (remind of those) will, won't, did—what might be useful to add on? Elicit 'did not'.

Teach *masen deshita* with all verbs known. Make sentences together.

4 Add in the *masen deshita* cards to the packs of cards used earlier and students work individually to make sentences—reading out the sentence when it is complete and putting it out on the desk for the partner to check, read and give the English.

They keep going until they have used all the cards they can possibly use. The winner out of each pair is the one who makes the last possible sentence.

5 Choose activities from page 129.

Homework

Check vocabulary and review textbook to page 130 for a test next lesson.

Dismissal: Students give an example of something they did not do yesterday as they leave.

Lesson Thirty-one (Evaluation lesson)

Aims and objectives

- To test retention of vocabulary and structures and ability to communicate and understand ideas about daily activities.

Introduction

Explain the need to check up from time to time on what students remember, to help them to keep up with the work and to give them a feeling of satisfaction that they have made progress

Main theme

(15 minutes)

1 TAPE. Listen to passage.
Read passage alongside tape.
(Listening, reading or comprehension)
A poor, hardworking student tells you about his week.

Senshuu watashi wa mainichi gakkoo ni ikimashita. Mainichi benkyoo shimashita. Kore wa watashi no shukudai deshita. Kiite kudasai.
Getsuyoobi, eigo to nihongo no shukudai o shimashita.
Kayoobi, kagaku to rekishi no shukudai o shimashita.
Suiyoobi, chirigaku to FURANSUgo to eigo o shimashita.
Mokuyoobi, eigo to suugaku to kagaku no shukudai or shimashita.
Kinyoobi, suugaku to nihongo to shakai o shimashita. Eigo o shimasen deshita.
Doyoobi, shukudai o shimasen deshita Juuji ni BAREEBOORU o shimashita, hon o yomimashita.
TEREBI o mimashita, TEEPU o kikimashita, Hisako san to Kenichi kun ni denwa o shimashita, watashi no inu ni hanashimashita.
Nichiyoobi, machi ni ikimashita. Rokuji ni DANSU no PAATII ni ikimashita. Nichiyoobi ni shukudai o shimasen deshita.
Ashita shimasu.

Answer the questions.

1 What subjects does the student study?
2 Did the student do homework every day?
3 Was there any light relief in the student's life?
4 Who did the student communicate with on Saturday?
5 What time was sports time?
6 What will happen tomorrow?
7 What languages does the student learn?
8 How many times a week does the student have English homework?
9 What did the student not do on Friday?
10 What do you think the student enjoys, but does not have time for in the week?

Verb Cards

The following pages of verb cards may be used in many ways:

1 Photocopy onto think card and cut up into small cards for students to use as a pack of cards turning up one at a time to make a sentence with that verb.

2 Photocopy and cut up cards tense by tense as your students learn the form.

3 Use them as a complete sheet for showing students the overall patterns of the verbs they have learned.

4 Use them for quiz questions.

5 Use them in conjunction with the vocabulary cards to play games in groups making sentences.

6 Use them for miming activities. Student takes a card and mimes activity.
Work out system for tenses, e.g.: arms crossed over face to show negative, hands behind to show past, draw a question mark in the air to show *mashoo,* go down on knees to show *kudasai,* cross arms behind head to show did not.

7 Students give each other spelling tests taking one card each at a time from the pile.

8 Give each student five cards to work out how to write it in *hiragana.* Then check with the textbook for main form and with the blackboard for endings.

NOTE: The students have only met some of the verbs in their instruction form, e.g.: *yonde kudasai.* It may be interesting as an extension activity to find out who can find the 'family' of verbs to which each *te kudasai* form belongs, and to practice making sentences with the whole 'family'.

Vocabulary cards

The following pages of vocabulary cards may be used in similar ways to verb cards. You can also use them in other ways:

1 Use for listening comprehension. Photocopy a sheet and call out ten words for identification.

2 Use for vocabulary quizzes.

3 Use for sentence making.

4 Use for guessing games.

5 Use for playing 'hangman' in Japanese.

Verb cards

kaerimasu	kikimasen deshita	kaite kudasai	ikimasen deshita	dewa arimasen deshita
ikimasu	renshuu shimashita	shimete kudasai	hanaashimashita	dewa arimasen
kikimasu	mimasen	akete kudasai	yomimashita	shimasen
benkyoo shimasu	kaerimashoo	benkyoo shimashita	mimasu	kikimashita
desu	ikimasen	deshita	kimasu	benkyoo shimasen
hanashimasu	yomimasen deshita	shimasen deshita	shimasu	mimashita
yomimasu	yomimasen	shimashita	renshuu shimasu	ikimashoo

Times

rokuji ni	shichiji ni	rokujihan	shichijihan
goji ni	juuniji ni	gojihan	juunijihan
yoji ni	juuichiji ni	yojihan	juuichijihan
sanji ni	juuji ni	sanjihan	juujihan
niji ni	kuji ni	hijihan	kujihan
ichiji ni	hachiji ni	ichijihan	hachijihan

Topic Two Vocabulary Cards

dore	jin	kore o kudasai	PEN	
doozo	janai desu	kore	NOOTO	yoochien
chuugakkoo	isu	kokuban	monosashi	tsukue
chizu	hako	keshigomu	manga	sore
BOORUPEN	gomibako	kami	mado	shoogakkoo
are	fudebako	kaite kudasai	kyooshitsu	shinbun
akete kudasai	e	juku	kootoogakkoo	shimete kudasai

Topic Three Vocabulary Cards

DOITSUgo	hanashimasen	kikimasu	nanigo	REKOODO
chiri	hanashimasu	kendoo	SUPEINgo	rekishi
chigaimasu	GITAA	karate	kun	RAJIO
benkyoo shimasu	gakkoo	kagaku	FUTTOBOORU	SAKKAA
BASUKETTO-BOORU	FURUUTO	juudoo	koohai	PIANO
BAREEBOORU	FURANSUgo	ITARIAgo	kirai desu	ongaku
BAIORIN	eigo	ikebana	kikimasen	BEISUBOORU

renshuu shimasu	senpai	shakai	shimasu	shimasen	soo desu	soo desu ka
suki desu	suki janai desu	SUPOOTSU	suugaku	taiiku	KASETTO TEEPU	TENISU
ya	yomimasu	yomimasen				

Topic Four Vocabulary Cards

doo itashimashite	HAIKINGU	ikimashoo	juuichi	juuhachi
doyoobi	hachi	ikimasu	juu	juunana
doko	go	ie	jikan ga arimasen	juuroku
denwa bangoo	getsuyoobi	ichi	jikan ga arimasu	juugo
BIDEO GEEMU	eki	hyaku	-ji	juuyon
ban	eiga	heisei	itsumo	juusan
ashita	ee	han	itsu	juuni

konshuu	. . . mashita	ni	raishuu	shichi
kinyoobi	. . . masen deshita	nanyoobi desu ka	PUURU	shi
kinoo	mainichi	nanaban desu ka	PIKUNIKKU	senshuu
kimasu	machi	nana	OOKURANDO	sanjuu
kayoobi	kyuu/ku	mokuyoobi	nijuuichi	san
kaerimasu	kuji	mimasu	nijuu	roku
juukyuu/ku	kooen	. . . mashoo	nichiyoobi	rei

uchi	ZERO
toshokan	zero
tasu	yon
suiyoobi	yoji
shukudai	yakyuu
shoowa	NYUUYOOKU
SHIDONII	umi

Topic Five Vocabulary Cards

atsui	haru	kiri	samukunai	Ame deshoo ka
atatakakunai	hanami	kaze	samui	yuki
atatakai	Rosanzerusu	kara	Otenki	warui
ame	fuyu	kaminari	ne	tsuyu
aimasu	baiu	ka	naze desu ka	suzushikunai
aki	atsukunai	ii Otenki desu	natsu	suzushii
akauri	Atsui deshoo ka	ii	mushi atsui	shimo

ni	o	wa	ga	ka
ni	o	wa	ga	ka
ni	o	wa	ga	ka
ni	o	wa	ga	ka
ni	o	wa	ga	ka
ni	o	wa	ga	ka
ni	o	wa	ga	ka

Times and Activities

In groups of three, find out from two classmates what they study and what musical instruments or games they play. Find out what times on what days they do these activities. On the board collate the numbers for each activity as the information is reported to the group. Each student will need two of the following forms to fill in and stick into their notebooks when completed.

Ask:	*O namae wa nan desu ka*
	Nani o benkyoo shimasu ka
	Nani ga suki desu ka
	Nani ga kirai desu ka
	Ongaku o shimasu ka
Find out what kind-	*PIANO desu ka*
	GITAA desu ka
When do you do it?	*Itsu shimasu ka*
What kind of sport?	SUPOOTSU *o shimasu ka*
	Donna SUPOOTSU *desu ka*

Seito no namae wa _____ *desu*

Benkyoo wa _____ *desu*

_____ *wa* (Study liked) *suki desu*

_____ *wa* (Study disliked) *kirai desu*

Ongaku wa _____ *o renshuu shimasu*

(Itsu) _____

SUPOOTSU *wa* _____ *o shimasu*

(Itsu) _____

(15 minutes)

2 Dicomm survey activity to evaluate students' ability to ask for and give information.

(15 minutes)

3 Prepare a role play (see outline for photocopying). Depending upon confidence of the class ask them to perform it in front of a small group or the whole class next lesson and to practice in their own time between this lesson and the next (While one group is showing their play to you and a group, others can keep practicing quietly, until you have worked your way around to them.)

Homework

Writing Practice page 130.
Check exercises (Teacher's choice)

Dismissal: Sing song *Musunde hiraite* together (TAPE).

Lesson Thirty-two (Roleplay lesson)

Aims and objectives

• To give students an opportunity to show their prepared roleplays to the class.

Introduction

Sing *Musunde hiraite* with TAPE to relax students.

Main theme

(5 minutes)

1 Practice roleplays for five minutes only.

2 Do roleplays either in front of small group or whole class at teacher's discretion. Outline:
   • Meet a friend or a stranger.
   • Greet each other.
   • Introduce with name, nationality. Use *nan desu ka, desu* and *dewa arimasen*.
   • Tell about school life.
   • Tell about out of school activities and when they do them, likes and dislikes.
   • Ask each other what they did yesterday/last week.
   • Ask if they played tennis yesterday.
   • Reply: No didn't play.
   • Suggest playing tomorrow.
   • Say goodbye.
   Those listening keep a tally every time the pair do one of the things they were asked to do and give a total mark for communicating the information asked for, for giving more than asked for, for an enjoyable performance. The important thing is whether they understand what the pair are communicating, not whether it is totally accurate all the time.
   (This ensures that everyone listens carefully.)

Compliment for quality of work. Find something good about every roleplay to boost confidence and keep students willing to try.

Encourage to make up lots of mini-plays to show class. Remind that in the real situation they won't have time to look up books and practice so they will gradually be given practice so that they can do roleplays 'off the top of their heads'.

Homework

Students write the script of their role play for teacher to evaluate accuracy of sentence patterns and spelling.

Dismissal: Hold up *hiragana* flash cards, allow to leave in groups as they read the syllables together.

Roleplay checklist

- Meet a friend or a stranger.
- Greet each other.
- Introduce each other with name and nationality.
- Use *nan desu ka, desu, dewa arimasen.*
- Tell each other about your school life.
- Talk about your out-of-school activities, and when you do them.
- Tell each other your likes and dislikes.
- Ask each other what you did yesterday, and what you did last week.
- Ask if you played tennis yesterday.
- Reply—No, I didn't play.
- Suggest that you play tomorrow.
- Say goodbye.

TOPIC FIVE
Lesson Thirty-three (Introduction & Unit 1, page 134)

Aims and objectives

- To teach the students adjectives to describe the weather and the names of seasons.
- To teach the difference between adjectives and nouns.

Preparation

Teru teru boozu page 136.
Temperature chart showing *atsui* at top and *samui* at the bottom—other temperatures between.
Pictures of the seasons or calendar.
Pictures of good weather, bad weather with appropriate labels (children's reading books are often a good source of pictures).

Introduction

Greet the class, commenting on the weather today, exaggerating the temperature. Ask *samui desu ka* (shivering as you do so), *atsui desu ka,* mopping brow. Elicit response from students.

Main theme

(5 minutes)

1 Show pictures saying *ii otenki desu, atsui desu, warui otenki desu, samui desu* appropriately. Elicit the same information from students as you show several pictures to them several times in different order (ask *samui desu ka/Otenki wa nan desu ka* etc. to get as much mileage out of the pictures as possible).

(5-10 minutes)

2 Talk about the way weather is usually a topic of conversation in any country and that people have sayings and superstitions connected with the weather. Show the students a *teru teru boozu* (page 136). Hang it in the window to wish for fine weather tomorrow.
Draw on board a snowman, a cloud, half a sun, a big sun. As you are drawing say *samui desu, suzushii desu, atatakai desu, atsui desu,* appropriately.
Go through them once or twice. Dodge around the pictures randomly to elicit the temperature words from the students.

(5 minutes)

3 Show calendar months appropriately for your part of the world and say *natsu desu—atsui desu, aki desu—suzushii desu, fuyu desu—samui desu, haru desu—atatakai desu.*
Elicit how to say 'It is'—*desu.*
What therefore does *atsui desu* mean?
Explain that the *ne* is a noise that asks for agreement from the other person.
Practice saying *atsui desu ne, samui desu ne, fuyu wa samui desu ne,* etc.

(5 minutes)

    4 Have fun with *atatakai* using it as a tongue-twister and *Atatakakunai.*

(5 minutes)

    5 Demonstrate good and bad and write them up, good at the top, bad at the bottom of the board. Show students pictures and charts and go through the vocabulary.

    Ask students to write the new vocabulary in their books with their own picture associations.

(15 minutes)

    6 TAPE. Listen to tape conversation and understand (page 139)

    Students make up a role play in pairs in which they greet someone they haven't seen for a while, talk about the weather, suggest doing something together at a particular time.

    Say they will or won't do the suggested activity.

    Each pair splits up and goes to find a new person with whom to have a similar conversation. This time they will have to listen very carefully as they don't know what the other person will say and try to make appropriate responses.

    Teacher circulates listening and making sure students are really making an effort to communicate in Japanese by having conversations with students to the same pattern while circulating.

Homework

Learn new vocabulary.
Study pages 136–138. Find out how to say 'not hot' etc.
Do the matching activity on page 139.

Dismissal: Each student makes a comment about the weather when leaving

Lesson Thirty-four (Unit 2, page 141)

Aims and objectives

- To consolidate last lesson.

- To teach weather nouns and their usage patterns.

Preparation

Pictures of weather conditions.

Introduction

Greet. Ask about the weather today.

Main theme

(5-7 minutes)

    1 TAPE. Listen to conversation from page 139 again.

    Check understanding by asking questions in Japanese.

Weather Symbols

Weather and Activities

Photocopy six sheets of weather symbols and cut up into cards. These may be used simply for *Otenki wa nan desu ka, Otenki wa nan deshoo ka,* or for an activity similar to the following:
Photocopy onto thin card the activity cards that follow. Cut up.

1 Each group needs a set of weather symbols and activity cards. Place weather cards face downwards on desk. Spread out activity cards face upwards on the desk. Students take one weather card and find one activity that they can do in those weather conditions, and one that they can't do. Say when the weather will be or is in that state, then put them together and read out the sentences made, e.g.: *kyoo atsui desu kara eiga ni ikimasen, umi ni ikimasu.*
Each person keeps the cards if they have made sentences that the others agree to be sensible. Each person takes a turn until it is impossible to make a sensible sentence with the remaining cards. The winner is the one who has the most cards.

2 Use a checker board. Students throw dice to see how many squares they can move depending on the number value of the weather card they pick up. They must say what the weather state is and suggest a suitable activity before being allowed to move their counter along the board. Winner is the first to reach the other side of the board. (Students may like to make up their own board games with similar themes.)

3 Extension: Place activity cards face down on the desk. Each student picks up a card and puts in into the past tense.

Weather

Use weather symbol cards from previous activity. Photocopy enough sheets for your class (1 sheet to 3 students).
Groups or whole class listen as teacher or student reads out the day and weather randomly from a master sheet, ticking off the ones read out as they go. Students listen and find the relevant pairs of information. Cover with appropriate weather card to prove all have been correctly covered. Student reads out information and gives English equivalent of the weather cards. Information is checked against master sheet to see if it has in fact been read out.

suiyoobi / atatakai deshoo	ka yoobi / samui deshoo	getsuyoobi / atsui deshoo
doyoobi / yuki deshoo	kinyoobi / mushi atsui deshoo	mokuyoobi / suzushii deshoo
ashita / ii otenki desu	kyoo / kaze deshoo	nichiyoobi / ame deshoo
getsuyoobi / taifuu desu	ashita / tsuyu desu	kyoo / iya na tenki desu
nichiyoobi / hare deshoo	suiyoobi / atsui desu	kayoobi / kumori deshoo

(5-7 minutes)

2 Show students pictures of weather conditions. Give Japanese word.

Ask *donna otenki desu ka* (don't worry about explaining *donna*, just tell them it means 'What kind of').

Elicit word. Play a fast game with them calling out the weather as you quickly show pictures.

(10 minutes)

3 Go through pages 137–138 quickly. Teach what adjectives and nouns are if students are not clear about them.

Write up two lists from the new vocabulary with the help of students: the nouns in one and the adjectives in the other. Point out that today's vocabulary—rain, snow, etc.—are nouns. Write in noun list.

(10 minutes)

4 Work back over the past week and record the weather for each day with the pattern *getsuyoobi wa ii otenki deshita, kayoobi wa atsui otenki deshita,* etc.

(10 minutes)

5 Students draw up a weather chart in their notebooks on which to record the coming week's or month's weather. Write in the names of the days in Japanese. Start a key of symbols used with the Japanese name alongside. Have a competition to see who can maintain a record every day, accurately for a specified period of time (decide on a time of day for noting weather).

Homework

Learn new vocabulary and patterns.
Read introduction to the weather topic page 135.

Dismissal: Students tell you if they are hot cold warm or cool as they leave.

Lesson Thirty-five (Unit 3, page 143)

Aims and objectives

- To teach *deshoo* with nouns and adjectives only.

- To consolidate *hiragana* learned.

Preparation

Pictures of weather conditions: rain, snow, cloud.
Write up words of song in *hiragana* large enough for whole class to read leaving space below to add *roomaji* later.

Introduction

(5 minutes)
TAPE. Listen to song as they enter.
Greet, write date and ask students for present weather and temperature.
Write under date.

Main theme

(10 minutes)

1 Listen to song, try to pick up words. The tape will play it three times.
Teach song, explaining that they don't need to translate it, just enjoy it!
It's about snow in winter. Can anyone read any of the *hiragana?*
As they offer, write up syllables in *roomaji* under the *hiragana.*

(5 minutes)

2 Divide class into two teams. Call out *hiragana* syllables from those known. Students race to be first to write called syllable on the board.
Which of the temperature words can they write in *hiragana? (atatakai) (atatakakunai)*
Remind to keep practicing the *hiragana.*

(5 minutes)

3 In pairs practice answering the questions on page 144.

(10 minutes)

4 Ask the questions around the class, each student asking a question in turn, of any other person. The person who answers takes the next turn to question. Questions may be taken out of order but should not be repeated until all ten have been used. Anyone who repeats a question is 'out'. After ten questions, start again until all have a turn. Encourage students to try to work out the answers in their heads while listening to other people's answers.

(10 minutes)

5 On the weather chart fill in today's weather together.
Fill in names of days in Japanese, writing them in carefully copied *hiragana.*
(Later they will be able to tell you how to double the *o* when writing *hiragana* from the unconscious absorption.)

Dismissal: Sing the song looking at the *hiragana* syllables. A group at a time leave at your signal.

Lesson Thirty-six (Extension unit, page 145)

Aims and objectives

- To teach *naze desu ka*.
- To encourage speed learning.
- To listen for specific items.

Preparation

TAPE.

Introduction

Greet.
Put up date and weather.
Check homework and weather charts.

Main theme

(5 minutes)

1 Listen to tape of conversation very carefully. What was the new word?

(10 minutes)

2 Open book. Practice conversation with a friend until they can say everything without looking at the book. Who are the first pair who are word perfect? They prove their claim. Reward!

(5 minutes)

3 Teach *desu kara*, pages 145–146.
   Do activities

(5 minutes)

4 Teach *aimasu*, pages 146–147

(20 minutes)

5 Choose activities from pages 147–148.

Homework

Vocabulary check.
Hiragana check.

Dismissal: Students tell you when they will meet someone and what they plan to do (e.g.: *BEN san ni aimasu. TENISU o shimasu*).

Pair work activity

(May also be used for listening comprehension)

Pairs receive a sheet each, A or B, and keep sheets hidden from each other. Teacher explains the following and puts up possible questions on the board.

Two students meet at the end of the holidays and catch up on what their friends are planning to do or have done recently. Each has information about Dan and Mariko. The other student knows about Nicky and Masao. Offer the first sentence on your sheet and then wait for questions. Ask each other questions like these to find all the information that your partner has.

Ask:

Kyoo doko ni ikimasu ka	*Senshuu doko ni ikimashita ka*
Nanji ni ikimasu ka	*Itsu ikimashita ka*
Nani o shimasu ka	*Nanyoobi ni ikimashita ka*
Dare ni aimasu ka	*Nani o shimashita ka*
	Itsu ... san ni aimashita ka
	Otenki wa nan deshita ka

If you don't know the answer, say *wakarimasen* (I don't know!)

Try to follow up with questions that find out more information when you are given some information, e.g.: If someone tells you they have been to Australia, ask where or when, or when they came home.

If your partner runs out of questions before you have given all the information you have, give it voluntarily. Don't forget to make noises like *soo desu ka* and *soo desu* to show that you are interested!

Student A

Find out the following information about Nicky and Masao:

  What are they doing today?
  What time will they do it?
  What did they do last week?
  Where will they go? Where have they been?
  Who will they meet? Who have they met?
  What is the weather like? What was it like?
  Any other information?

Reporting to the group:
  Be prepared to tell the group at least one sentence in Japanese about the personalities of the people you have been finding out about.

Here is what you know about Mariko and Dan:
  Kyoo ii otenki desu kara Mariko san wa sanji ni kooen ni ikimasu.
  TENISU o shimasu Kenji san ni aimasu. Mainichi Kenji san ni aimasu.
  Mainichi Kenji san to Mariko san wa TENISU o shimasu.
  Senshuu Mariko san to Kenji san wa eiga ni ikimashita.
  Kyoo DAN san wa nihingo o benkyoo shimasu. Nijihan ni to shokan ni ikimasu.
  DAN san wa itsumo to shokan ni ikimasu. Mainichi nihongo no hon o yomimasu.
  Itsumo SUPOOTSU o shimasen deshita. Senshuu NYUUYOOKU ni ikimashita.
  Kinoo kaerimashita.

Student B

Find out the following information about Mariko and Dan:

  What are they doing today?
  What time will they do it?
  Who will they meet? Who have they met?
  Where will they go? Where have they been?
  What did they do last week?
  What is the weather like? What was it like? When?
  Any other information?

Reporting to the group:
  Be prepared to tell the group at least one sentence in Japanese about the personalities of the people you have been finding out about.

Here is what you know about Nicky and Masao:
  Kyoo no ichiji ni NIKKI san wa OOSUTORARIA ni ikimasu.
  SHIDONII ni ikimasu. Senshuu no getsuyoobi ni ame deshita.
  NIKKI san to watashi wa eiga ni ikimashita.
  Mariko san to Kenji san ni aimashita. Eiga ga suki deshita.
  Masao san wa kinoo nihon ni kaerimashita. Kyoo nihon no gakkoo ni ikimasu.
  Mainichi Masao san wa eigo o benkyoo shimasu. Ii seito desu ne!
  Senshuu NIKKI san to Masao san wa umi ni ikimashita. Ii Otenki deshita.

Activity cards

BASUKETTO-BOORU o shimasu	Umi ni ikimasen	KASETTO TEEPU o kikimasu	Toshokan ni ikimasu	E o mimasu
TENISU o shimasen	Umi ni ikimasu	Manga o yomimasen	HAIKINGU ni ikimasen	Yakyuu o shimasen
TENISU o shimasu	Eiga ni ikimasen	Manga o yomimasu	HAIKINGU ni ikimasu	Yakyuu o shimasu
REKOODO o kikimasen	Eiga ni ikimasu	Kooen ni ikimasen	Eki ni ikimasu	BIDEO GEEMU o shimasu
REKOODO o kikimasu	Machi ni ikimasen	Kooen ni ikimasu	Mise ni ikimasu	PUURU ni ikimasen
Hon o yomimasen	Machi ni ikimasu	RAJIO o kikimasen	Mise ni ikimasu	PUURU ni ikimasu
Hon o yomimasu	BASUKETTO-BOORU o shimasen	RAJIO o kikimasu	KASETTO TEEPU o kikimasen	Toshokan ni ikimasen

GITAA o renshuu shimasen				
GITAA o renshuu shimasu				
Ongaku o renshuu shimasu				
Uchi ni kaerimasu	DOITSUgo o benkyoo shimasen			
E o kakimasen	FURANSUgo o benkyoo shimasu			
E o kakimasu	Eigo o rehshuu shimasu			
E o mimasen	Nihongo o benkyoo shimasu			

Ano hito no namae wa nan desu ka (A)

Greet each person. Ask for the information you need. Say thank you and goodbye.

Ano hito no namae wa nan desu ka. Doko no kata desu ka.
Ano hito no namae wa .... desu. ....jin desu.

Maria san wa.

_____

_____

Maria   Eliza san wa.

AMERIKAjin desu. Kookoosei desu.

NYUUYOOKU ni sune imasu.

Eliza   Simon san wa.

_____

_____

Simon   Lucy san wa.

DOITSUjin desu. HANBURUGU ni sunde imasu.

Daigakusei desu.

Lucy   Jared san wa.

_____

_____

Jared   Tom san wa.

Chuugokujin desu. Kookoosei desu.

HONKON ni sunde imasu.

Tom

Ano hito no namae wa nan desu ka (B)

Greet each person. Ask for the information you need. Say thank you and goodbye.

Ano hito no namae wa nan desu ka. Doko no kata desu ka.
Ano hito no namae wa .... desu. ....jin desu.

Maria san wa.

NYUUJIIRANDOjin desu.

OOKURANDO ni sunde imasu. Kooloosei desu.

Maria Eliza san wa.

_____

_____

Eliza Simon san wa.

OOSUTORARIAjin desu.

Daigakusei desu. SHIDONII ni suned imasu.

Simon Lucy san wa.

_____

_____

Lucy Jared san wa.

FURANSUjin desu. Chuugakusei desu.

PARI ni sunde imasu.

Jared Tom san wa.

_____

_____

Tom

TOPIC SIX—Myself and others

Lesson Thirty-seven (Introduction and Unit 1, page 150)

Aims and Objectives

- to teach how to ask age with *nansai*.
- to teach about some festivals connected with age: *Shichi Go San* and *Seijin No Hi*.
- *Hiragana:* teach *shuu, juu, issai, hassai, kyuu,* and doubling letters in words like *gakkoo.*

Preparation

Decorate the classroom as for a birthday party, display birthday cards, 2–3 balloons, etc. Label with *Tanjoobi.*

Put the picture of four birthday cakes up on the wall during the lesson:

One with 20 candles labeled *Seijin No Hi* and *hatachi,*

Three others with 3, 5, and 7 candles respectively, labeled *Shichi Go San.*

If possible take in a cake and candles to use for demonstration. Hide until required.

Rewards for quiz (balloons maybe, if you don't use a cake).

Introduction

(10 minutes)

Tape music for entry. Greet. Put up date. Is it anyone's birthday? If so use *O tanjoobi ..omedetoo gozaimasu.* Sing Happy Birthday to that student (in English!)

Who has had a birthday recently? What difference has it made to their lives?

Talk about birthdays and their importance to people.

Elicit from students information about the relevance of certain birthdays to them. Different families and nationalities will have different ages for privileges and responsibilities, such as:

      becoming a teenager

      being allowed certain privileges—

          going to movies

          use of make-up

          dating

          bedtime

          driving a vehicle

          voting

          getting married

Discuss traditional ways of marking these milestones in students' own society.

Talk about the Western system of counting in months from birth up to the first birthday and then explain the *kazoedoshi* method in Japan (Page 151).

Talk about two Japanese special birthdays:

Show pictures of children going to the shrine for a blessing just after birth. Link with christenings and dedications at church.

Show pictures of the next important birthdays in Japan: *Shichi Go San* held on November 15. Boys of five and three and girls of three and seven are taken to shrines to receive a blessing and to give

---

thanks for good health. It is a joyful occasion and thousands of families flow through the shrines on that day with their children all dressed in beautiful new *kimono,* carrying *chitose ame* as a symbol of long life. Why do students think all the children of those ages go on the same day? (*kazoedoshi*) Have they got anything similar in their society or is it all individual dates?

Talk about *Seijin No Hi*—another time when all those who have had a particular birthday (become twenty in the previous year) celebrate a day together. Teach the word *hatachi* for twenty years old. It is such a special occasion that it merits a special word.

Draw a large key on the board to symbolize 20 being the age for getting the key of the door and adult responsibility and write up *hatachi* by the side.

Students think: What would be the advantages and disadvantages?

Compare own society's ages for responsibility with those of Japan.

Make a chart to put on the wall. (page 151)

Show the word *tanjoobi* and elicit from students what they think it may mean (looking at the classroom displays and perhaps having heard the birthday greeting to one of the class).

Main theme

(5 minutes)

1 Review numbers. Who will volunteer to give the numbers to ten? Have a game around the class, each student giving the next number as fast as they can until someone makes a mistake, OR

Count in twos, threes, fours, etc. (use table square if you wish).

Ask student volunteers to write the numbers one to nineteen on the board. Teacher writes the *hiragana* beside the *roomaji.*

(5 minutes)

2 Introduce the word *sai* as the counter for ages. Explain that when you want to give an age it is necessary to adjust some of the number words to make the sound more agreeable:

They cannot use *ichisai* but must say *issai* for one year old.

Which other number do they think will need to be changed if they follow that rule?

Elicit *hassai* instead of *hachisai.*

Teach *jussai* for ten years old, and then go through the words for ages to twenty, putting up the ages alongside the numbers to twenty previously written, so that students can see the relationship.

(5 minutes)

3 Pick out a group of students who are friends, demonstrating *? san wa, ? san no tomodachi desu; ? san wa, ? san ga suki desu; ? san wa ? san no tomodachi desu; kochira wa ? san no tomodachi no ? san desu.*

Elicit the meaning from the students.

Ask students to tell you who ?'s friend is.

Ask *(Ken) san, (JON) san wa nansai desu ka … Juuissai desu ka. Juunisai desu ka. Juusansai desu ka* until Ken gives the answer required.

Ask him his age with *nansai desu ka.*

(10 minutes)

4 Bring out a picture of a person or draw a figure on the board.
Introduce the person with *ano hito wa (...) san desu.*
(...) san wa watashi no tomodachi desu. (...) san ga suki desu.
Kyoo wa (...) san no tanjoobi desu.
Bring out cake with no candles on it.
Explain: *(...) san no tanjoobi no KEEKI desu.*
If you have no cake draw one on board and get students to draw candles as you proceed.
Ask students: *Dare no desu ka, (...) san wa dare desu ka.*
Elicit name and try to get response: *Anata no tomodachi desu,* or *(...) san wa anata no tomodachi desu.*
Ask, pointing to the cake: *Nan desu ka.*
Elicit: *KEEKI desu and tanjoobi no KEEKI desu,* and *(...) san no tanjoobi no KEEKI desu.*
Invite a student to light the candles one by one.
Ask the students after each candle is lit: *(Ano hito wa) nansai desu ka.*
Students chorus ages until you arrive at thirteen/fourteen (age of majority of your class).
Blow out the candles.

(5 minutes)

5 Student volunteers read dialogue to class.

6 Quick written answer quiz:
  What is the name of Kennichi's friend?
  Has Kimiko met her before?
  What time of day is it?
  How old is Kimiko?
  How old is Yumiko?
  How old is Kennichi?
  How many have answered all correctly?
  Reward (with a piece of birthday cake or other).

(5 minutes)

7 Teach *watashi no tomodachi no (Yumiko)chan desu, (JON)kun desu.*
Ask students who have not had a reward yet to come out and tell you the name of their friend using that pattern and giving the friend's age. Reward the first two or three to volunteer without warning them of your intention (with a small piece of cake). (If they come out voluntarily those who are not sure have time to practice before their turn arrives). The rest of class listen carefully to answers. Randomly question the class on the information you have just been given to keep them listening with *(name of student) no tomodachi no namae wa nan desu ka (name of student) no tomodachi no (... kun/chan) wa nansai desu ka.*

(5 minutes) (Finish writing for homework if necessary.)

8 Conclusion. Students practice asking the ages of 5 other people's friends. Write down the answers in their books after heading *Nansai desu ka.*

Homework

Practice the new *hiragana.*
Do the reading exercise on page 156.

Answers

1. Watashi wa nihongo ga suki desu.
2. Ima nanji desu ka.
3. Juuji ni aimasu.
4. Hana ga suki desu ka.
5. Michiko san wa hassai desu.
6. Kasa desu.
7. Zasshi desu.
8. Yumiko san wa juuhassai desu.
9. Sore wa ki desu.
10. Kyoo wa umi ni ikimasu.

Ask students to start collecting material about Japan (news and magazine articles), finding out what books on Japan are in their local libraries—folklore, customs, crafts, geography, history—to be used later in the term.

Dismissal: Students tell you their age and say goodbye as they file past.

Lesson Thirty-eight

Aims and objectives

- to review some of the achievements from first five topics of Basic Japanese.

Preparation

Photocopy accompanying sheets for students.

Introduction

(5 minutes)
Tape. Greet and put up date. Choose situations from earlier lessons to check.
Explain need in language learning (because it is cumulative) to keep checking that previously learned material is still spontaneously available for use and that today new material will be added to it.

Main Theme

(20-25 minutes)
Suggestions:
Photocopy sheet for students. Check over to make sure students are not consolidating incorrect patterns.
Conclusion

(15 minutes)
Roleplay an introduction between adult stranger and student, adding weather comments. The stranger drops something and the student gives it back. The stranger is pleased and asks how old the student is and what the student studies at school. He is pleased that the student is learning Japanese. They say goodbye.
Practice quickly and efficiently. Show to class.
Comment on plays and point out the building process. Each lesson more can be added on.

Homework

Check over vocabulary from earlier lessons.

Dismissal: Introduce next student in line to teacher.

The following are some of situations you learned earlier in Basic Japanese.
With a partner work through them and check that you still know how to say these things.
If there are some you have forgotten, check in your notebook or ask your teacher for help.
After you have checked that you are correct, test each other until you are both perfectly sure that you know them well.

1 How would you introduce yourself to someone your own age and say goodbye
   a) informally
   b) formally

2 How would you introduce yourself to a complete stranger for the first time?
   Greet each other. Introduce yourself with phrases appropriate to the time of meeting. Give your nationality. Ask the stranger's nationality. Comment on the weather today. Say goodbye formally.

3 How would you ask if someone thinks the weather will be fine tomorrow? Rainy? Cold?

4 What would you say to find out what someone studies at school?

5 How would you tell someone what you study?

6 How would you tell someone what you like and dislike?

7 What would you say to ask someone if he/she had read a book about Japan yesterday?

8 How would you find out who the pencil you had just picked up belonged to?

9 How would you tell someone the pencil is yours?

Lesson Thirty-nine (*Atarashii seito desu ka,* page 158)

Aims and objectives

  • to teach how to explain what year student you are.
  • to introduce *atarashii/atarashikunai.*
  • to review particle *no.*
  • to teach writing of own and friends' names in *katakana.*
  • to review previously learned structures.
  • notes about the use of *san, chan* and *kun.*

Preparation

Something old and something new.
Name cards of students' names in *katakana* to put on students' desks for familiarization. Collect in each lesson. (Next lesson put cards out and ask students to find own desk.)

Introduction

Greet and put up date.

Put up, in students view, two objects—new and not new with labels alongside.

Talk about being new. Ask class what it feels like and how they think they would feel:

1 if thousands of miles from home,

2 in a country with a different language.

Work on the idea that people are usually very glad to find someone to talk to from their own culture or language even though they may be keen to immerse themselves in the new culture. Explain that when in a country with a different language there are always things you don't understand clearly. It is often necessary to make a thoughtful guess. Ask them to do that while listening to the teacher reading the conversation before they open their own textbooks or listening to the tape, and see how much they understand.

See if they can pick out the words they haven't heard before and make some sort of guess at them.

Who can make some sort of guess at the link between the two objects on the desk and the discussion you've just had?

Main theme

Listen to tape of conversation on page 158.

How much do they understand? Which words are a puzzle?

Comment on the understanding.

They may have worked out *atarashii* by this time. Consolidate.

Show new object to class and contrast it with something not new using *atarashii desu* and *atarashikunai desu*. If you have a new student, introduce to the class with *atarashii seito desu.*

Contrast with others in class who are not new.

Write up the new words and ask if the class can think of any other words they know that end the same way (*ii* or *kunai*). Elicit the weather adjectives learned in Topic Five.

Point out that all are adjectives and take the ending *kunai* in the negative.

Talk about the word *atarashii*. It can mean new or fresh. They need to use the context to decide which is appropriate.

What was another new word? (*ichinensei, ninensei*). Did class remember *chuugakkoo*? If so, commend.

SHIKAGO ni sunde imasu. Comment and learn just as a phrase.

Try to elicit the meanings of these words by writing on the board your class followed by *Nihongo no ichinensei,* and the following year class—*Nihongo no ninensei.*

OR

Put up the names of well known students in three consecutive year classes and the words *ichinensei, ninensei,* etc.

Students know *ichi* and *ni*.Show them *sei(to)* and see if they can make the connection themselves. Explain that this is an important skill to develop as they continue their study, but it will come slowly. They must not be discouraged if some students seem to be able to make connections more quickly than they do.

Can they make any guesses about *SHIKAGO ni sunde imasu* after you have drawn a sketch map of your country with a town marked clearly, by which there is a house. Tell the students it is your house: (name of town) *ni sunde imasu*.

(The principle we are working on is to make the words and phrases memorable and meaningful by demonstration and to let the students themselves make the connections. Just feeding them the vocabulary lists does not encourage the same consciousness.)

Teach the other new phrases using the same principle.

What do they think will have to happen when the bell rings?

What do people usually say in English when they need to break off a conversation?

What would they be likely to say to each other as they part?

Listen to or read the dialogue again and students can have the pleasure of understanding everything easily. Point out that this is a common feature of learning a new language. At first it is just a jumble of meaningless sounds. Gradually, partial understanding occurs followed by full comprehension if they are patient and keep going.

Do the Study section on page 160 together.

Conclusion

Choose two activities from page 161.

Homework

Learn how to write own name in *katakana*.

Read over pages 158–162. Do the first activity on page 161,

OR

Make a list of all the questions they now know how to ask.

Dismissal: Say what year student they are as they pass—*Watashi wa kootoogakkoo no ichinensei desu (Chuugakkoo no ichinensei desu)* depending on your school system. *Nihongo no ichinensei desu.*

Lesson Forty

Aims and Objectives

- to review order of words in questions and statements.
- to give the students the opportunity to use questions and answer questions within the framework of their present vocabulary and structures.

Preparation

Photocopy sheets of questions for pairs of students or groups.
Choose activities from list below.
Scissors.

Introduction

(10 minutes)
Tape. Greet, put up date.
Remind of sentence order in making questions.
Do a few examples on the board.
Prepare questions for quiz. (Team game or homework, or use the ones given below).
Divide class into teams or groups.
Who can come up with the longest list of questions in ten minutes?
Number the neatly written list.
Who had most?

(25 minutes)

1 Group work. Students ask each other the questions prepared, turn by turn, to ensure all the students in that group can answer their own question list.

2 Teams read out their questions and challenge other teams to answer. Teacher is the arbiter.

    OR

    Quickly cut up all questions from each group and put in box.
    Extract questions one by one for students to answer, in groups, or individually.

Question list

(There will be many more possibilities as students combine different elements but here are the most important.) It's quite impressive!
(Examples of matching exercise. Find the question to which these could be the answers.)

O namae wa nan desu ka	*Yon go san no yon ni roku desu*
Denwa bangoo wa nan desu ka	*Neko ga kirai desu*
Nanban desu/deshita ka	*Hai enpitsu desu*
Nan desu/deshita ka	*Nanajuu deshita*
(enpitsu) desu/deshita ka	*Hai soo desu/Soo desu ka*
Itsu desu/deshita ka	*Watashi no namae wa (SUE) desu*
Dare desu/deshita ka	*Getsuyoobi desu*
(Neko) desu/deshita ka	*Hai, neko desu*
Nani ga kirai desu ka	*Kyoo desu*

A further list of possible questions:

Dare ga suki desu ka	*Dare no (inu) desu ka*
Watashi no desu ka	*Anata no (hon) desu ka*
Anata no desu ka	*Dare no desu ka*

Dare ga kirai desu ka *Nani ga suki desu ka*
Doko no kata desu ka *Anata no tomodachi desu ka*
Tomodachi no desu ka *... san no desu ka*
... san desu ka *Kore desu ka/Sore desu ka*
Ano hito wa dare desu ka *Ano hito wa doko no kata desu ka*
Ima nanji desu ka *Nanji ni (gakkoo ni) ikimasu/ikimashita ka*
Nanji ni kaerimasu/kaerimashita ka *(Ichiji) ni ikimasu ka* (Many verb possibilities)
Dare ga kimasu/kimashita ka *Dare ga ikimasu/ikimashita ka*
Dare ga kaerimasu/kaerimashita ka *Doko ni ikimasu/ikimashita ka*
Nanijin desu ka *(FURANSU) jin desu ka*
Ogenki desu ka *Doko ni sunde imasu ka*
(Hon) o yomimasu/yomimashita ka *(REKOODO) o kikimasu/kikimashita ka*
Jikan ga arimasu/arimashita ka *Nani o shimasu/shimashita ka*
Nani o benkyoo shimasu/shimashita ka *Nani o renshuu shimasu/shimashita ka*
Nanigo o hanashimasu/hanashimashita ka *Nanigo o benkyoo shimasu/shimashita ka*
Nanigo o renshuu shimasu/shimashita ka *Nansai desu ka*
(Ichi)nensei desu ka *(SUPOOTSU) o shimasu/shimashita ka*
(Eigo) a benkyoo shimasu/shimashita ka *(Ongaku) o renshuu shimasu/shimashita ka*
(Eiga) o mimasu/mimashita ka *(Kooen) ni ikimashoo ka*
(TEREBI) o mimashoo ka *(BIDEO GEEMU) o shimashoo ka*
Kaerimashoo ka *(REKOODO) o kikimashoo ka*
(Manga) o yomimashoo ka *Nanyoobi desu/deshita ka*
(Raishuu) ikimashoo ka *(Ii) otenki desu ka*
Atsui deshoo ka *Ame deshita ka*
Naze desu ka

Plus many more combinations with time words.
Save all questions to use on other occasions.

Conclusion

(5 minutes)

Give students a selected number of questions from the box or from the list below to answer in writing.

Homework

Students write a selected number of questions and answers from the sheet of questions.

Dismissal: Teacher chooses a question to ask each student.

VARIATIONS on the use of the students' questions and question sheet are given below:

1 Students make their own list and later compare with the list given.
   Find the number the same, the number different.
   Add into their own list the ones from the sheet that they did not have.
   Check that the different ones are structurally correct.

2 May also be used as an exercise for students to give answers (written or oral) or to match against possible answers in listening comprehension or reading comprehension.

3 As a team game, each team uses questions prepared turn by turn for the other teams to answer with a correctly structured answer. If their answer proves they understood the question but is grammatically incorrect they receive one point. If it is correct, two points.

4 Teams give questions for the other team to translate.

5 Students take part of the list and work out answers. When answers have been checked, lists of questions and answers are jumbled and re-written. Students test or challenge each other.

6 If answers are written on one sheet of paper in random order and questions on another, students read question for partner to find matching answer on his/her paper. (See example below.)

7 Use as an oral/aural test. Student One has questions. Student Two has nothing, and does not know in which order the questions will be asked. Student Two must try to come up with a reasonable answer to each question. (They may sometimes seem a bit strange as they are odd questions out of context, but will show the listening teacher if the question has been understood and, also, the competence level of the replies.) Teacher sits by students and listens in to Student One's pronunciation as questions are read, and Student Two's replies. Students alternate after five questions.

Lesson Forty-one (optional lesson)

Continue with the ideas from last lesson, choosing other options from the variations given to really consolidate students ability to cope with question and answer with the material known.

If students are given the opportunity now, they should become so familiar with the questions that they can ask them spontaneously and by careful listening answer spontaneously too.

More practice at this point would also help to establish the sentence patterns.

Lesson Forty-two (Unit 3, page 163)

Aims and Objectives

- to teach *shoo joo ra hiragana.*
- to encourage students to read *hiragana* sentences.
- to practice listening and giving spontaneous replies.
- to consolidate use of *wa* and *no* particles.
- to remind about lack of particles between nouns and *desu.*
- to raise consciousness of *katakana* in two new words.
- to encourage students to sit alongside different people for at least part of the lesson.

Preparation

Tape. Textbook.
Provide card for students to make *hiragana* flashcards during lesson.
Put out *katakana* name labels on each desk randomly.

Introduction

(10 minutes)

Tape music (softly). As students enter ask them to sit in the desk where they find their name card even if it's not next to their friend!

While waiting for the lesson to begin, try to memorize the look of their neighbors' names in *katakana* to identify later.

Greet, put up date. Tell students that today is the first time they are going to be asked to try to read a *hiragana* dialogue. They are really making progress.

Review *hiragana* syllables known so far by brainstorming from the students which ones they may be expected to know. Those who have learned the whole chart may like to watch silently while the others go through their list.

Teach *shoo, joo* and *ra*. (page 163).

Students make sets of *hiragana* flash cards from vocabulary list (or all vocabulary lists in this book so far).

Play tape or read dialogue to students before they open their own books. Check their understanding. Did they guess the meaning of *PAATII?* Comment on the closeness of many *katakana* words to English and the fact that Julie becomes *JUURI*.

Main Theme

(25 minutes)

Students open books and cover *roomaji* version of the text.

In pairs they attempt to read the *hiragana* version of the dialogue.

Write *PAATII* and *JUURI* on the board in *katakana* and *roomaji* for reference.

If they have difficulty they should try to match the words from the word list before resorting to the *roomaji*.

How many managed without problems?

Cover the *roomaji* of the word list. Elicit words from volunteer students. Check that everyone understands how to make the combined sounds. Practice reading together for long sounds.

In pairs, students challenge each other to read words from the *hiragana* flash cards and to give their meaning. If they can read and give meaning they win the card. Highest number of cards wins.

Do the study portion on pages 164 and 165 together.
Anata no tanjoobi wa itsu desu ka, page 165.

Pairwork: Practice reading only from the *hiragana*.

Work together to remind of past tense of *desu—deshita*—and in pairs do the activity on page 166.

Conclusion

(10 minutes)

Check your understanding, page 166. Do individually as a written exercise or work in pairs orally. Practice listening and giving spontaneous replies:

Extend by asking students to take turns reading the questions and statements and to make some comment or reply. For example:

Getsuyoobi wa watashi no tanjoobi desu

Comment *soo desu ka,* or *soo desu.*

If there is a direct question, answer with fictional answer yes or no.

Collect in *katakana* name cards and hiragana flash cards for future use.

Homework

Review *hiragana*. Go through vocabulary list at back of book and pick out twenty words they can read and write without difficulty.

Write them out in a list to test friends with next lesson.

Remind that they are supposed to be looking for information on Japan/Japanese for later.

Dismissal: Tell teacher what day it is today and comment on weather:
kyoo wa (getsu)yoobi desu, (ame) desu.

Lesson Forty-three (review lesson, page 167)

Aims and objectives

- to teach *he be ri se ze o hiragana.*
- to review structures and situations taught previously.
- to interest students in more Japanese festivals.
- to give more practice in listening and reading.
- to encourage students again to sit next to different people.

Preparation

Tape. *Katakana* name cards.

Photocopy list of review questions for each group of four students (without the answers).

Cut up one list into strips.

Hiragana flash cards from last lesson for dismissal time.

Put out *katakana* name cards on desks randomly.

Introduction

(10 minutes)

Students sit where their own name card is.

Tape music.

Tell students that from time to time it's necessary to make sure things learned previously haven't been forgotten. Today is a review lesson. They must not open their textbooks until told to do so.

Check on last lesson's homework.

Students challenge each other in pairs or groups to read the words they have written in *hiragana*.

OR

Challenge. Divide into groups. Choose ten words from their individual lists and rewrite large enough to be seen from the front of the class. Each group challenges another to read ten of their *hiragana* words.

Teach *he be se ze ri o* from page 167.

Point out that the *o* is the *o* used for writing honorific *O* and elicit from students the words they know that have honorific *O*. Add to their list *O tanjoobi* for special politeness when asking about someone else's birthday. Remind that honorific *O* is never used for your self or your own family. Remind that particle *o* is always written with を .

Main theme

(25 minutes)

Divide into groups. Give each group a photocopied list of questions from pages 167 and 168. Each team takes five minutes to prepare answers for each of the review situations together, without looking at textbook. Add in questions about birthdays and using *atarashii*.

Put aside any notes. A representative from Group 1 takes out a question slip to ask Group 2. They reply and are awarded marks if correct. Group 2 take a slip for Group 3, and so on until all the slips have been used twice. If a group gets the same question twice, choose again.

Open textbooks, page 168.

Mini test

Cover the *roomaji* and alone or in pairs practice reading the *hiragana*. Check against the *roomaji*. Individually write the English equivalent. Mark.

Compliment those who did well. Encourage those whose results were disappointing to work out where and why they were incorrect and to ask for help if necessary.

Homework

Learn the new *hiragana well*. Make up ten questions to ask a partner next lesson.

Tell students they need to visit libraries, look in encyclopedias, ask friends if they may borrow books about Japan, look for news articles, etc., for lesson after next.

Dismissal: Show *hiragana* flash cards (from last lesson) as students file past. Student reads, gives meaning and says goodbye. Collect name cards.

Lesson Forty-four (page 169)

Aims and objectives

- to consolidate material learned previously.
- to teach *ge ga ru chi choo hiragana*.
- to research more Japanese festivals.

Preparation

Photocopy profile cards from page 170–71 (12 in a set), enough for each group of four.
Katakana name cards, put out cards on desks randomly.

Introduction

Tape.

Students sit where card has been placed and try to memorize the look of the *katakana* of neighbors cards while waiting for beginning of lesson.

Greet. Put up date. Today, listening to and answering questions and giving information spontaneously is the main objective.

Students try to think of some sort of relevant answer to every question even if they are not willing to offer it aloud.

(5 minutes)

1 Listen to tape questions (or teacher). Teacher asks for volunteer answers in the pauses.

Kyoo wa nanyoobi desu ka

Atsui desu ka

Kinoo wa nanyoobi deshita ka

Kinoo wa ii otenki deshita ka

Kinoo no yoru wa nani o shimashita ka

Kyoo wa anata no tanjoobi desu ka

Anata no tomodachi no tanjoobi wa nan desu ka

Kyoo wa nani o benkyoo shimasu ka

(5-10 minutes)

2 Find a partner. Move to sit together. Ask each other the questions worked out for homework last night. Try to answer after only one reading of the question. Do not use English to find out what the question meant unless absolutely unable to understand.

Main Theme

(15-20 minutes)

Giving information.

Give out the photocopied profile cards, one set per group.

Look at textbook page 170 for a model answer.

Listen to the teacher giving information about three people from the cards. Which two were the same age/same nationality/had a birthday the same day?

Ask for only two items of information unless your group are very confident.

1 Place cards face downwards in the center. Each student takes one card in turn and gives as much of the information as possible to the rest of the group in Japanese. If there is something that student can't say, the card must be offered to the next person to finish and he/she then wins that card and continues with own card. (Place card face up so that rest of group can check if the information being given is correct.) Continue until all cards have been used.

2 All cards are placed face upwards on the table and a student gives the group the information about one person. The group listens to be the first to identify which person is being described. Save the name and nationality until last, to make the identification more difficult. The one who guesses first wins and takes the next turn.

3 Team game, group against group. One team gives information and others have to guess which person is being described,

OR

4 Team game, spot the similarities (four students in a team). Each team chooses three cards and tells the information in Japanese. The other team spot the similarities and differences.
If there is time left over, ask students to make up similar profiles about someone in the class and they all try to guess who.

(5-10 minutes)

5 Written exercise. Students take one card and write all that they can about the person described. Practice the new *hiragana*.

Homework

Make up a profile adding in perhaps sports, interests, and subjects studied, about someone in the class. Class guess who it is next lesson. Review all *hiragana* up to date. Remind to find some resource books/material/newspaper articles about Japan if possible for next lesson.

Dismissal: Ask each student one question from the following:
Nansai desu ka/oikutsu desu ka.
Doko no kata desu ka.
Kyoo wa nani o shimasu ka.
Otenki wa nan desu ka.

Lesson Forty-five (page 172)

Aims and objectives

- to give more opportunity for listening carefully to information given.
- to find out more about Japanese festivals.
- to research material for themselves.

Preparation

Resource books about Japan and Japanese festivals if possible.
Paper for poster making.
Information about the festivals from pages 172–176.
If you can, display labeled pictures on the walls.
During lesson put up pictures brought by class.

Introduction

Greet, put up date.
Before beginning today's lesson find out who has really been taking note of the *katakana* cards.

Show *katakana* name cards. Ask who they belong to and ask students to come to collect them and then return to places. See if anyone in class can identify cards other than his/her own.

Main theme

Open textbooks at page 172.
Look at the pictures and discuss:
Have students anything similar in own society?
Suggest students find out their birth animal according to Japanese tradition (page 173).
Read or talk about the festivals and use your resource material, if you've been able to find some, for students to find out more about Japan and its customs.
Display all the resource material. Students who brought material have first choice to use their own material if they wish. If there is not much resource material, use the textbook and omit the next activity, moving straight to the quiz (part 2, below).

1 Give students five minutes to find out something interesting about Japan. Each student thinks of one question that he/she could ask to see if others were listening. After that students tell class what they found out.
   Class may make notes or just listen.

2 Have a quiz to see what they remember—each student offering a question.

3 Make posters to advertise the various festivals—don't forget *Shichi Go San* and *Seijin No Hi*—to display in the classroom.
   OR
   Make posters in their notebooks.

Lesson Forty-six (Unit 4, page 177)

Aims and objectives

- to teach months of the year.
- to give more practice in reading *hiragana*.
- to teach song 'Sakura Sakura'.
- to introduce line-ups (line-ups give students an excellent reason for using the target language many times).

Preparation

Tape.
Katakana name cards.
Large calendar.
Put up pictures of the seasons and label in *hiragana*.
Put up calendar pages on wall labeled in *hiragana* during lesson.
Poster paper to enter chart of class birthdays.

Introduction

(10 minutes)

Play tape song. Greet. Put up date.

Show calendar to class, month by month, giving first four months and see if students can supply the rest of the year. Point out the *odd* ones—*shi* not *yon* for April, *shichi* for July, *ku* not *kyuu* for September.

Point out the groups of months for the seasons in your own country and compare with Japan.

Students may remember the name *Haruko* and therefore know the word for spring.

Use the labeled pictures on the wall to elicit other season names.

Cover *roomaji* and English in textbook, page 177.

Students study and read the *hiragana* vocabulary.

Main theme

(25 minutes total)

Follow textbook.

Activity 3. (5 minutes)

Line up. Ask students to go around room asking *O tanjoobi wa nangatsu desu ka,* finding out in which month each person's birthday occurs, and slotting themselves into a line around the classroom that starts in January and ends up with December birthdays.

When all are in line, students answer teacher's question *O tanjoobi wa nangatsu desu ka* OR *anata no tanjoobi wa nangatsu desu ka* until all have been checked and students move if necessary to be in the correct place in the line.

From this line up, a chart may be made of the group's birthday months to put on the wall.

Hold up *katakana* name card for that student to recognize and give birth month in Japanese. (3–4 students.)

Ask *dare desu ka.*

Check your understanding, page 180. Match the sentences.

Answers

1. c	6. j
2. d	7. h
3. b	8. f
4. e	9. g
5. a	10. i

Quiz. Written or oral.

Learn song *'Sakura Sakura'*, and comment on the importance of blossom time emotionally for Japanese people—the end of winter and cold weather and being cooped up inside for leisure time. Also point out the importance of beauty in the lives of Japanese people.

Homework

Writing practice. Find out what *mikka* and *yokka* mean (leave students to find out—they occur in next lesson).

Write meaning of words in writing practice alongside their own writing.

Dismissal: Students give birth month as they file out with *watashi no tanjoobi wa ...gatsu desu.*

Lesson Forty-seven (Unit 5, page 182)

Aims and objectives

- to teach how to give dates in Japanese.
- reading practice.

Preparation

Tape for dialogue.
Katakana name cards.
Large writing, list of dates to put up when students are doing the line up, for reference.

Introduction

Who can remember the months of the year?
Volunteer student gives list.
Compliment with *joozu desu ne, yoku dekimashita,* showing exaggerated approval to get over the idea of *joozu.*
Ask students what they guess the meaning to be.

Main theme

1 Talk about the next step in giving calendar information—the actual dates. Point out the difference between date and day.
   Look at the special date names in Japanese and reassure that students don't need to learn all of them at this time!

2 Lineup. Go around room asking *anata no tanjoobi wa nangatsu nannichi desu ka.* Put themselves in line according to birthdate.
   Going from front of room to back, students give own birthday month and date. Check that all are in correct position in line.

3 Hand out one *katakana* name card to each student.
   Each student then goes to find the owner of the card, showing card and asking *anata no namae desu ka* until they find the owner then ask *Otanjoobi wa nangatsu nannichi desu ka.*
   All stand still and silent when task completed and report each other's birthdates to the class to be added to last lesson's chart.
   Listen to dialogue and read. Work out meaning with partner.

4 Study (page 184).

5 Choose an activity from page 186.

Homework

Check your understanding.

Dismissal: Tell teacher birthdate in full.

Lesson Forty-eight (optional lesson)

It may be valuable to pause here and consolidate numbers and times learned so far.

Aims and objectives

- to remind of Chinese numbers.
- to remind of how to give telephone numbers.
- to remind of telling time in hours and half hours.
- to consolidate months, dates and days and other time words that should be known.

Preparation

Pack of number cards for the class. Photocopy time work sheets.

Introduction

(10 minutes)
Tape music
Greet. Put up date.
Give each student a number randomly around class. Students do not show other people their number. Each one must find the correct position for him/herself in a line around the class by asking people *anata wa, nanban desu ka (juu desu),* and slotting into the line. Ask students to do this really fast. Each student then calls out number *ichi ni san,* etc. Class listen to check that people are in the correct order.

Main Theme

(30 minutes)
1 Remind of other uses of numbers.
   Each student writes own telephone number secretly on a piece of paper without their name. Slips of paper are given to the teacher who then redistributes them quickly.
   Students' task is to find the person who has their telephone number and stand with that person quickly, by asking *anata no denwa bangoo wa nan desu ka,* until they find the one that answers with the number they are holding. Winners are first to find each other but all wait quietly until the last pair finish.
2 Play game *ima nanji desu ka* that they may remember earlier. Decide on the time for dinnertime, e.g., *rokuji han desu.* Student calls out times from the front of the class and last one to sit when dinnertime is called is out.
   OR

Student secretly chooses a time for an activity, e.g.:
Niji ni TENISU o shimasu. Student says *kyoo (TENISU) o shimasu* (or activity chosen).
Class ask the time *...ji ni (TENISU) o shimasu ka* etc.
Person who guesses takes over.
Use clock exercise.

3 Months of the year, days of the week, general time words quiz. Brainstorm on board as answers are given.
Conclusion

(5 minutes)
Students make a table of number and time words in their books.
Homework
Finish chart. Review all number and time words. Prepare ten numbers to challenge someone with next lesson.

Dismissal: Students give teacher own phone number to write down for reference.

Lesson Forty-nine (Unit 6, page 188)

Aims and objectives

- to review verbs and tenses known.
- to teach particle *mo*.
- reading and listening practice.

Preparation

Enlarge New Year card (on page 187) on photocopier to put on wall.

Introduction

(10 minutes)
Tape music. Greet, put up date.
Students may now be able to give you the whole date.
Go through last lesson's homework (pages 186–187).

(2-3 minutes)
Discuss New Year card that they will have seen while doing homework.
Students may be able to guess which writing is the name (*Yamaura*).
This card was sent in the year of the horse. (Which year was that?)
New Year cards have the animal sign of the year rather than any other decoration but there are manydifferent styles of showing them. The greeting is usually written very beautifully, often by a professional calligrapher.

Main Theme

(15 minutes)

1 Ask two or three students their age. When two the same age have answered, tell class *(JON) san wa juusansai desu, (AN) san mo juusansai desu.* Ask what students think the *mo* may mean? If no ideas, give more examples.

Listen to or read the conversation. Those who think they can cope cover the *roomaji* and try to follow the *hiragana*.

After the reading, allow students time to read through again on their own before asking the following questions (*OR* you may like to use the following for reading comprehension with written answers):

> *Sensei no namae wa nan desu ka.*
> *Atarashii seito no namae wa nan desu ka.*
> *AN san wa nansai desu ka.*
> *AN san wa doko no kata desu ka.*
> *JEMUSU SUKOTTO san wa doko no kata desu ka.*
> *SUKOTTO san wa nansai desu ka.*
> *Minasan wa nani o benkyoo shimasu ka.*
> *Kyoo wa nangatsu nannichi desu ka.*
> *Dare ga AMERIKAjin desu ka.*
> *AN san mo AMERIKAjin desu ka.*

Now let's study as the people in the conversation were about to do.

(5 minutes)

2 Study (page 189)—use of *mo*.

(10 minutes)

3 Divide into teams. Each team has 5 minutes to write down all the verbs they can remember in all 5 forms known plus meaning in English of the stem. Which team has the most?

Each team reads out list. Others check each verb if they have it, and teams one by one offer the extra ones they may have.

Warn of a mini test on the verbs next lesson.

4 If time, start to prepare a role play as page 190.

Homework

Read over pages 188 to 192. Be sure that all is thoroughly understood.
Review verbs for test in near future (after next two lessons).

Dismissal: Leave in twos. First student says 'I will study well' and other says 'I will study too'.
Remind of *yoku* meaning well as in *yoku dekimashita.* Apply it to the following study, too:

> *Watashi wa yoku benkyoo shimasu.*
> *Watashi mo yoku benkyoo shimasu.*

Lesson Fifty (Unit 7, page 193)

Aims and objectives

- to teach how to describe physical characteristics.
- to teach one use of particle *ga*.
- to introduce color adjectives and two color nouns.

Preparation

Pictures of people, preferably large and in color.
Wall label for stories. *Hanashi.*
Labels of color adjectives and color nouns to fix to articles during lesson, or chart of colors and color names.
Colored origami paper or similar.

Introduction

(10 minutes)

In groups of four or five, students test each other on verbs.
Students help each other to fix up mistakes, checking with teacher if not sure.
Teacher monitors and asks each group to pick their best story to be put on the wall for everyone to read.
Commend and comment on the fact that it would be good to be able to add in descriptions of what people look like as well as what they do, and that is what they'll learn this lesson.
Hand in pictures found for homework.
They have just been reminded of many things to say about people but now they need to learn the names of colors and parts of the body to be able to describe physical characteristics.

Main theme

(5-10 minutes)

1 Teach colors (page 193).

   Some ideas:

   Give students pieces of origami paper or similar, telling student the color as they receive a piece. Ask each student the color they received, e.g., *akai desu ka.*
   Students tell each other what color they have received. *Watashi no kami wa ... desu,*

   OR

   Put out color samples on desk or on wall, labeled in Japanese, for students to learn colors by association,

   OR

   Show students papers or fabrics of different colors. Tell color. Elicit Japanese color name from students,

   OR

Go around room describing hair color of several students until students may have registered *kuroi/chairo/BURONDO/akai.*

Point out things in the room of different colors and label as you go.

OR

Students make 6 illustrations in notebooks—flowers, balloons, etc. Number them 1-6.
Teacher calls out color for each in turn.
Check to see if students are correct.

(5-10 minutes)

2 Pick out two or three tall students and two or three short students, and place them on opposite sides of the room. Tell students *... san wa se ga takai desu,* demonstrating how tall for all but one of the tall students. Elicit same sentence about the last.
Do the same with the short students: *...san wa se ga hikui desu.*
Students are thanked and sit down.
Question class about other students: *Se ga takai desu ka/Se ga hikui desu ka.*
Pick out a student and ask class his/her height. Then give names of parts of the body, demonstrating with this student, *atama desu,* asking class *nan desu ka ashi desu,* etc.

OR

Use pictures of people brought in earlier to point out parts of body and to describe.
Class draw a figure and label appropriately.

OR

Take a picture to put in their notebooks. Give pattern for description of part of the body—*Me ga aoi desu. Kami no ke ga chairo desu.*

(5 minutes)

3 Game: *Minasan tatte kudasai. Me ga aoi seito, suwatte kudasai* all the blue–eyed students, sit down. Last one of that description to sit is out. Vary with *minasan, suwatte kudasai* to keep everyone on their toes.

(10 minutes)

4 Two more words we need are long and short: *nagai* and *mijikai.* Apply to the lines of students and to lengths of colored wool to impress that these words are used for length.
Point out that *hikui* is low and *takai* is high or tall.
Short in length is always *mijikai.*

5 Put up words *BURENDA* and *OOSUTORARIA* on board in *katakana.*
Cover the *roomaji* and read the information on page 193 about Brenda. Check understanding.
Do the study section together.

Homework

Draw a person and label parts of the body given in vocabulary list, color eyes and hair, and put on colors and long and short appropriately.
Draw three quick figures of different school students and label with *onna no ko, otoko no ko* and school level. Put glasses on one and label.
Read over textbook. Study pages 194–195.

Dismissal: Tell teacher something about the student who is following them with the pattern: *(me) ga (aoi) desu.*

Lesson Fifty-one (page 196)

Aims and objectives

- reading practice.
- consolidation of patterns.
- give students the opportunity to use their reading skills and see how well they have learned vocabulary and structures used so far.

Preparation

Tape.
Introduction
Tape. Greet. Put up date, eliciting information from students.

Main theme

(10-15 minutes)

1 Reading profiles of three people. Do individually or in pairs.

OR

Divide class into three groups. Each group reads and takes in the information about their character. Close textbooks. They then take it in turns to tell about him/her in Japanese offering one or two sentences each.

The listening groups make quick notes while they are speaking. Within each group compare notes on information gathered.

Each group then tries to be the first group to answer the questions (page 198).

Answers

1. The same birthday.
2. Girls.
3. They are both boys.
4. Piano.
5. Rae and David are tall. John is short.
6. Watches TV.
7. David.
8. John and David.
9. David.
10. David, with an Australian friend.

(10 minutes)

2 Textbook. Alone think of ten questions to ask a partner about the three people in Japanese. Find a partner. Question each other. Answer in English.

3 C as textbook, page 198.

(15-20 minutes)

4 D as textbook, page 199.

Homework

C Page 49. If you wish, warn students of review coming up at the end of Topic Six. Suggest they find time to do some review.

Dismissal: Students go as teacher calls out physical characteristics (no need to explain *dete* at this point, it will be obvious to students what they should do and they unconsciously assimilate another verb). *Me ga chairo seito, dete kudasai, se ga takai seito,* etc., until all have gone.

Lesson Fifty-two

Aims and objectives

* to test understanding of tenses.
* to practice roleplay.
* to encourage students to listen to each other.

Preparation

Photocopy of test if you want to give it as a written exercise.
Photocopy of evaluation sheet (number of groups) for each student if wanted.

Introduction

(10 minutes)

Mini Test. Listen very carefully for the tense. Give the English equivalent:

> *Nihongo o benkyoo shimasen*
> *JONsan wa hanashimashita*
> *Neko dewa arimasen*
> *Ame deshoo ka*
> *Watashi no hon desu*
> *Kinoo PAATII deshita*
> *Uchi ni ikimasu*
> *PAATII ni ikimasen deshita*
> *Uchi ni kaerimashita ka*
> *TEREBI o mimasu*
> *Kinoo wa hon o yomimasen deshita*

TENISU o shimashoo
GITAA o renshuu shimasen
BENsan ni aimashita
Hachiji ni gakkoo ni ikimashita
Nihongo ga suki desu

Suggest 2 marks for entirely correct answer, 1 only for verb correct or other vocabulary correct.

(10 minutes)

Check sentence patterns have been remembered by asking pairs of students to make as many sentences as possible in five minutes using present and present negative tense.

Teacher walks around checking accuracy.

Pair with highest number of sentences read them out to class for check on accuracy.

Winners are the pair with greatest number of correct sentences.

All pass sentences to another pair who will put as many as possible (depending on time) into the past and past negative appropriately as fast as possible.

Teacher asks class to stop.

Pair with highest number finished at that time read out sentences. Class check accuracy.

Main theme

(25 minutes)

Activity (page 190). Students have 15 minutes to prepare a simple roleplay. When they perform it for the class they may not read it, so will have to try to listen to each other and keep going without a script. Therefore they need to use their time well so that they get as much practice as possible in the fifteen minutes.

Suggest that students use as many as possible of the verbs they know but the most important thing is to get their message across and to really stay in role.

Take about 10 minutes to watch the roleplays and see how different each one is even though following the same idea.

Students often need to have a purpose apart from enjoyment, to ensure they really listen to each other. At the end of each role play they need to be prepared to answer two or three questions in English or Japanese to prove their understanding and that they have been listening.

It is sometimes a good idea to give them an evaluation sheet to fill in as they watch and listen to make them more attentive.

The next page shows an example of an evaluation sheet for this case.

Names of students taking part:

_____

Was the introduction correct for people meeting for the first time? Yes/No

Who were the students?

_____

What did each student study?

(Student One) _____

(Student Two) _____

What were the things they liked?

(Student One) _____

(Student Two) _____

What extra information did they give?

_____

Commend for participation and any especially good plays.
Pick out common mistakes to comment on afterwards.

Homework

Activity (page 191). Story of own life to tell group next lesson.
Bring pictures of people for next lesson (from magazines, newspapers, etc.)

Dismissal: Teacher says he/she likes something and asks (Name) *mo ... ga suki desu ka.*
Student replies *hai watashi mo ... ga suki desu* OR *watashi wa ... wa sukijanai desu.*

Lesson Fifty-three (Unit 8, page 200)

Aims and objectives

- to teach more names of parts of the body.
- to give interview practice.
- to describe people.

Preparation

Photocopied profiles from page 202 to allow one profile card per student.
Large picture of a person, parts of body labeled in *hiragana* and *roomaji* to put on wall for reference.
Some pictures of people brought in by students previously.

Introduction

(5 minutes)
Greet. Elicit date from students and write on board.
Students read stories written for homework to group, who take notes in English on the information.

Main theme

(5-10 minutes)

1 Describing people. Open textbooks at page 200. Look at the illustrations of more names of parts of the body. Quickly read over the information about Henry (page 201).
Leave books open for reference to new vocabulary and point out wall illustration for reference, too. Together work out what could be said about some of the pictures of people you have.

(15 minutes)

2 Group activity. Divide class into groups of four or five. They nominate one student from their group to describe to the rest of the class and each offer some information about him/her. They may use him/her to point out names of parts of the body—*atama desu/ashi desu,* etc., and then try to give a few items of information like *SAMUsan wa se ga takai desu ne,* or ask class questions about their friend, e.g.: *kami no ke ga mijikai desu ka nagai desu ka.*
Class join in to ask questions like *doko no kata desu ka, seito no namae wa nan desu ka* to find out as much as possible.

OR

They may like to line up and give the information and then ask class which one of them they have been describing. Class may ask extra questions if they can't guess straight away.

OR

Use pictures of people putting them out for all to see, describing one. Class guess which one is being described.

(15 minutes)

3 Activity. Place profile cards face down on desk. Students take turns to pick up a card and give the information to the group except for name. First student to guess person's name wins card. Use textbook complete set for reference. Note: Please alter *Mario* to *Maria* on the first card!

OR

Group find out name by questioning. By looking at the textbook complete set they can work out which questions would be relevant. Possible questions are:

Otoko no hito desu ka/Onna no hito desu ka.
Nansai desu ka.
Se ga takai desu ka/Se ga hikui desu ka.
Kami no ke ga nani iro desu ka.
Nani ga suki desu ka/Nani ga kirai desu ka.
Doko no kata desu ka.
Nani o benkyoo shimasu ka.
Doko ni ikimashita ka.

Homework

"Wanted" posters. Make posters in Japanese about one person on the chart.
Learn new *hiragana* pages 203–204.
If you wish, warn about evaluation of Topic Six coming up at end of this unit. Suggest students find time to review.

Dismissal: Tell teacher what student is going to do after school today.

Lesson Fifty-four

Aims and objectives

- to practice descriptions.
- to learn *Jankenpon* as a way of choosing who goes first in activities, etc.

Preparation

Sheets of plain paper for drawing to instruction.
Paper for doing drawings of strange creatures.

Introduction

(10 minutes)
Greet. Put up date. Take in Wanted posters.
Do Activity One, page 204.

Main Theme

(10 minutes)
1 Look at new vocabulary bottom of page 204, and do page 205.

(5 minutes)
2 Students draw creatures of own design.

(5 minutes)

3 Learn *Jankenpon.*

(15 minutes)

4 Do Activity Two, page 206. Choose who will start with *Jankenpon.*

Homework

Topic Six Review, pages 208 and 209. Write answers in notebooks.
Do Activity One page 206.

Dismissal: Students tell teacher what they did yesterday evening using *sakuban nani o shimashita ka. Sakuban ...*

Lesson Fifty-five (review lesson, pages 208–209)

Aims and Objectives

• to check students' understanding and productive use of Topic Six material.

Preparation

Read through pages 208–209 as well as the material below and decide what you'd like to use and how.

Main theme

Use material below. May be done orally: whole class/in pairs/individually as a self check, or maybe students could test each other.
The stories in Check 3 are on the tape if you want to use them for listening comprehension, or could be read to your students. The same short passages may be used for reading aloud for pronunciation using the *roomaji* version or for testing of ability to read *hiragana* or reading comprehension.

Homework

Check over mistakes and make a list of things to ask teacher about if still not understood.

Topic Six, Check 1

How would you say or write the following in Japanese?

A

1. My name is Derek.
2. I'm fourteen years old.
3. I'm a New Zealander.

4. I like sports.
5. I am tall.
6. I have long legs.
7. My eyes are blue.
8. My hair is short.
9. I don't wear glasses.
10. I am a boy.

B

(You are allowed to use the chart of dates for this exercise!)

1. My birthday is on the first of July.
2. Is your birthday the second of May?
3. Graham's birthday is the third of June.
4. I went on the fourth of January.
5. The party is on the fifth of February.
6. I saw Ken on March sixth.
7. Did you read April seventh's newspaper?
8. The ninth of August I go to Australia.
9. I won't go to town on the tenth of September.
10. I'll meet you at nine o'clock on the eighth of November.

Answers (Topic Six, Check 1)

A

1. *Watashi no namae wa DEREKU desu.*
2. *Juuyonsai desu.*
3. *NYUUJIIRANDOjin desu.*
4. *SUPOOTSU ga suki desu.*
5. *Se ga takai desu.*
6. *Ashi ga nagai desu.*
7. *Me ga aoi desu.*
8. *Kami no ke ga mijikai desu.*
9. *Megane o kakemasen.*
10. *Otoko no ko desu.*

B

1. *Shichigatsu tsuitachi watashi no tanjoobi desu.*
2. *Anata no tanjoobi wa gogatsu futsuka desu ka.*
3. *GUREAMU (Graham) san no tanjoobi wa rokugatsu mikka desu.*
4. *Ichigatsu yokka ni ikimashita.*
5. *PAATII wa nigatsu itsuka desu.*
6. *Sangatsu muika KEN san ni aimashita.*
7. *Shigatsu nanoka no shinbun o yomimashita ka.*
8. *Hachigatsu kokonoka OOSUTORARIA ni ikimasu.*
9. *Kugatsu tooka machi ni ikimasen.*
10. *Juuichigatsu yooka no kuji ni aimasu.*

Topic Six, Check 2

A

Describe yourself as fully as possible to a new penpal to whom you are writing for the first time. (Your own answers)

B

Imagine that the following three-legged creature has been reported found in the Southern Alps. Read about this animal and draw its physical characteristics as described:

どうぶつ は あたま が おおきい です。みみ が おおきい です。かみ
の け が ながい です。かみ の け が あかい です。くち だ
ちいさい です。め が あかい です。め が ちいさい です。おなか が
おおきい です。あし が みじかい です。あし が あおい です。

Doobutsu (animal) wa atama ga ookii desu. Mimi ga ookii desu. Kami no ke ga nagai desu. Kami no ke ga akai desu. Kuchi ga chiisai desu. Me ga akai desu. Me ga chiisai desu. Onaka ga ookii desu. Ashi ga mijikai desu. Ashi ga aoi desu.
(Own answers but facts must be correct.)

C

Write a profile of your best friend, giving as much information as possible, for an article in the school magazine.
(Own answers)

Topic Six, Check 3

The following may be used for reading comprehension, listening comprehension or translation.

A

わたし は おとこ の こ です。せ が ひくい です。わたし の なまえ
は ロブ です。じゅうよんさい です。ニュージーランドじん です。
(ロブ   ROBU   Rob)

Watashi wa otoko no ko desu. Se ga hikui desu. Watashi no namae wa ROBU desu. Juuyonsai desu. NYUUJIIRANDOjin desu.
Give four facts about Rob.

B

せ が たかい です。じゅうごさい です。みみ が ちいさい です。め
が あおい です。あし が ながい です。わたし の なまえ は ウノキ
です。スポーツ が すき じゃない です。

(ウイキ *WIKI* Wiki) (スポーツ *SUPOOTSU* sports)

Se ga takai desu. Juugosai desu. Mimi ga chiisai desu. Me ga aoi desu. Ashi ga nagai desu. Watashi no namae wa WIKI desu. SUPOOTSU ga suki janai desu.

How many things can you say about Wiki in English, without referring to the passage?

C

わたし は マオリじん です。えいご と マオリご を になします。
マオリご と にほんご を べんきょう します。せ が ひくい です。かみ
の け が くろい です。ながい です。おんな の こ てす。
じゅうよんさい です。

(マオリ *MAORI* Maori)

Watashi wa MAORIjin desu. Eigo to MAORIgo o hanashimasu. MAORIgo to nihongo o benkyoo shimasu. Se ga hikui desu. Kami no ke ga kuroi desu. Nagai desu. Onna no ko desu. Juuyonsai desu.

Give five items of information about this person.

D

ボール です。きょう ちり と すうがく の しゅくだい を します。
しゅくだい が きらい です。テレビ が すき です。でんわ が すき
です。よる わたし は ともだち に でんわ します。

(ポール *POORU* Paul)

POORU desu. Kyoo chiri to suugaku no shukudai o shimasu. Shukudai ga kirai desu. TEREBI ga suki desu. Denwa ga suki desu. Yoru watashi wa tomodachi ni denwa shimasu.

1 Do you know who is giving this information? How can you tell?
2 Do you know the age of the person?
3 Do you know the nationality?
4 Give three other items of information about this person.

E

わたし は リデア です。じゅうごさい です。にほんご ⌒ さんねんせい
です。
にほんご が すき です。わたし は フランスご も べんきょう します。
オーストラリアじん です。ろくがつ に ニュージーランド に いきます。
(リデア　　RIDEA　　Lydia)
(フランス　　FURANSU　　France)
(オーストラリア OOSUTORARIA　　Australia)

Watashi wa RIDEA desu. Juugosai desu. Nihongo no sannensei desu.
Nihongo ga suki desu. Watashi wa FURANSUgo mo benkyoo shimasu.
OOSUTORARIAjin desu. Rokugatsu ni NYUUJIIRANDO ni ikimasu.

How old is Lydia?
What does Lydia plan to do? When?
What languages does she study?

TOPIC SEVEN
(Families and Friends, page 210)

During this topic it is suggested that students prepare a magazine about the class and its activities, in Japanese, illustrating it with photos, etc, if possible.

The idea is to give the students a really relevant reason for writing Japanese.

Optional lessons are therefore included to allow time for this to be done. The information gathered will also prove a very good way of consolidating sentences patterns and vocabulary.

The lessons giving time for this have been incorporated with the flow of lessons but some teachers may prefer to go straight through the book, finish teaching the structures and vocabulary of this year, leaving the magazine idea as an end of year special activity which will review the year's work.

NOTE: In topics seven, eight, and nine, the *katakana* name cards may be put out on desks at the beginning of each lesson to encourage students to recognize *katakana* syllables informally.

Each lesson find time for a quick recognition activity, for example:

- After the students are seated, tell them to have a good look at their neighbor's card. Collect cards from one row at a time spread out on a desk. Ask a student from that row to come and collect a card he/she can read (other than own!), hold it up, and read it to the class. Reward if correct.
- Tell students as they enter, they can sit with anyone they like today if they can find and read each other's cards without help.
- Use cards to pick out specific students for leaving the room first or to collect things to give out etc. Hold up card. That student may stand and leave etc.
- Use cards to group students for activities.
- Mix up cards and pick out the number needed for a group randomly.
- Students recognize own name and group accordingly for that activity. Teacher holds cards and reads out names as soon as students have grouped to check that group is correct. Put pile of cards with that group for reference if necessary as sometimes students try to switch groups to be with friends.
- Use the cards to show which students you want to talk with specifically each lesson. Put cards on wall before students come in and they will soon get used to checking the wall to see if they or their friends have a turn with you.
- Use the cards to show students who have done well that week. Put them up on the wall under a suitable title. Students will eagerly read to find their own and their friends' names and to see who is being complimented.

Family A

Label the family with appropriate names and ages. Do not tell your partner what you have written.
Describe 'your' family to your partner. Decide which of the family is yourself.
When you have described the family to your partner, make a list of the things they have in common, if any.

Family B

Label the family with appropriate names and ages. Do not tell your partner what you have written.
Describe 'your' family to your partner. Decide which of the family is yourself.
When you have described the family to your partner, make a list of the things they have in common, if any.

Lesson Fifty-six (Unit 1, page 214)

Aims and Objectives

- to use more genuine conversation with students in an informal way.
- to make students aware of traditional and present day Japanese family life in comparison with their own.
- to teach how to introduce own mother and father.
- to teach how to enquire about someone else's father and mother.

Preparation

Photocopy pictures of families for each student.
Photos of families or mothers and fathers to put on wall with appropriate labels under a title of *kazoku*.

Introduction

(5-10 minutes)

Play Tape—Japanese national anthem as students enter.
Comment on the weather. Ask such things as *sakuban TEREBI o mimashita ka, kinoo wa nani o shimashita ka, sakuban yoku benkyoo shimashita ka.* Comment on new things like new hair styles, school bags ... *ga suki desu,* good students etc.

Ii seito desu as you return homework.
Try to use as much Japanese as possible in commending and commenting.
Greet and put up date.
Read about and discuss Japanese families pages 210–213.

Main Theme

(10 minutes)

1 Talk about the fact that the Japanese have different words for members of your own family and those of others and also have different words for 'I' for males and females.
   Remind of *san, chan* and *kun* and demonstrate that a girl would introduce herself as *watashi* and a boy as *boku,* so if you are reading a passage it is easy to see whether a boy or girl is speaking.
   Show students *kanji* for *haha/okaasan* and *chichi/otoosan* (page 215). Use *chotto matte kudasai* to excuse the pause while you draw quick pictures of people alongside each word to illustrate. Excuse yourself again to get pictures from your desk with *chotto matte kudasai.*
   Give out pictures of families. Students label the first father and mother with both *otoosan/chichi* and *okaasan/haha* and the 'other' family *otoosan* and *okaasan.* Explain the difference in usage.
   Keep pictures to stick in book and use during future lessons.
   Question students about the mother and father figures.

   > *Otoosan no namae wa nan desu ka*
   > *Otoosan wa se ga takai desu ka/Se ga hikui desu ka*
   > *Otoosan wa nansai deshoo ka*
   > *Otoosan wa nani ga suki desu ka*

   Students answer as if it is their own father with *chichi.*

2 In pairs students ask each other similar questions about each other's real mother/father, remembering to use the correct labels.

Each student reports to the group one fact discovered about friend's father or mother.

Put pattern on board to help students:

... san no okaasan no namae wa ... desu.

... san no otoosan wa se ga takai desu, etc.

(15 minutes)

3 Now open books and read or listen to the dialogue.

Matching the words in the title who can give you the name for family?

Whose father is Sam talking about when he uses *otoosan? chichi?*

Do any students remember you using the phrase *chotto matte kudasai?* Think back. What do they think it would have meant in context?

Read through new word list. Can students come up with ideas to help them to remember the new words? (Associations/pictures etc)

Work through the Study page 215.

Sometimes it is easier to understand things your own way.

In this Unit students take the onus to understand without help from teacher.

Pairwork: Ask students to work through textbook from page 216–222, taking parts appropriately to read the dialogues aloud and to help each other with understanding.

Teacher is available to answer questions and to move around making comments like '*ii desu ne/yoku dekimashita* (Error on page 218: *Mariko san ga kimasu – ga* has been incorrectly omitted.)

Choose two or three pairs to say what they thought of to say about the photos in the unit.

Together work out descriptions of the pictures of mothers and fathers on the wall.

Homework

Writing Practice pages 221–222.

Write a profile of someone as if they are own parent (it doesn't have to be the truth). Introduce. Give age, physical description, say what they like/dislike, do/don't do, etc. Try to write at least ten sentences.

Dismissal: Each student tells one thing about own father or mother. Teacher comments with *soo desu ka/soo desu ne/omoshiroi desu,* etc.

Lesson Fifty-seven (optional lesson)

Aims and Objectives

- to review earlier lessons and Topic Six material.
- to produce the first part of a class magazine.

Preparation

Tape.

Set up room for interviews with three or four desks out at the front facing the class.

Camera to take photos of interviewees (either in class or doing one of their activities). Students may like to bring their own cameras and do this.

Introduction

Greet. Put up date.

Listen to interview on tape.

Introduce the idea of group interviews.

Three or four students volunteer to be interviewed by the class, who will ask them as many questions as they can about their lives for a class magazine about the personalities of this class.

Interview. The volunteers take their places in front of the class. The rest of the class get out their notebooks and take down the information they glean about each student.

They question the volunteers in any way they wish but try to follow up on questions asked by others. For example, if one person has been asked when his birthday is, the next question may be the same but to another interviewee. This gives less confident students the opportunity to repeat questions made by others, that they know will be relevant and acceptable.

Give as much time as seems appropriate and either keep going with same panel or change over to give others a turn.

Conclusion

At the end of the interviews, students compare notes with a group on one of the people interviewed, make sure facts are correct, then each group writes up an article for the magazine on that person, adding in the information they have observed on physical features politely stated. Photos could be taken perhaps to illustrate the article.

Homework

Each person writes up own profile of one person interviewed.

Dismissal: Each student tells teacher one fact about one of the people interviewed.

Lesson Fifty-eight (Unit 2, page 223)

Aims and objectives

- to teach use of *kochira* and *doozo*.
- to teach labels for own young sister and own older brother.
- to give more reading practice from *roomaji* and *hiragana*.
- to consolidate own family patterns.
- to give roleplay practice.

Preparation

Tape to record students' playlets and tape recorder with record facility, 'OR' video camera.

Introduction

(5 minutes)

Ask after students' mothers and fathers as they enter.

Otoosan wa ogenki desu ka, etc. Be careful only to choose students who have mothers and fathers living with them.

Comment on the weather. Comment on something you like or ask if a book is new, etc. Greet. Put up date.

Remind of own family labels/other family labels for mothers and fathers and introduce own little sister/own older brother labels.

Have a mini–quiz on Topic Six and Seven vocabulary.

Main Theme

(20 minutes total)

1 Students imagine they are auditioning to be the actors in a T.V. Japanese lesson. Divide class into groups of six.

(5 minutes)

2 Read through pages 223–224 together, correcting pronunciation and checking comprehension.

Answers

1. Five.	4. Sixteen
2. Kathy.	5. Younger sister.
3. Winter.	6. A dog.

(5 minutes)

3 Do the study page together.

(10 minutes)

4 Each group then has 10 minutes to produce their *play.*

(10 minutes)

5 Students perform playlet without books.
Teacher records for students to listen to or watch own performance later.
Class vote on best performance—the group that made the situation seem most true to life.

10 minutes

6 Students take turns watching or listening to own performance while others do Reading practice in pairs A and B on pages 227–228. Pairs find out the answers and write them down ready for a check at end of activity.

Homework

Writing practice page 227.

Reading practice pages 228–229. Re-read ones done in class and read the passage on page 229. Answer the questions.

Read over pages 223–229 and understand.

Add in *ani* and *imooto* on picture of own family

Lesson Fifty-nine (optional lesson)

Aims and Objectives

• to produce more information for the class magazine.

• to consolidate material learned in a different way.

Preparation

Tape.

Introduction

Greet. Put up date.

Listen to an interview on the tape. What was understood?

Students interviewed others recently, but there are many people who did not have the opportunity either to interview or to be interviewed.

This lesson that can be remedied.

Main Theme

Students interview each other aiming to find out as much as possible to end up with profiles of each member of the class.

Those who were previously interviewed interview the class on other topics, eg:

Find out how many people have older brothers? Younger sisters?

What do people do with their older brothers, younger sisters?

What don't they like about them or like about them?

Give the reasons where possible.

Plans for next week: Do a survey about who will go where, for what purpose, with whom?

Conclusion

Students write up the information and put it safely together to compile later into the magazine.

Homework

Finish writing up the information to be checked by teacher before it is put in the magazine. Learn new vocabulary.

Dismissal: Students give teacher an item of information, eg, *otooto ga imasu, ane mo imasu.*

Lesson Sixty (Unit 3, page 230)

Aims and objectives

- to teach own family labels for younger brother, older sister.
- to review reasons for using particles *wa o ni ga to mo.*
- to continue policy of using as much Japanese as possible in asking about students' lives, the weather, etc.

Preparation

Tape.
Photocopies of pictures on page 234 sufficient for groups of three or four if choosing that activity. Small rewards.

Introduction

(5 minutes)

Tape. Greet. Put up date

Ask some students how they are. Comment on the weather. If someone has been absent from school use *ohisashiburi desu ne.*

Ask *ima genki desu ka.* Comment *ii desu/dame desu ne,* etc, in genuine response. Ask a few students what they plan to do tomorrow, if they played sports yesterday, etc. (These enquiries must be genuine to play their part in showing the students that Japanese is an everyday language to be used even though they are limited by what they have learned. Information about students gathered during the first term's surveys and interviews will help you to have some background knowledge of your students interests.)

Main theme

(20 minutes)

1 TAPE. Listen while reading the passage about *NIKKU* on page 230. How many particles have been used in the passage? Check through to see who was correct.

Work through the Study on page 232 to remind about the uses of *wa, ni, to.* Work through the passage about *NIKKU,* getting students to tell the class why they think each particle has been used in that place. (This will help you to see who has not really understood the particles yet and discussing them together may help to sort them out.)

Students then read the passage about Melissa and try to be the first to tell you why the writer particularly likes Melissa. (She does his homework)

Do the writing and reading practice on page 232, asking volunteers to read the *hiragana*—word by word or sentence by sentence. Who can tell the class what the passage was about?

Who can read the next sentence and tell the class its meaning?

(5 minutes)

2 Work through the Study on page 233.

(15 minutes)

3 Choose an activity from below:

Students have five minutes to find out how much they have in common with another student that they don't know very well.

Choose partners. Brainstorm the sort of things they could tell someone about themselves quickly eg:

- *Ongaku ga suki desu*
  PIANO o renshuu shimasu
  Neko ga kirai desu. Anata wa
  Kinoo wa eiga ni ikimashita
  Kyoo wa SUPOOTSU o shimasu

  Answer with *mo* if making agreement or make a relevant comment like not doing something or not liking something using *soo desu ka,* etc, to try to have a genuine exchange of information.

- Pairs compete to keep talking to each other the longest, telling each other what they do, study, like, dislike, show photos of family if they have them, and describe, etc.

  They may keep a record of the number of sentences if they wish.

  They may not record repeated questions or statements.

- The students imagine that they have never met their partner before and have five minutes to find out as much as possible about what they have in common. If they run out of things to say to each other they should sit silently and listen to others.

  When time is up choose two or three pairs to report what they have in common to the rest of the class who note the similarities between each pair in their notebooks.

- Teacher keeps record too, and afterwards reads out correct information so that class can mark their answers. (Useful information about students for use in short exchanges of conversation with them later may be gathered at times like these. Students will often be surprised that you remember and appreciate your interest in them as people.)

  Commend the good listeners.

OR

Activity 1, page 234.

Divide class into groups of three or four. Each group takes one set of pictures and places them face upwards on the desk. One student chooses a picture secretly and describes.

Choose first person in each group to start with *Jankenpon.*

Homework

Activity 2, page 234. Writing and Reading practice pages 235–236.

Dismissal: Pairs leave together each telling teacher of something they do or like, family member they have, as in last activity and partner tells teacher if he/she is the same.

Lesson Sixty-one (optional lesson)

Aims and Objectives

- to work on the magazine production.
- to consolidate material taught previously.

Preparation

Material already written for magazine.

Introduction

(10 minutes)

Greet. Put up date.

Collect in material and start to put the magazine together.

Groups make a list in Japanese about what will be included under titles and headings, eg:

Nani ga suki desu ka

Konshuu nani o shimasu ka

Kazoku

Seito

Doobutsu

Gakkoo

Together decide by consensus what the headings can be. Do this in Japanese by calling out the heading and getting a show of hands for inclusion.

Main theme

(25 minutes)

Students decide which area to work on. Finding out about members of people's families, their pets, the subjects it is possible for them to study at school, and a survey on the popularity of the various subjects, etc. Do as much by interview and verbal survey as possible.

Teacher monitors and makes sure all are busily occupied.

Conclusion

(25 minutes)

Write information neatly for teacher to check before putting it into the magazine in the next magazine lesson.

Homework

Check magazine article and finish writing it up neatly. Think about illustrations to put with it.

Dismissal: Tell teacher an item of information.

Lesson Sixty-two (Unit 4, page 237)

Aims and Objectives
- to teach how to ask about other's families.
- to teach how to count people.

Preparation
Tape.
Words of song large enough to be seen from the back of the room.
Labels for counting people to put up on wall under a line of pictures of people.

Introduction
(10 minutes)
TAPE. Sing 'Ten Little Indians' song in English and in Japanese.
Put up words in large *hiragana*. Ask students to tell you how people are counted in Japanese.
Go through list—*hitori, futari, sannin* etc. Remind of other counters that they know:

Age—*sai*
Hours—*ji*

and other suffixes:

Nationality—*jin*
Languages—*go*.

Demonstrate the *kanji* for people and numbers to ten.
Students make pictures in notebooks of ten little Indian boys (or others) and label appropriately with people counters written in *hiragana and kanji*.

Main theme
(10 minutes)
1 Explain that today they will learn how to speak about other people's families. Remind of the two sets of words mentioned previously.
Elicit from students for whom they use *san*.
Teach the names for other people's families and fill in on photocopied sheet already in students' books.
Work through the Study section quickly on page 238. Listen to tape of dialogue and follow *hiragana* in books. Practice reading in pairs.
Pairs work out meaning of dialogue together.
Together work out how to ask about each other's families, following the patterns in the dialogue.

(10 minutes)
2 Survey. Each pair takes a copy of half a class list and approaches each person on their list to ask how many people are in that family, taking turns to ask:
... san, go kazoku wa nannin imasu ka.
Make a quick graph in note books.

---

3 Do the activities 2, 3, 4 on page 240.

Note *yonin* carefully—only one *n*.

Teach students how to say *I have one brother* etc. with *ani ga hitori imasu,* etc., explaining carefully that the number of people must be put in front of the verb with no particles between. (Students should not worry unduly about this at present as it will be offered again later, but if they would like to use it, good.)

Do activities 5 and 6, page 240 orally.

Working in the same pairs as for the survey above, one pair of students question another pair of students about their brothers and sisters (avoid asking about parents as it may be embarrassing for some of them), asking *Oniisan ga imasu ka* etc., and remembering to answer with *ani ga futari imasu* or *ani wa imasen.*

Find out as much as possible about one person from each family (age, physical characteristics, likes, dislikes, activities, etc.).

Choose two or three students to tell group what they found out (in English).

Homework

Activities 5 and 6 on page 240. Check your understanding page 240, and the Writing Practice.

Answers

1. e	6. g
2. a	7. h
3. c	8. d
4. j	9. i
5. f	10. b

Dismissal: Students tell teacher if they have an older brother or sister appropriately, as teacher asks *Oneesan ga imasu ka/imootosan ga imasu ka.* Teacher listens for those who have remembered to use own family labels in reply.

Lesson Sixty-three (Unit 5, page 242)

Aims and Objectives

* to teach *HANSAMU, joozu* and *kirei* with *desu/dewa arimasen/janai desu, deshita, dewa arimasen deshita.*
* to review adjectives in present and present negative.
* to raise consciousness of accepting differences between languages.
* to teach use of *ni aimasu* vs. *mimasu.*
* to review verbs and *kore sore are.*
* to practice using in different ways all they are able to say.
* to demonstrate the power students have to communicate ideas in Japanese. (Within the limits of the course this far, by recombining material, they are capable of making interesting short dialogues and stories.)

Preparation

Tape.

Paste or glue and poster paper for mounting work produced for the wall.

Photocopy enlarged of ugly, handsome, beautiful, objects and animals.

Photocopy and cut up sheets of short dialogues and stories.

Suggestion: The shorter stories may be given to less able students inconspicuously so that they have the chance of completing their task in the same time as more able students.

Introduction

(15 minutes)

Greet as students enter, indicating student who is in front of them ... *san wa kirei desu ne* ... *san wa HANSAMU desu ne*. Put up date.

Ask students to *mite kudasai*.

Put up new words *HANSAMU* and *kirei*.

Comment on the way you met students today.

Discuss the fact that we don't always agree on these labels.

In Japanese words that tell 'what kind of' are a special group of words called qualitative nouns (some people call them quasi adjectives). The impressive labels are not important but it is important to remember that they are 'not adjectives' and behave in a different way. Page 243.

Brainstorm the adjectives known—*ii, atsui, suzushii, atatakai, samui, mushi atsui, ookii, chiisai, akai, aoi, kiiroi, kuroi, shiroi, nagai, mijikai, takai, hikui* (remind that *hikui* actually means 'low').

If some students are finding sentence making difficult, they may benefit from some time going over sentences with you while the more confident students read the dialogues on the photocopy sheet.

If you decide to split the class, the more able students could read the stories individually or in pairs and work out the meaning, then compare notes with each other after they have done each one. It will extend them and give you time to work with the others.

They could then be set to constructing some of their own, trying to use as many adjectives and qualitative nouns from their repertoire as possible.

HANSAMU desu ka, kirei desu ka

NAN

KEN

JAN

BOBU

MORI

SUU

Dore ga suki desu ka, Dore ga kirai desu ka.

joozu desu ka

MIRANDA : GITAA

SAMU : BEISUBOORU

Mariki : Koto

MAIKU : PIANO

JON : Juudoo

FUREDDO : Suugaku

Take the opportunity while they are busy to have informal conversations in Japanese with a few students to find out about their interests and families. You may like to give them the chance to question you to find out more about you as a person.

Main theme

(15 minutes)

1 Sentence making practice. Study page 243.

In Japanese there are often things that seem strange to an English speaking person's way of looking at things, e.g.: meeting a person—Japanese always meet TO a person (page 243), not just meet a person.

Students offer some sentences using the new material.

Write on board and comment on the structures, elicit why the particles were chosen etc.

English speaking people say 'see' a person as well as 'meet', but in Japanese this is not possible. We must be tolerant and understanding of the differences. They are part of what makes language learning interesting.

Practice making sentences with *ni aimasu* and *mimasu*.

Review other verbs briefly by brainstorming a list to help students in next activities.

Remind of *kore sore* and 'are.'

Together discuss how the following short dialogues could be expressed in Japanese:

A Is that your older brother?
B Yes, it is.
A He's handsome, isn't he!
B No, he's not!

A I saw Mary yesterday.
B She's beautiful.
A Yes, she is. She's clever too.

A Is that your car?
B Yes.
A Is it new?
B No, it's not new.

A Have you seen Dan this week?
B No. He went to Canada.
A I like Dan. Do you?
B No I dislike him. He hates my dog.
A Your dog is clever. I like it.

The possibilities are amazing! It is not necessary to make long dialogues but it will be interesting to see what the students can achieve working together.

(10 minutes)

2 In pairs take ten minutes to construct similar short dialogues. Show to teacher for checking.

Here are dialogues and short passages to use in many ways:
(Also on TAPE for listening.)

1 To read for enjoyment. Students should gain satisfaction from being able to read them quite easily. It should prove to them how much progress they have made.

2 Listening comprehension.

3 Reading comprehension.

4 Students construct questions for other students to answer. It saves the teacher a lot of work and is better practice for the students. Questions may be worked out in groups too. Each group has a different story or dialogue to work on.
Groups then challenge each other to answer their questions.

5 Students may use the dialogues and stories as ideas for own stories or dialogues.

Inevitably the stories students can tell, like these examples, will be rather stilted because they have not learned how to join sentences and describing words but it is amazing how much they are able to communicate. They should be encouraged to see how well they are able to express ideas after such a short time of study and not to feel irritated by the limits.

Short dialogues

Jan	*Aa MEERI san, konnichi wa. O genki desu ka.*
Mary	*JAN san, Ohisashiburi desu ne. Genki desu. Doko ni ikimashita ka.*
Jan	*MEKISHIKO ni ikimashita. MEKISHIKO wa kirei desu ne.*
Mary	*Soo desu ka. Itsu kaerimashita ka.*
Jan	*Senshuu kimashita. Konshuu KANDI chan ni aimashita ka.*
Mary	*Hai. KANDI san no kami no ke ga chairo deshita. Ima BURONDO desu.*
Jan	*Soo desu ka. Kirei desu ka.*
Mary	*Iie. Kirai desu.*
Jan	*Raishuu akai deshoo!*

Teacher	*KEN san, oniisan ga imasu ka.*
Ken	*Hai, ani ga futari imasu.*
Teacher	*Nansai desu ka.*
Ken	*TOMU wa juurokusai desu. DEBIDO wa juuhassai desu.*
Teacher	*Ii seito desu ka.*
Ken	*TOMU wa atama ga ii desu. Ii seito desu. DEBIDO wa TENISU ga joozu desu.*
Teacher	*Oniisan wa se ga takai desu ka.*
Ken	*Hai, se ga takai desu. Haha to chichi mo se ga takai desu.*

Paul	*Kinoo machi ni ikimashita. RISA san o mimashita.*
Ben	*RISA san wa kirei desu ne.*
Paul	*Soo desu ne.*
Ben	*RISA san ni aimashita ka.*
Paul	*Iie. BEN kun wa?*
Ben	*Watashi no ane no tomodachi desu. Itsumo RISA san wa watashi no uchi ni kimasu.*
Paul	*RISA san ga suki desu ka.*
Ben	*Hai. Taihen suki desu. Ashita RISA san ni hanashimasu ka. RISA san wa anata go suki desu.*
Paul	*RISA san ni hanashimasen. Aimasen. RISA san wa atama ga ii desu. Watashi ga atama ga warui desu.*
Ben	*POORU san, anata wa atama ga ii desu. Ashita watashi to RISA san ni aimasu ka.*
Paul	*... Jaa, ... ashita deshoo.*

Glen shows his friend Stephanie a black and white photo of his penpal, and is then relieved to find a way of diverting her attention from it!

Glen	*Kore wa watashi no atarashii tomodachi desu.*
Stephanie	*Se ga takai desu ne ... Me ga aoi desu ne...*
Kami	*no ke ga nagai desu ne ... san ga suki deshoo. HANSAMU desu ne.*
Glen	*Hai soo deshoo ... san wa SUPOOTSU ga suki desu.*
Stephanie	*Donna SUPOOTSU o shimasu ka.*
Glen	*SAKKAA ga joozu desu.*
Stephanie	*SAKKAA ga kirai desu......Doko no kata desu ka.*
Glen	*KANADAjin desu.*
Stephanie	*Nansai desu ka.*
Glen	*Juuyonsai desu. Watashi mo juuyonsai desu.*
Stephanie	*Watashi mo juuyonsai desu*
Glen	*Soo desu ka. Anata no tanjoobi wa itsu deshita ka.*
Stephanie	*Kyoo desu.*
Glen	*Soo desu ka! O tanjoobi... omedetoo gozaimasu.*
Stephanie	*Arigatoo.*

Marian, an American girl, is talking to a Japanese woman who is staying at their house who understands no English. (Remember that Japanese people prefer to use names instead of 'you'.)

Kazuko	*Kyoo wa MARIAN san no tanjoobi no PAATII desu. Anata no ii tomodachi ga uchi ni kimasu ka.*
Marian	*Hai, yonin kimasu.*

Kazuko	Tomodachi no namae wa nan desu ka.
Marian	KIMU to KURISU to NIKKI to SUZAN desu.
Kazuko	Minasan wa onna no ko desu ka.
Marian	Chigaimasu. KIMU san to KURISU san wa otoko no ko desu. NIKKI san to SUZAN san wa onna no ko desu.
Kazuko	Dookyuusei desu ka.
Marian	Hai, soo desu. Minasan wa nihongo o benkyoo shimasu.
Kazuko	Ii desu ne. Minasan wa AMERIKAjin desu ka.
Marian	Chigaimasu. NIKKI san to KURISU san wa AMERIKAjin desu. KIMU san wa IGIRISUjin desu. SUZAN san wa KANADAjin desu. KIMU san wa se ga hikui desu. Kami no ke ga kuroi desu. Me ga kuroi desu. Okaasan wa Nihonjin desu. KIMU san wa Nihongo ga joozu desu.
Kazuko	Ii desu. Watashi wa KIMU san to nihongo o hanashimasu. Arigatoo gozaimasu.

Short stories

Watashi no inu.
Watashi no inu no namae wa TIMI desu. TIMI wa watashi no ii tomodachi desu.
Kirei desu. Atama ga chiisai desu. Ashi ga mijikai desu. Chairo desu.
Mimi ga nagai desu. Mimi ga shiroi desu.
Watashi wa TIMI to mainichi no yoji ni kooen ni ikimasu.
Kinoo watashi no tomodachi to TERESA san ni aimashita.
TERESA san no inu wa taihen ookii desu. Kuroi desu.
Atama ga ookii desu. Namae wa KIRAA desu.
TIMI to KIRAA wa BOORU to SAKKAA o shimashita.
Joozu deshita.

KAREN san.
KAREN san wa watashi no dookyuusei desu. Sukijanai desu.
Se ga hikui desu. Kami no ke ga nagai desu. Me ga ookii desu.
Aoi desu. Kirei desu.
KAREN san wa itsumo sensei ni hanashimasu. Itsumo toshokan ni ikimasu.
Eiga ni ikimasen. REKOODO o kikimasen. Zasshi o yomimasen.
SUPOOTSU o shimasen. Itsumo hon o yomimasu. Itsumo benkyoo shimasu.

Watashi no tomodachi wa itsumo benkyoo shimasen. Eiga ga suki desu.
Mainichi TEREBI o mimasu.
Doyoobi to nichiyoobi ni SUPOOTSU o shimasu.

Kinoo yama ni ikimashita. Otoosan to okaasan to imooto to ikimashita. Yuki o mimashita. Kirei deshita. Yuki ga suki desu.
Samui otenki deshita.
Yoji ni yuki deshita kara uchi ni kaerimashita.

Raishuu no suiyoobi ni gakkoo no SUPOOTSU no hi desu.
Watashi wa SUPOOTSU ga joozu desu kara SUPOOTSU no hi ga suki desu.
Watashi no tomodachi no AN san wa SUPOOTSU ga kirai desu.
AN san wa hon to ongaku ga suki desu. PIANO ga joozu desu.
Mainichi PIANO o renshuu shimasu. SUPOOTSU no hi ga kirai desu.

MAIKU kun wa watashi no dookyuusei desu. Ii tomodachi desu.
Mainichi MAIKU kun wa watashi no uchi ni kimasu.
Mainichi MAIKU kun to shukudai o shimasu. TEREBI o mimasu.
BIDEO GEEMU o shimasu. Doyoobi ni eiga ni ikimasu.

Conclusion

(5 minutes)
Read the dialogues over quickly. Stick them all on to a large poster for everyone to read after the teacher has checked them. Keep them carefully so that they are available when material is being chosen for inclusion in the class magazine.

Homework

Write a short dialogue or story about any subject.
For those who need ideas to get them started suggest 'My pet', 'My older brother', etc., as starting points.

Dismissal: While students sing 'Ten Little Indians' song, teacher indicates who may leave.

Lesson Sixty-four (optional lesson)

Aims and objectives

- to give students a free story-writing session.
- to work further on last lesson's new material.

Preparation

Photocopied stories from last lesson.
Paper to mount students work.
Scissors, glue.

Introduction

Greet. Put up date. Listen again to textbook stories from last lesson.
Volunteers read aloud some of the stories written for homework and hand them in for checking.

Main theme

Class work individually on stories for the magazine, choosing between writing for a fiction section and a cartoon dialogue section. If they choose the cartoon they must produce the dialogue first before beginning the artwork, otherwise some never achieve a finished product!

After writing their own story they find someone else who has finished and get them to check it before showing it to the teacher.

Teacher is available for consultation and checking of structures and spelling.

Conclusion

In pairs, groups, or whole class, share as many as possible of the finished stories and correct together.

Homework

Write up neatly in *hiragana* if it has been checked.
Think of ideas for other stories or dialogues.

Dismissal: Use *katakana* name cards, held up one by one. As students recognize their own name, they may leave, saying thank you and goodbye to the teacher in Japanese.

Lesson Sixty-five (Unit 5 [continued], page 242)

Aims and Objectives

- to encourage comment on statements made.
- to practice use of the family labels.
- to practice questioning.
- to find out about each other's families and the teacher.

Preparation

Happy Family cards. Photocopy on thin card a set for each group.

Introduction

(10 minutes)

Collect homework for checking and keeping. It could be displayed on the wall now, and later best pieces selected for the magazine.

As well as finding out some facts it's good to be able to make some comment.

Listen to and read the dialogue on page 242.

What other comments could the two speakers have put in to show that they were listening and interested?

Listen to the dialogue again and hear some of the additions that could have been made to enrich the conversation.

OR

Make additions to the dialogue and share them with the class.

It's important that we try to make real conversation as soon as possible and one way of doing it is to add comments as well as asking direct questions.

Main theme

(10 minutes)

1 Do Activities 1 and 2 on page 244, making comments in response to the information given. Teacher monitors and picks out a good pair to demonstrate for the others.

The 'Smith and Brown families' worksheets

Suggestion for use:

1 Pairwork/Group work/General class discussion.
Describe the Smith's home.
Imagine that you visited them yesterday. The illustrations show what they did while you were visiting.
Which one of the family did you spend time with? What did you do?
Which members of the family do you like/dislike?
Say where each person was when you arrived.
What was the weather like?
After discussion in Japanese, 2 or 3 students (randomly chosen) report their pair/group's information to the class.

2 Use for question and answer activities.
Pointing to pictures,
    Dare ga imasu ka,
    Doko ni imasu ka,
    Doko de TEREBI o mimashita ka, etc.

3 Describe the family's physical characteristics, or question to elicit physical characteristics, age, likes/dislikes, etc.

NOTE: After students have completed later books, the same illustrations may be re-used for the *te* form and position words.

The Smith family

Otoosan	*Okaasan*	*TIMU*	*DION*
52	40	14	22

The Brown family

The Butcher family

JON   *Okaasan*   *Otoosan*
14   43   44

(10 minutes)

  2 Do Activity 3 on page 244.

(15 minutes)

  3 Play Happy Families. Instructions on pages 247, 248.

    OR

    Take turns to give information about each person in a family. Students listen to find something in common with cards they are holding and make appropriate comment, e.g.: *HERENA san no otoosan mo yonjuuissai desu* etc.

    If they can make a comment about a similarity, they win a point.

Homework

Puzzles on page 245. Writing practice page 249.

Answers to words puzzles on p. 245
- Imperial Goddess *Amaterasu*
- The present emperor *Akihito*
- Name of this period in Japan *Heisei*
- also/neither *mo*
- my own father *chichi*
- my own mother *okaasan*
- I/me *watashi*   *boku*
- father *otoosan*
- mother *okaasan*
- Ten words that belong to family relationships:
  - *kazoku*
  - *chichi*
  - *ani*
  - *imooto*
  - *haha*
  - *ane*
  - *oniisan*
  - *otooto*
  - *watashi*
  - *boku*
- 1 (Temperature) *suzushii*
  - *atsui*
- 2 (Animal) *inu*
  - *neko*
- 3 (Present) *hana*
- 4 (Numbers) *shi*
  - *go*
- 5 (Places) *kooen*
  - *umi*

Dismissal: Students make a comment about the lesson as they file past.

Lesson Sixty-six (checks 1, 2, and 3)

There are many ways to use the check exercises. Please use them in any way you wish. The following is one way of using them.

Aims and Objectives of check exercises

- to give students practice in writing answers to formal exercises.
- to talk about a family member to a given format.
- to read and understand a letter written in *hiragana*.
- to check use of *kore sore are*.
- to check family labels
- to check adjectives in present and present negative.
- to check ages.
- to check use of some verbs.

Preparation

Go through check exercises and decide what you would like to use/reject and how you'd like to use those you choose.

Topic Seven, Check 1

A

Families. Write the English equivalent of the following:

1. *Sore wa chichi desu.*
2. *Are wa haha desu.*
3. *Kore wa watashi no kazoku desu.*
4. *RISA san wa watashi no tomodachi desu.*
5. *Watashi no otoosan no namae wa JIMU (Jim) desu.*
6. *Okaasan no namae wa CHIERI (Cherry) desu.*
7. *Haha dewa arimasen.*
8. *Haha no tomodachi desu.*
9. *Boku wa JIEKU (Jake) desu.*
10. *Chotto matte kudasai.*

B

Use the following sentences for translation, listening comprehension, or reading aloud.

1. *Okaasan, mite kudasai.*
2. *Otoosan, kiite kudasai.*
3. *Dewa, chotto matte kudasai.*
4. *Uchi wa ookii desu.*
5. *Watashi no kazoku wa ookii desu.*
6. *Kazoku wa ookikunai desu.*
7. *Okaerinasai.*
8. *Otoosan to okaasan desu.*
9. *Haha wa se ga takai desu.*
10. *Otoosan wa se ga hikukunai desu.*

Answers (Topic Seven, Check 1)

A

1. That is my father.
2. That is my mother over there.
3. This is my family.
4. Lisa is my friend.
5. My father's name is Jim.
6. My mother's name is Cherry.
7. It's not my mother.
8. It's my mother's friend.
9. I am Jake.
10. Please wait a minute.

B

1. My family is not big.
2. Welcome home.
3. It's my mother and father.
4. My mother is tall.
5. My father is not short in height.
6. Please look/watch Mom.
7. Please listen, Dad.
8. Well then, please wait a minute.
9. The house is big.
10. My family's big.

Topic Seven, Check 2

A

How would you say the following in Japanese?

1. This is my family. (boy speaking)

2. Is that so/Really?
3. Is that your father over there?
4. Who is that?
5. What is your mother's name?
6. This is me. (girl speaking)
7. This is my friend Francis.
8. Is it Lisa's mother?
9. Is Ken your friend?

B

1. My older brother's name is Dev.
2. My younger sister's name is Diane.
3. My older brother is eighteen.
4. My younger sister is eleven.
5. My father is fifty.
6. My mother is forty-three.
7. My father cleans the car.
8. My mother's birthday is May 5.
9. Dad watches TV every day.
10. My mother is French.

Answers (Topic Seven, Check 2)

A

1. *Boku no kazoku desu.*
2. *Soo desu ka.*
3. *Are wa otoosan desu ka.*
4. *Dare desu ka.*
5. *Okaasan no namae wa nan desu ka.*
6. *Kore wa watashi desu.*
7. *Kore wa watashi no tomodachi no FURANSESU desu.*
8. *RISA san no okaasan desu ka.*
9. *KEN san wa anata no tomodachi desu ka.*

B

1. *Ani no namae wa DEBU desu.*
2. *Imooto no namae wa DAIAN desu.*
3. *Ani wa juuhassai desu.*
4. *Imooto wa juuissai desu.*
5. *Chichi/otoosan wa gojussai desu.*
6. *Haha/okaasan wa yonjuusansai desu.*
7. *Chichi/otoosan wa kuruma o sooji shimasu.*
8. *Haha/okaasan no tanjoobi wa gogatsu itsuka desu.*
9. *Chichi/otoosan wa mainichi TEREBI o mimasu.*
10. *Haha/okaasan was FURANSUjin desu.*

Topic Seven, Check 3

A

You have been asked to speak about your younger brother. You decide to tell the class the following:
My younger brother's name is Steven. He is twelve years old. He is a junior high school intermediate school student. He plays soccer. Every day he practices guitar. He studies math, social studies, English (and other things). He doesn't study Japanese. He likes comics. he reads comics every day. His birthday is the first of April.
How would you say it in Japanese?

B

You received a letter from your penpal in which she tells you all about her older sister. As your friend doesn't understand Japanese, you translate it for him.

こんにち は。きょう は あつい です。あね と じゅうじ に うみ に
いきました。あね の なまえ は すみこ です。じゅうろくさい です。
こうこうせい です。あね が すき です。せ が ひくい です。かみ の
け が ながい です。
めがね を かけます。スポーツ が きらい です。ピアノ が
すき です。まいにち ピアノ を れんしゅう します。しゅくだい が
きらい です。わたし も しゅくだい が きらい です。あなた は。
どようび に あね と えいが に いきます。かいて ください。さよなら。
きみこ。

(スポーツ   *SUPOOTSU*   sports)   (ピアノ   *PIANO*   piano)

Konnichi wa. Kyoo wa atsui desu. Ane to juuji ni umi ni ikimashita. Ane no namae wa Sumiko desu. Juurokusai desu. Kookoosei desu. Ane ga suki desu. Se ga hikui desu. Kami no ke ga nagai desu. Megane o kakemasu. SUPOOTSU ga kirai desu. PIANO ga suki desu. Mainichi PIANO o renshuu shimasu. Shukudai ga kirai desu. Watashi mo shukudai ga kirai desu—anata wa? Doyoobi ni ane to eiga ni ikimasu. Kaite kudasai. Sayonara. Kimiko.

Answers (Topic Seven, Check 3)

A

おとうと の なまえ は ステ・ベン です。じゅうにさい です。
ちゅうがくせい です。ラグビー を します。まいにち ギター を
れんしゅう します。すうがく や しゃかい や えいご を べんきょう
します。にほんご を べんきょう しません。まんが が すき です。
まいにち まんが を よみます。たんじょうび は しがつ ついたち です。

(スティベン *SUTIBEN* Steven)　(ギター *GITAA* guitar)

Otooto no namae wa SUTIBEN desu. Juunisai desu. Chuugakuse desu. RAGUBII o shimasu. Mainichi GITAA o renshuu shimasu. Suugaku ya shakai ya eigo o benkyoo shimasu. Nihongo o benkyoo shimasen. Manga ga suki desu. Mainichi manga o yomimasu. Tanjoobi wa shigatsu tsuitachi desu.

B

My older sister's name is Sumiko. She's sixteen. She's a high school student. I like my older sister. She's short. Her hair is long. She wears glasses. She hates sports. She likes the piano. Every day she practices piano. She hates homework. I hate homework too. How about you? On Saturdays we go to the movies. Please write. Goodbye. Kimiko.

Introduction

(5 minutes)

Comment to students as they enter. Greet. Elicit date and write it up on board.

Explain the way in which you would like students to work in this lesson which is more formal than usual. It will give them a chance to evaluate their own progress and see where they need to put in some extra time.

Reassure that it is not a test that they need to feel anxious about, merely a way to find out what they have really absorbed without being warned to review.

Explain that the purpose is not competitive. It will help the teacher to see what needs to be re-taught, and should help them to know what has not yet sunk in so that they can remedy the problem before it mounts up into too much work.

Main theme

(10-15 minutes)

1 Students set their own pace through the check exercises 1 and 2, and mark them when finished. There is no point in them cheating if they have taken in the purpose of the lesson.

(15 minutes)

2 As they finish teacher places them in groups of four. Members of a group test each other in Check 3. One student reads out what the student being tested needs to say, in English. While the student is giving the answers, the other members of the group listen and mark the following:

Has the information been stated correctly?

Were there minor mistakes?

Did the student need to make more than one attempt?

Did the student give a fluent, quick answer?

They discuss and compliment each other on what was well done and help each other to correct minor mistakes.

Each member of the group takes a turn, learning from the previous student's mistakes. Teacher monitors group activity.

By the end of this activity the information should be being given like clockwork.

(10 minutes)

3 Reading exercise from *hiragana* to be followed by questions and answers in English. Cover *roomaji*. Students read through passage alone silently. Look up words they couldn't read in the *roomaji* version.

They then follow the *hiragana* information in the book as questions are asked to find the information.

Quickly write answers in notebooks.

Referring to the *hiragana* passage

1 What is the weather like?

2 Who went to the beach?

3 At what time did they go to the beach?

4 How old is the older sister?

5 What is her name?

6 What is her height?

7 What do you know about her hair?

8 Does she wear glasses?

9 What does she like?

10 What does she dislike?

11 How often does she practice?

12 What do they do on Saturdays?

13 What question does the writer ask her penpal?

14 What is the name of the writer?

15 When did they go to the beach?

Students mark work.

If all correct—fantastic.

Compliment on more than half correct.

Suggest that students below that mark need to talk to you to find out where they are having problems, unless they can now see where they had difficulties—not reading *hiragana* well enough yet, not knowing the vocabulary, not noticing tense, etc.

Homework

Check the exercises over and make sure that if the check was done again they could improve their mark/get everything correct.

Dismissal: Collect notebooks open at test page to see how students got on. Ask how they got on, varying phrases—*yoku dekimashita ka, joozu desu ka.* If you know they did well, compliment. If they didn't do too well use *gambatte kudasai* (Keep trying).

Lesson Sixty-seven (Unit 6, page 250)

Aims and Objectives

• to teach *mo ... mo*—both ... neither.

Preparation

Tape.

Introduction

(10 minutes)
Tape.
Greet. Comment on results of check lesson positively.
Students open textbooks at pages 246–247.
Use the Happy Family cards used previously. Ask students to find similarities and differences between people. Report the items they find in English.
Discuss the words we use in English—either, both, neither.
Explain that today they will learn how to give that information in Japanese.

Main Theme

1 Study (page 250). Go through the material carefully.

2 Do the activities on page 251 in Japanese.

3 Taking turns each pair gives information about family members.

Topic Six Vocabulary cards

ashita	itsu	kinoo	konshuu	kyoo
NYUUYOOKU	NYUUYOOKU	KANADA	to	sorosoro shitsurei shimasu
atarashii	ichinensei	mata	ninensei	AMERIKA
jussai	juuissai	juunisai	juusansai	hatachi
gosai	rokusai	nanasai	hassai	kyuusai
sai	issai	nisai	sansai	yonsai
chan	kochira	tomodachi	Oikutsu desu ka	nansai desu ka

nangatsu	nannichi	yoko dekimashita	tsuitachi	futsuka
juugatsu	juuchigatsu	juunigatsu	joozo desu ne	kodomo no hi
gogatsu	rokugatsu	shichigatsu	hachigatsu	kugatsu
nangatsu	ichigatsu	nigatsu	sangatsu	shigatsu
aki	fuyu	haru	natsu	O tanjoobi Omedetoo Gozaimasu
suiyoobi	mokuyoobi	kinyoobi	doyoobi	nichiyoobi
raishuu	senshuu	tanjoobi	getsuyoobi	kayoobi

saa	akai	akakunai	aoi	aokunai
nijuuhachinihi	nijuukunichi	sanjuunichi	sanjuuichinichi	mo
nijuusannichi	nijuuyokka	nijuugonichi	nijuurokunichi	nijuunananichi
juuhachinichi	juukunichi	hatsuka	nijuuichinichi	nijuuninichi
juusannichi	juuyokka	juugonichi	juurokunichi	nuunananichi
yooka	kokonoka	tooka	juuichinichi	juuninichi
mikka	yokka	itsuka	muika	nanoka

mimi	onaka	te	sooji shimasu	WASHINTON
takakunai	ashi	atama	hana	kuchi
onna no ko	otoko no ko	se	shoogakusei	takai
kami no ke	kookoosei	me	megane o kakemasu	megane o kakemasen
chuugakusei	hikui	hikukunai	ichinichijuu	iro
nagai	nagakunai	chairo	midoriiro	ashi
aokunai	kiiroi	kuroi	mijikai	mijikakunai

sakuban	nezumiiro	murasakiiro	momoiro	jankenpon	doobutsu	daidaiiro

For example, Student One says 'Both my mother and my father play tennis. How about yours?' *(Anata no otoosan to okaasan wa).*

Student Two follows up with 'My mother plays tennis' or 'Neither my mother nor father play tennis' or 'Both my mother and my father play tennis' as a genuine reply.

They try to think of five things to comment on.

Write down the best sentences made, to use when reporting to the group on the similarities or differences between their families.

4 Using the Happy Family cards, have a group competition to find and be able to give the most similarities and differences offered by the cards.

5 minutes preparation time.

Each group 'stockpiles' information and must be able to express it in Japanese.

Each group then takes a turn to offer information in Japanese.

May offer two items of information each turn.

Other groups check against information on cards and allow a point for each correct.

Continue with whatever time available.

Count up scores and announce the winners.

Conclusion

Compliment on participation level. Encourage higher participation level from quiet or less enthusiastic students.

Homework

Go through Check your understanding (page 251). Writing practice (page 252).

Lesson Sixty-eight (page 252)

Aims and objectives

- to give students sentence building practice with *mo.*
- to practice roleplay using *mo.*
- to group the students in arbitrary groups to encourage them to work with different partners.

Preparation

Photocopy onto thin card vocabulary cards sufficient for 5 groups.
Put out in packs the vocabulary cards made previously for earlier lessons.
Photocopy and cut up into cards page 253.

Introduction

(10 minutes)
Greet. Elicit date.
Check on homework success rate by asking randomly selected students to tell the class how to say the items in the homework set without reference to their notebooks or the textbook.

Student or teacher calls out a name and reads an item. Named student answers, then takes responsibility for choosing the next person.

Main theme

(10 minutes)

1 Explain that on page 252 there are several activities that they are to complete in groups. Divide into groups by counting around class *ichi, ni, san, shi, go,* and repeating until all class have been numbered with numbers one to five.

Tell all students numbered *ichi* to group in one corner, *ni* in another, etc., until the groups have been clearly segregated.

Go around and count numbers in each group with *hitori, futari, sannin,* etc., to check that groups are even in number.

Give out to each group a list of verbs they should know and two packs of vocabulary cards. Give each group the verb list.

Do Activities One, Two and Three. Take turns to use the next verb on the list. If a student can't make a sentence the next person in the group takes the card to work with and takes the next verb in the list as well. Each correct sentence gains one point.

Teacher monitors as students work. Which activity, which verb have they got to when you stop them? Compliment the team who have worked most efficiently and carefully. Who were the winners from each group?

(10 minutes)

2 Start again and with the vocabulary cards quickly go through the pile giving the English. Any they have forgotten go in a separate pile. Winning group is the one with fewest cards in the *forgotten* pile.

(20-25 minutes)

3 Groups role play the situation in Activity 4.

Don't plan, just let it happen. Each student takes responsibility for offering something until all the framework has been covered.

One person from each group sits aside to note whether all the points are covered and to comment on the group's performance, picking out something particularly good (in English).

OR

With groups or pairs of own choice, play Happy Families in Japanese/Test each other on *hiragana*/ Make word searches/Make code puzzles in *hiragana* for others to do/Make Japanese posters/ Do *origami,* etc., at their choice.

Homework

Vocabulary—study from the vocabulary lists at the back of the book up to Topic seven Unit 7,

OR

the free choice section above.

Writing practice. Go through *hiragana* chart and see how many they know well/how many still to learn. Set a target for knowing them. Students bring in card for making games next lesson if possible.

Dismissal: Use *katakana* name cards. Hold up a card. Students recognize and leave politely with *soro soro shitsurei shimasu* (I'm sorry I must be leaving).

Lesson Sixty-nine (Unit 7, page 255)

Aims and Objectives

- to teach students how to talk about occupations

Preparation

If chosen as an activity:
Photocopy Family Tree. Paper for family tree posters (or could be done in notebooks).
Paper for results of surveys.
Paper or card for competition (see below).

Introduction

Tape.
Greet. Elicit date.
Ask about the names for jobs that students would need if they wanted to tell people about their families' jobs.
Students draw family members, label and put symbols for their job, e.g.: hammer for a carpenter, nurses cap, doctor's stethoscope, etc.
Look at list or dictionary to find the job names needed.
Point out that in Japan a very large number of people work in transportation jobs, particularly trains, because the transportation system is so good, to explain why *ekiin* has been included.
Listen to the tape or teacher or students reading dialogue.

Main theme

Read through the dialogue to demonstrate how the survey of their class could be done and for reading practice.
Make sure class are happy with their own and other's family labels before continuing.
Choose activities from pages 256–257.
Competition:
Plan a board game/quiz game/matching games/dicomm activity (in pairs or individually) that would give practice in using the Japanese that everyone in the class should know.

Family Tree

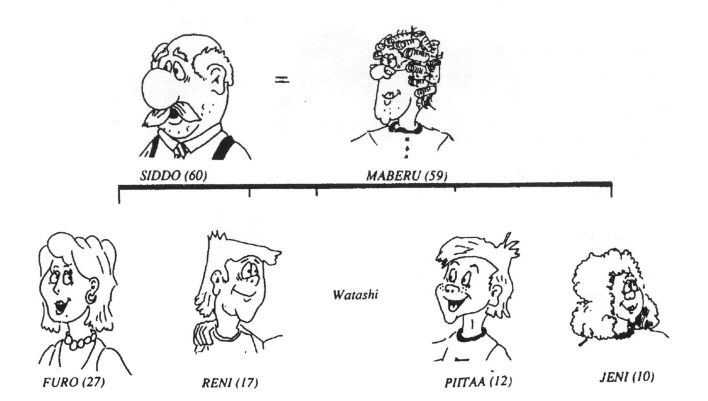

SIDDO (60) = MABERU (59)

FURO (27)   RENI (17)   Watashi   PIITAA (12)   JENI (10)

Family Tree

JAKKU (41) = MERII (40)

FIRIPU (14)   MARIA (16)   WARU (19)   *Watashi*

Homework

Work on games started above. Writing practice page 258.

Dismissal: Tell teacher the job of one member of family.

Lesson Seventy (Unit 8, page 259)

Aims and Objectives

• to consolidate and remind of introductions.

Preparation

Tape.

Introduction

Listen to tape.

Cover *roomaji* and read the *hiragana* in pairs, finding the *katakana* if necessary from the vocabulary list. Remind of different introductions—to strangers (formal and informal), to friends, to friends you haven't seen for a while.

Students were reminded last lesson of how much they can now say about themselves and their friends.

Main theme

(5-10 minutes)

1 Do activity 1, adding in genuine information about themselves to extend the conversation. Use the checklist on page 257 and add in information accordingly, making comments of interest as they listen to each other. Don't plan it first. Start with the given dialogue, substituting own names, nationalities, and activities. Add in the information from the list on page 257 that has not been offered.

Allow five to ten minutes. Which pair manages to keep going longest? As students finish they sit and wait silently, listening until the last pair run out of things to say.

2 Choose another activity *OR* give students time to work on games, aiming to finish production this lesson or this lesson plus homework time.

Conclusion

Students study picture page 261.

Think of something they could say about the people or the place or the time to nearest hour, as they leave the room.

Homework

Finish games. Be prepared to explain them (in English) lesson after next.

Dismissal: Tell teacher something about the picture (page 261), e.g.: *otoko no ko wa kookoosei desu, otoko no ko wa eki ni imasu, otoko no ko wa hitori megane o kakemasu, seito wa se ga takai desu, nihonjin desu, nihon no eki desu, densha wa kimasen,* etc.

Lesson Seventy-one (Unit 9, page 261)

Aims and Objectives

- to give more practice in listening comprehension.
- to give more reading practice from *hiragana*.
- to give more practice in questioning and understanding passages.

Preparation

Tape.

Photocopy the worksheets for this lesson (*Maishuu Tomokochan to, nani o shimasu ka*).

Read through textbook, deciding which activities to use and how to use them: Is your need for *hiragana* reading practice, or for quick understanding of the passage? Choose *roomaji* or *hiragana* to suit your purpose, or for practice in reading aloud.

Is your students' need for listening comprehension? If so listen to the tape version which takes the passage in short sections and asks questions after each.

Is your need for a passage to discuss structures from? Why have those particles been used? Order of sentences/use of adjectives and qualitative nouns, etc.

Exercises for speedy recognition of *hiragana* (or *roomaji*):

1 Ask students to read the first passage alone silently and understand. Each student thinks of at least one question to ask the class about the passage. Question around the class. To ensure class listen intently, no question may be repeated. If it is, have a fun penalty.
   (Ask students to cover the *roomaji,* questions and answers provided before you begin.)

2 Ask students to read aloud together, in pairs, or around the class one sentence each for pronunciation practice.

3 Use passage for skim reading to find specific words quickly. Students read quickly to be the first to find the word called out.

Maishu Tomokochan to, nani o shimasu ka

getsuyoobi   _____ *ji* _____ *masu*   月

kayoobi   _____ *ji* _____ *masu*   火

_____

_____

_____

suiyoobi   _____ *ji* _____ *masu*   水

mokuyoobi   _____ *ji* _____   木

kinyoobi   _____ *ji* _____   金

doyoobi   _____ *ji* _____   土

nichiyoobi   _____ *ji* _____   日

_____

_____

_____

How many things did the writer do with Tomoko in the course of a week?

_____

4 Hunt the *hiragana:* A student calls out a combined sound *hiragana,* e.g., *da/cha.* Others hunt the passage to find how many times it occurs.

5 Which sentence has the greatest number of particles? How many different particles have been used in the passage?

6 Listening comprehension. Listen to the tape. Stand every time a member of the family is mentioned. Sit down again quickly ready for next.

OR when a time is mentioned

OR a day

OR an activity, at teacher's choice. (Students enjoy 'bobbing up and down'.)

7 Make diary entries for the writer, listing times and activities.

Introduction

Tape music—Songs learned previously
Sing along with tape
Play tape dialogue
Answer questions asked in English in Japanese.

Main theme

Follow pages 261–265, choosing activities. Use worksheet from this lesson for pages 264 and 265.

Conclusion

Code captions on page 266.

Homework

Make sure games are ready to play lesson after next.
Check that the games work and that instructions are really clear.
Bring to school next lesson for teacher to check.

Dismissal: Tell code caption or its meaning.

Glenn's trip to Washington

Circle the correct answer as you listen. The story will be read twice.

When did Glenn go to Washington?

Senshuu   Konshuu   Raishuu

Who did he go with?

Mother   Older brother   School friends   Sister's friends

On what day did he see the capitol?

Saturday   Sunday   Monday   Tuesday

What Sport did he practice?

Baseball   Rugby   Soccer   Basketball   Volleyball

What was the weather like on Tuesday?

wet   good   hot   cold   humid

On Wednesday what was the weather like?

Hot and good   cold and wet   windy and wet

What day did they return to New York?

Thursday   Friday   Saturday   Sunday

What time did they return to New York?

five o'clock   six o'clock   seven o'clock   eight o'clock

Who did he meet in New York?

Mother   sister   brother   father

Kathy's Trip to Paris

Where does Kathy normally live?

    Japan   France   America   England

How many people are there in Kathy's family?

    hitori   futari   sannin   yonin   gonin

Kathy has

    an older brother   an older sister   a younger brother   a younger sister

How old is Kathy?

    Twelve   Thirteen   Fourteen   Fifteen   Sixteen

What language does she study?

    French   German   Italian   Japanese

When did sho go to Paris

    January   February   March   April   May   June

Why may she want to return to Paris based on the information in the passage?

    to see friends   to swim   to lie in the sun   to study French

Lesson Seventy-two (optional lesson)

Aims and objectives

- to add more material to the class magazine.
- to write code captions, games, and puzzles.

Preparation

Small reward

Introduction

(5 minutes)
Greet. Put up date.
Put up code message using code on page 208 to ask students to bring homework to you. Reward the first student to do as asked.

Main theme

(25 minutes)
While the teacher is busy checking through games produced last lesson with the students who made them, the class have time, working individually or in pairs, to make puzzles, code captions (using the key on page 208 or their own), *hiragana* word searches or to continue their cartoons from last magazine session.

Conclusion

(10 minutes)
Share the finished products and check them to see if they work.

Homework

Check them over again and write up neatly for the magazine.

Dismissal: Show teacher what was produced this lesson—*kore o mite kudasai.*

Lesson Seventy-three (game lesson)

Aims and objectives

- to give time for students to use the games or activities made.
- to give time for student interaction of a different sort.

Preparation

Have Happy Family cards available and packs of vocabulary cards in case some students have a gap between activities and need something to do.

Introduction

Greet. Elicit date. Sing a song (Tape: *Musunde Hiraite*)

Students show their activities to the class briefly.

Comment on the work students have put in and the need to participate willingly to give the best chance of the activities working well.

Some activities will take a very short time to do. Sort them out accordingly. Divide class into groups or pairs and give several short activities to one or two groups to do while others are doing longer ones.

Main theme

Use activities made, changing over after ten or fifteen minutes.

Try to give all students a turn at as many activities as possible.

If anyone finishes early and has run out of activities, offer vocabulary cards and ideas for patience, e.g.: Putting words in piles of nouns, particles, adjectives, qualitative nouns, verbs.

Go through pack one by one. Can only put a card down in its correct turn in the sequence.

If several students are at a loose end, offer Happy Families or making stories, posters or roleplays to make sure that everyone stays happily occupied.

Conclusion

Vote on the most enjoyable activity. Vote on the activity that gave best practice of Japanese. Were the two the same?

Homework

Write an outline of activities for a day or a week like *Tomoko*'s (page 262) saying when, where and with whom.

Dismissal: Students tell teacher what they think they will be doing at five o'clock tonight.

Lesson Seventy-four (Unit 10, page 268)

Aims and objectives

- this is a bridging lesson between the two topics of families and friends, and homes.
- to teach how to describe own home and where students live.
- to remind of adjectives in present and present negative and position in sentence.

Preparation

Tape.
Photocopies of maps of Japan with major cities marked.

Introduction

(5 minutes)

Greet. Elicit date. Thank students for efforts made for last lesson.

Main theme

(5 minutes)

1 Look at picture on page 269. Discuss the way houses have been squeezed into the space, style of houses, making use of land, narrowness of street, and the fact that most Japanese people spend their lives in a cramped environment—crowded into trains, in large classes, in crowded towns, in small houses, etc. Compare with own situation. Comment on the way Japanese people therefore feel about the large houses, gardens and spaciousness of some other nationalities' surroundings. (Remember that not all Japanese live in cramped surroundings but the large majority do.) Write up new words: *hiroi* and *semai*. Ask students to think of good ways to remember which is which.

(15 minutes)

2 Study—Using adjectives. Activities 1–4 (pages 269–270).

(10 minutes)

3 Talking about where you live.
   Reintroduce map of Japan. Students stick map into notebooks for reference.

4 Do Activity 5. Add in information from imagination about the homes the people live in.

Conclusion

(5-10 minutes)

Guessing games about where people live.

Put up list of fictitious names on board.

Choose a student to come out and choose a name and to secretly decide on the place where he/she lives.

Write it on paper and give to teacher to avoid changing mind!

Japan: the country

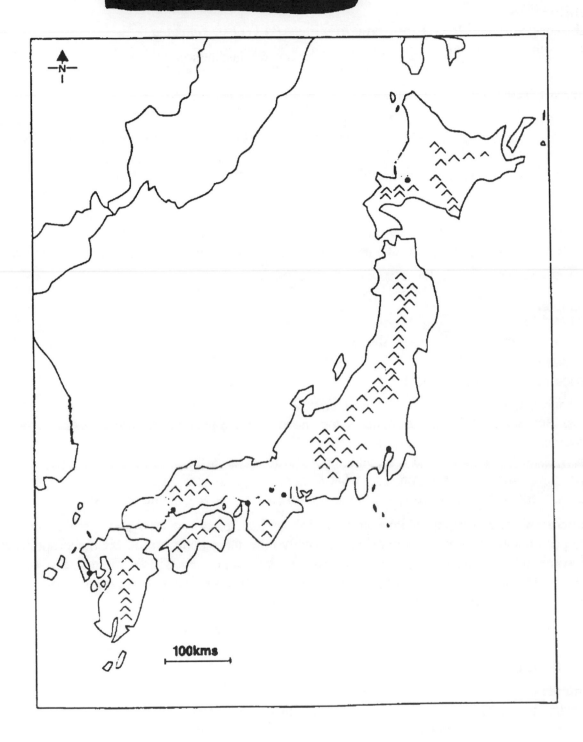

100kms

Other students take turns to ask ... *san wa (Sapporo) ni sunde imasu ka*.
Answer *iie, chigaimasu*, or *hai, soo desu*, until the place is guessed.
Person who guesses takes next turn.

Homework

Read dialogue (page 268). Learn how to write *APAATO* in *katakana*.
Write about an imaginary friend (in *hiragana*) who lives in Japan, giving physical description and telling where he/she lives, similar to oral descriptions done in class.

Dismissal: Tell teacher whether own home is spacious or cramped.

Lesson Seventy-five (Unit 10, page 268)

Aims and objectives

• to consolidate descriptions of families and friends and introductions.
• to encourage towards more spontaneous roleplay.

Preparation

Tape. Photocopy student answer sheets.

Introduction

Tape music. Greet. Elicit date and weather.
Discuss the amazing ability the students now have to make genuine conversations about a number of everyday subjects.
Discuss the ways in which good genuine conversation takes place:
By listening with genuine interest to what someone says to you.
By answering with follow up questions or comments to show genuine interest.

Comment on conversations. If you tell someone an item of information and there is only a grunt or the person starts talking about something totally unconnected, you think him/her impolite. If you think something important enough to tell someone you hope they will be interested if only out of politeness. The best conversations are where the comment sparks off a real discussion about something. Sometimes a disagreement follows but at least it is genuine interaction.

Today's lesson is a starting point for having good conversations expressing your own interests.

Main theme

(15 minutes)

  1 Listen to the tape or read the dialogue on pages 268–269.
    Even though it is simple, do the participants appear to be listening to each other before making a reply?
    How does the conversation move away from the photos being shown without rudeness?
    Listen to or read the dialogue on page 271–272.

Does it sound as if Hiroko is interested in the photos?
How could she have extended what she said? (After the first photo she may have commented on physical characteristics or asked where Ann met him or where he lives, etc.)
Explain *ga*—but, (page 272) and then read dialogue on pages 272–273.
Listening carefully and making relevant replies is today's focus.

(20 minutes)

2 Activity (page 273).
Whole class read the following example together.
Here is a possible starter sentence. Think of a situation:

It's holiday time. Brendan has had a visitor to stay who has now gone home.
Kenichi is the son of Brendan's mother's friend. They don't know each other well because they are not in the same class. In the course of conversation Brendan tells Kenichi:
Watashi no tomodachi no DION san wa OOSUTORARIA ni sunde imasu.
Kinoo kaerimashita.

Here is an example of the way the conversation went from there:
Kenichi asked: *DION san wa nansai desu ka.*

From the 'student worksheet', read in turn and find out where the conversation leads...

A *Juuyonsai desu. Watashi mo juuyonsai desu. Anata wa.*
B *Watashi wa juugosai desu.*
A *Otanjoobi wa nangatsu nannichi desu ka.*
B *Shichigatsu nanoka desu.*
A *Soo desu ka. Sore wa nihon no tanabata desu ne.*
B *Soo desu ka. Nihongo o benkyoo shimasu ka.*
A *Hai soo desu.*
B *Nihongo ga suki desu ka.*
A *Hai taihen suki desu. Nanigo o benkyoo shimasu ka.*
B *DOITSUgo o benkyoo shimasu.*
A *DOITSUgo ga suki desu ka.*
B *Iie, kirai desu. Suugaku mo kirai desu.*
A *Watashi mo. TENISU o shimashoo ka.*
B *Hai soo shimashoo.*
A *Nanji ni kooen ni ikimashoo ka.*
B *Yojihan ni (ikimashoo).*
A *Yojihan ni ... Ja mata.*

Other responses to start from may have been (among many other possibilities):
DION san wa KANADAjin desu ka
Doko ni aimashita ka
Itsu DION san ni aimashita ka (Answer which month or date)
Anata wa KANADA ni ikimashita ka
DION san wa SUPOOTSU o shimasu ka

Choose one and follow it through as in the example above.
Just listen carefully and think of a relevant response.
Write down your responses and be prepared to read them to the class. It will be interesting to

see how different the dialogues will be. If your conversation peters out quickly don't worry. Choose a different starter response and try again.

Starter information:

Watashi no tomodachi no DION san wa KANADA ni sunde imasu.

Starter response: (Choose from the five above)

How far past ten can you go? Use the back of the paper too if you like!

Conclusion

Choose as many as possible to read aloud and put all of them on the wall for others to read later. Read the short caption on page 275. Think up a question to ask about it.

Homework

Read teacher's choice of the passages on pages 275–276. Answer the questions and do the crossword in own notebooks.

Dismissal: Ask teacher the question about the photo as they leave. (Caption: Today my family's friends came from Mexico. The weather in Seattle today is good. It's hot.)

Lesson Seventy-six (check lesson)

Aims and objectives

- to check understanding of structures in Topic Seven.

Preparation

Go through exercises and decide what would be appropriate for your class (if any) and how you would like to present it.

Main theme

Teacher's choice from Topic Seven Checks below.

The intention is to give a straightforward formal lesson.

One idea would be to go through the sections together orally, then to do Check Seven as a written exercise, each student working alone for a formal assessment.

Homework

Vocabulary check of Topics Six and Seven.

Topic Seven, Check 1

A

Families. Write the English equivalent of the following:

1. *Sore wa chichi desu.*
2. *Are wa haha desu.*
3. *Kore wa watashi no kazoku desu.*

---

4. *RISA san wa watashi no tomodachi desu.*
5. *Watashi no otoosan no namae wa JIMU (Jim) desu.*
6. *Okaasan no namae wa CHIERI (Cherry) desu.*
7. *Haha dewa arimasen.*
8. *Haha no tomodachi desu.*
9. *Boku wa JIEKU (Jake) desu.*
10. *Chotto matte kudasai.*

B

Use the following sentences for translation, listening comprehension, or reading aloud.

1. *Okaasan, mite kudasai.*
2. *Otoosan, kiite kudasai.*
3. *Dewa, chotto matte kudasai.*
4. *Uchi wa ookii desu.*
5. *Watashi no kazoku wa ookii desu.*
6. *Kazoku wa ookikunai desu.*
7. *Okaerinasai.*
8. *Otoosan to okaasan desu.*
9. *Haha wa se ga takai desu.*
10. *Otoosan wa se ga hikukunai desu.*

Answers (Topic Seven, Check 1)

A

1. That is my father.
2. That is my mother over there.
3. This is my family.
4. Lisa is my friend.
5. My father's name is Jim.
6. My mother's name is Cherry.
7. It's not my mother.
8. It's my mother's friend.
9. I am Jake.
10. Please wait a minute.

B

1. My family is not big.
2. Welcome home.
3. It's my mother and father.
4. My mother is tall.
5. My father is not short in height.
6. Please look/watch Mom.
7. Please listen, Dad.
8. Well then, please wait a minute.
9. The house is big.
10. My family's big.

Topic Seven, Check 2

A

How would you say the following in Japanese?

1. This is my family. (boy speaking)
2. Is that so/Really?
3. Is that your father over there?
4. Who is that?
5. What is your mother's name?
6. This is me. (girl speaking)
7. This is my friend Francis.
8. Is it Lisa's mother?
9. Is Ken your friend?

B

1. My older brother's name is Dev.
2. My younger sister's name is Diane.
3. My older brother is eighteen.
4. My younger sister is eleven.
5. My father is fifty.
6. My mother is forty-three.
7. My father cleans the car.
8. My mother's birthday is May 5.
9. Dad watches TV every day.
10. My mother is French.

Answers (Topic Seven, Check 2)

A

1. *Boku no kazoku desu.*
2. *Soo desu ka.*
3. *Are wa otoosan desu ka.*
4. *Dare desu ka.*
5. *Okaasan no namae wa nan desu ka.*
6. *Kore wa watashi desu.*
7. *Kore wa watashi no tomodachi no FURANSESU desu.*
8. *RISA san no okaasan desu ka.*
9. *KEN san wa anata no tomodachi desu ka.*

B

1. *Ani no namae wa DEBU desu.*
2. *Imooto no namae wa DAIAN desu.*
3. *Ani wa juuhassai desu.*
4. *Imooto wa juuissai desu.*
5. *Chichi/otoosan wa gojussai desu.*

6. *Haha/okaasan wa yonjuusansai desu.*
7. *Chichi/otoosan wa kuruma o sooji shimasu.*
8. *Haha/okaasan no tanjoobi wa gogatsu itsuka desu.*
9. *Chichi/otoosan wa mainichi TEREBI o mimasu.*
10. *Haha/okaasan was FURANSUjin desu.*

Topic Seven, Check 3

A

You have been asked to speak about your younger brother. You decide to tell the class the following:
My younger brother's name is Steven. He is twelve years old. He is a junior high school student.
He plays soccer Every day he practices guitar. He studies math, social studies, English (and other
things). He doesn't study Japanese. He likes comics. he reads comics every day. His birthday is the
first of April.
How would you say it in Japanese?

B

You received a letter from your penpal in which she tells you all about her older sister. As your
friend doesn't understand Japanese, you translate it for him.

こんにち は。きょう は あつい です。あね こ じゅうじ に うみ に
いきました。あね の なまえ は すみこ です。じゅうろくさい です。
こうこうせい です。あね が すき です。せ だ ひくい です。かみ の
け が ながい です。
めがね を かけます。スポーツ が きらい です。ピアノ が
すき です。まいにち ピアノ を れんしゅう します。しゅくだい が
きらい です。わたし も しゅくだい が きら です。あなた は
どようび に あね と えいが に いきます。かいて ください。そよなら。
きみこ。

(スポーツ *SUPOOTSU* sports) (ピアノ *PIANO* piano)

Konnichi wa. Kyoo wa atsui desu. Ane to juuji ni umi ni ikimashita. Ane no namae wa Sumiko desu.
Juurokusai desu. Kookoosei desu. Ane ga suki desu. Se ga hikui desu. Kami no ke ga nagai desu.
Megane o kakemasu. SUPOOTSU ga kirai desu. PIANO ga suki desu. Mainichi PIANO o renshuu
shimasu. Shukudai ga kirai desu. Watashi mo shukudai ga kirai desu—anata wa? Doyoobi ni ane
to eiga ni ikimasu. Kaite kudasai. Sayonara. Kimiko.

Answers (Topic Seven, Check 3)

A

おとうと の なまえ は スティベン です。じゅうにさい です。
ちゅうがくせい です。ラグビー を します。まいにち ギター を
たんしゅう します。すうがく や しゃかい や えいご を べんきょう
します。にほんご を べんきょう しません。まんが が すき です。
まいにち まんが を よみます。たんじょうび は しがつ ついたち です。

(スティベン *SUTIBEN*   Steven)   (ギター   *GITAA*   guitar)

Otooto no namae wa SUTIBEN desu. Juunisai desu. Chuugakuse desu. RAGUBII o shimasu. Mainichi GITAA o renshuu shimasu. Suugaku ya shakai ya eigo a benkyoo shimasu. Nihongo o benkyoo shimasen. Manga ga suki desu. Mainichi manga o yomimasu. Tanjoobi wa shigatsu tsuitachi desu.

B

My older sister's name is Sumiko. She's sixteen. She's a high school student. I like my older sister. She's short. Her hair is long. She wears glasses. She hates sports. She likes the piano. Every day she practices piano. She hates homework. I hate homework too. How about you? On Saturdays we go to the movies, Please write. Goodbye. Kimiko.

Topic Seven, Check 4

A

Talking about your own family.
How would you say the following in Japanese?

1. John's a good student.
2. Kim's clever.
3. Frankie is a good older sister.
4. My younger brother's name is Dan.
5. My younger sister is Denise.
6. My older brother is nineteen.
7. Ben, my younger broker, plays volleyball.
8. My older sister went to Australia.
9. My younger brother read comics.
10. My older brother listens to records.

B

Give the following information in Japanese.

1. I have a younger sister.
2. I have an older brother.
3. I have a younger brother.
4. I have an older sister.
5. My family is small.
6. My family is big.
7. I haven't got an older brother.
8. I haven't got a younger sister.
9. I haven't got an older sister.
10. I haven't got a younger brother.

Answers (Topic Seven, Check 4)

A

1. *JON wa ii seito desu.*
2. *KIMU wa atama ga ii desu.*
3. *FURANKI wa ii ane desu.*
4. *Otooto no namae wa DAN desu.*
5. *Imooto wa DENISU desu.*
6. *Ani wa juukyuusai desu.*
7. *Otooto no BEN wa BAREEBOORU o shimasu.*
8. *Ane wa OOSUTORARIA ni ikimashita.*
9. *Otooto wa manga o yomimasu.*
10. *Ani wa REKOODO o kikimasu.*

B

1. *Imooto ga imasu.*
2. *Ani ga imasu.*
3. *Otooto ga imasu.*
4. *Ane ga imasu.*
5. *Kazoku wa chiisai desu.*
6. *Kazoku wa ookii desu.*
7. *Ani wa imasen.*
8. *Imooto wa imasen.*
9. *Ane wa imasen.*
10. *Otooto wa imasen.*

Topic Seven, Check 5

Other people's families.

A

1. How many people are in your family?
2. Have you an older brother?
3. Have you an older sister?
4. Have you a younger brother?
5. Have you a younger sister?
6. Have you one older brother?
7. Have you got two older sisters?
8. You have three older brothers, haven't you?
9. It's your younger brother, isn't it?
10. Your younger sister came yesterday.

- (Remember: *ne* can mean 'isn't it?'/'aren't you?'/'haven't you?')

B

Change the following sentences to ones that describe someone else's family. The first one is done for you.

1. *Ani ga futari imasu.*
   (Oniisan ga futari imasu.)
2. *Imooto ga hitori imasu.*
3. *Ane ga sannin imasu.*
4. *Otooto ga hitori imasu.*
5. *Kazoku wa sannin imasu.*
6. *Imooto wa imasen.*
7. *Otooto wa imasen.*
8. *Ani wa imasen.*
9. *Ane wa imasen.*
10. *Otoosan wa imasen.*

C

Make up sentences to use the words *HANSAMU, kirei, joozu, HANSAMU janai desu, kirei janai desu, joozu janai desu.*
Remember to put the person you are talking about first.

Answers (Topic Seven, Check 5)

A

1. *Gokazoku wa nannin imasu ka.*
2. *Oniisan ga imasu ka.*
3. *Oneesan ga imasu ka.*
4. *Otootosan ga imasu ka.*
5. *Imootosan ga imasu ka.*

6. *Oniisan ga hitori imasu ka.*
7. *Oneesan ga futari imasu ka.*
8. *Oniisan ga sannin imasu ne.*
9. *Otootosan desu ne.*
10. *Kinoo imootosan wa kimashita.*

B

1. *Oniisan ga futari imasu.*
2. *Imootosan ga hitori imasu.*
3. *Oneesan ga sannin imasu.*
4. *Otootosan ga hitori imasu.*
5. *Gokazoku wa sannin imasu.*
6. *Imootosan wa imasen.*
7. *Otootosan wa imasen.*
8. *Oniisan wa imasen.*
9. *Oneesan wa imasen.*
10. *Otoosan wa imasen.*

Topic Seven Vocabulary cards

taihen	warui	nin	hitori	futari
ane	atama ga ii desu	atama ga warui desu	ii	otooto
imooto	kochira e doozo	sooji shimasu	TEREBI	FIRIPPIN
mite kudasai	kiite kudasai	to	tomodachi	ani
okaasan	Okaerinasai	otoosan	ookii	ookikunai
kudasai	haha	ja	dewa	kochira
boku	chichi	chiisai	chiisakunai	chotto matte

semakunai	uchi	chiisai	chiisakunai	kara
APAATO	doko ni sunde imasu ka	hiroi	hirokunai	semai
GEEMU	kazoku	soshite	to issho ni	chan
HANSAMU janai desu	kirei	kirei janai desu	HAWAI	SAAFIN
kyoodai	oneesan	oniisan	otootosan	HANSAMU
hachinin	kyuunin	juunin	gokazoku	imootosan
sannin	yonin	gonin	rokunin	shichinin

SANFURAN-SHISUKO				
TORONTO				
chuugokujin				
ookikunai				
ookii				

TOPIC EIGHT

Lesson Seventy-seven (Introduction, page 277)

Aims and Objectives

- To introduce students to Japanese homes, names of rooms, appropriate behavior.

Preparation

If possible find pictures of Japanese homes to display alongside own country's homes. (real estate agents often have old advertisement posters and booklets with pictures and house plans that are useful.) Think through own experience of Japanese homes

OR

Read through information on Japanese homes in textbook and other resource books if they are available.

The beginning of the NHK (Japanese Public TV) language teaching video *YAN san* has a good introduction to a Japanese apartment.

The video from 'Japanese for Busy People' is also useful if you have access to it, showing Japanese natural situations in homes.

Try to organize a film about Japan or a Japanese visitor for the end of this topic.

Introduction

Music. Greet. Elicit and write up date.

Ask students, as they enter, questions about their homes, e.g.:

(namae) no uchi wa ookii desu ka chiisai desu ka,

(namae) no uchi wa hiroi desu ka semai desu ka,

(namae) no uchi wa APAATO desu ka.

Doko ni sunde imasu ka.

Comment on last lesson and return books.

Introduce new topic. Last lesson students learned to say one or two things about their homes and were reminded of those words when they came in today. Today they will learn about Japanese homes.

Main theme

Before opening textbooks:

Talk about houses in Japan, offering if possible interesting items of information from own experience or using information gathered from resources.

Compare with own homes. Make sure students realize the vast differences there are between homes as in any country but point out the traditional Japanese features which will be the same in most homes. Use resource pictures.

Draw a plan of a Japanese–style home. If it is two stories it will probably have the bath on the ground floor. Most often the toilet and bathroom will be close to the kitchen for plumbing convenience. If *Yan san* video is available, show it, pointing out traditional home features.

Conclusion

Students draw their own houses and label the rooms.
Draw different styles of houses: *APAATO, MANSHON, danchi,* 2–story home using illustrations in textbook as a guide.
Label appropriately.

Homework

Learn new vocabulary and be sure of how to write it in *hiragana* and *katakana*.
Read over pages 277–282.

Dismissal: Show work to teacher with some comment about the house they have drawn, e.g.: *ookii desu ne, chiisai desu ne, suki desu ka,* etc.

Lesson Seventy-eight (Unit 1, page 283)

Aims and objectives

- to teach particle *de* (location of activity).
- to teach how to describe own home simply.

Preparation

Pictures of homes from estate agents catalogues cut up,

OR

Pictures of homes as last lesson for reference or for students to base descriptions upon.
Pictures of homes labeled appropriately on walls to set scene.

Introduction

(15 minutes)
Today let's have a story. *Kiite mite kudasai.*
Point out a picture of an apartment on the wall if you have one as the focus. *Watashi no APAATO desu.*
Illustrate vocabulary by telling a story through sketches on board coupled with statements, putting in names as you draw. *Watashi no namae wa ... desu. Nagoya no APAATO ni sunde imasu. Nihonjin desu. Kore wa watashi no APAATO desu.*
Gradually build up a plan of a Japanese apartment.

Very small entrance area:	*Genkan desu. Taihen chiisai desu.*
Relatively large living room:	*Ima desu. Hiroi desu.*
Add another small room:	*Daidokoro desu. semai desu.*

Add next to it small rooms for toilet and bathroom.
Comment. Explain *watashi no APAATO desu.* Try to involve students all the way along by asking for comment, e.g.: *suki desu ka/ii APAATO desu ne* etc.

Add on 3 small bedrooms on the same level. *Shinshitsu desu. Watashi no heya desu. Okaasan to otoosan no shinshitsu desu. Imooto no heya desu.* Comment on relative size of rooms.
Sketch items and people into the rooms.
Avoid offering too many items at this time.
Other useful words may be added in next lesson.

Say *Watashi no APAATO wa kirei desu ka.* Elicit response.
Kirei desu/Kirei janai desu.
Explain *benri*—convenient, and that it is like *kirei,* a qualitative noun.
Watashi no APAATO wa benri desu.

Show a bus stop outside the apartment, a school close by, a station, shops, cinema, park, to demonstrate its convenient position, writing up the names as you point them out.
No need to interrupt story to explain *benri* at this point but be sure students heard it repeated several times.

Draw own room in detail.
Watashi no heya desu. Label.
Fill up with paraphernalia that students know, writing in the names of all the things in the room until the whole space has been filled with books, magazines, records, tapes, posters, bag, pens, maps, pictures, toy animals, etc. Ask students for things to put in there until it's bulging at the seams.
Comment without explanation—*gocha gocha desu. Itsumo gocha gocha desu! Daisuki desu,* showing your emotion in your voice.

Draw little sister's room.
Very tidy, only a bed with a doll on it and a cupboard with books and items beautifully stacked.
Gocha gocha dewa arimasen. Kore wa ningyoo desu.
Draw a poster on the wall. *POSUTAA desu. POSUTAA ga suki desu. (David Bowie) desu. Omoshiroi desu ne.*
Imooto no heya wa gocha gocha dewa arimasen.
Leave sketches on board.

Main theme

(30 minutes)

1 Elicit from students what they think the new words you have used mean: *gocha gocha, ningyoo* and *daisuki.* Teach *omoshiroi* and *oya.*
   Now the house itself has been described, but new structures are needed to explain what is in the house and where you do things.
   Teach *de*—location of activity. Remind of negative of adjectives and difference between them and qualitative nouns. Demonstrate with *benri.*
   Introduce *futsuu.*
   (Study section page 286)

2 If students had to show someone around their house, could they do it in Japanese?
   Look at textbook to see how a student coped with that situation:
   Open books at page 283.
   Listen to or read through the dialogue on pages 283–285.
   Comment on improving pronunciation.
   Listen again.
   Read through in pairs.

Conclusion

Pairwork. Students imagine taking partner through their own house. Working from the entrance through room by room drawing a sketch map as they explain, **OR** choose a real estate agent's picture and plan and imagine it to be own house. Partner tries to make appropriate comments as the house is described.

Homework

Choose a small picture of a house. Imagine its rooms.
Stick it into notebook and describe it and its rooms. At least ten sentences.

OR

Do it on paper to put on the wall.
Learn new vocabulary and read over again page 286 study.

Dismissal: Students make some comment about the drawing on the board.

Activity 1: Listening comprehension. *Dare? Doko? Nani?*

Draw lines to link the person to the activity as you listen to what the members of my family did yesterday afternoon.

Otoosan wa	kooen de	sooji o shimashita
Okaasan wa	genkan de	REKOODO o kikimashita
Otooto wa	heya de	TEREBI o mimashita
Imooto wa	tomodachi no uchi de	TENISU o shimashita
Ani wa	gakkoo de	hon o yomimashita
Ane wa	toshokan de	benkyoo shimashita
Watashi wa	ima de	shinbun o yomimashita
	shinshitsu de	SUPOOTSU o shimashita

Circle the correct answers to the questions below:

What day will they go to the beach?

      Monday   Thursday   Friday   Saturday   Sunday

What day will they go to Auckland?

      Monday   Thursday   Friday   Saturday   Sunday

What is going to Auckland?

      Mother   Older brother   Older sister   Little brother   Little sister

Activity 2

Nani o shimasu ka.
Doko de shimasu ka.
Dare to shimasu ka.
Itsu shimasu ka.

Nani o shimasu ka.
Doko de shimasu ka.
Dare to shimasu ka.
Itsu shimasu ka.

A

What will these friends do? Where? When?
Ask your partner the questions above to fill
in the missing information on your sheet.
Read carefully to see what information
you need to complete your sheet and ask
the relevant questions:

1 *TENISU o shimasu.*
  Niji ni shimasu.
  Tomodachi ni aimasu.
  Kooen de TENISU o shimasu.

2 _____
  _____
  _____
  _____

3 *TEREBI o mimasu.*
  Tomodachi to TEREBI o mimasu.
  Ima de TEREBI o mimasu.
  Goji ni TEREBI o mimasu.

4 _____
  _____
  _____
  _____

B

What will these friends do? Where? When?
Ask your partner the questions above to fill
in the missing information on your sheet.
Read carefully to see what information
you need to complete your sheet and ask
the relevant questions:

1 _____
  _____
  _____
  _____

2 *REKOODO a kikimasu.*
  Tomodachi to REKOODO a kikimasu.
  Tomodachi no uchi de REKOODO o kikimasu
  Sanjihan ni REKOODO o kikimasu

3 _____
  _____
  _____
  _____

4 *Shukudai o shimasu.*
  Tomodachi no imooto san to shukudai o shimasu.
  Tomodachi no heya de shukudai o shimasu.
  Rokujihan ni shukudai o shimasu.

Activity 3: Places and activities

Here are some activities and the place in which they were done.
On your own sheet:
Cross out two of the activities (things you decide you did not do).
Circle the rest of the activities one by one and join them with a line to a place.
Do not show your partner.
Take turns to ask your partner questions to find out what he/she did in the holidays. Choose a possibility from the list on your sheet. Ask (for example) *eiga ni ikimashita ka/tomodachi ni aimashita ka.*
Circle the answer.
Ask again *doko de .... o shimashita ka,* and circle the answer.
Link the two you have circled with a line.
If you did not do that activity you must tell your partner ... *wa shimasen deshita/ ... ni ikimasen deshita* etc.
Find out which activities your partner did not do.

Kooen de	*tomodachi ni aimashita*
Uchi de	*GITAA o renshuu shimashita*
Toshokan de	*zasshi o yomimashita*
Ima de	*TEREBI o mimashita*
Shinshitsu de	*BIDEO GEEMU o shimashita*
Watashi no heya de	*HAIKINGU ni ikimashita*
Gakkoo de	*PIKUNIKKU o shimashita*
PUURU de	*SAAFIN o shimashita*
WASHINTON de	*eiga ni ikimashita*
TORONTO de	*hon o yomimashita*
Yama de	*BASUKETTOBOORU o shimashita*
FURANSU de	*PARII o mimashita*
AMERIKA de	*FURANSUgo o benkyoo shimashita*
KANADA de	*okaasan ni aimashita*
APAATO de	*nagai inu o mimashita*
HAWAI de	*akai doobutsu o mimashita*

Lesson Seventy-nine

Aims and objectives

- to consolidate use of *de*—location of activity.

Preparation

Photocopy Dicomm sheets A and B sufficient of each for half the class.
Photocopy Sheet Dicomm Activity 2.
Photocopy Listening comprehension answer sheets.

Introduction

(20 minutes)
Greet, put up date.
Remind of *de*—location of activity
Listen to tape.
Who did what, where?
Tape: Teacher's script for listening comprehension
Read each sentence twice.

1 *Otoosan wa ima de shinbun o yomimashita.*
2 *Okaasan wa kooen de TENISU o shimashita.*
3 *Otooto wa tomodachi no uchi de REKOODO o kikimashita.*
4 *Imooto wa genkan de hon o yomimashita.*
5 *Ani wa toshokan de benkyoo shimashita.*
6 *Ane wa heya de sooji o shimashita.*
7 *Watashi wa gakkoo de SUPOOTSU o shimashita.*
8 *Kyoo wa doyoobi desu kara minasan wa umi ni ikimasu.*
9 *Getsuyoobi ni otooto wa ane to OOKURANDO ni ikimasu.*

(10 minutes)
Activity 2.
Teacher selects 5 student volunteers to make sentences combining all the information for each activity.

(10 minutes)
Activity 3.

Conclusion

(5 minutes)
Report to another pair who can say 'we did that too,' etc.
Each student takes it in turn to read out five activities.
Quickly establish who did the same with *watashi mo*.
Ask *doko de shimashita ka*. Establish if anyone did it in the same place. If so, note.
Make a list of the activities that all did in the same place, if there were any.
Report to the whole class. Find out how many other groups did the same activity in the same place.

Homework

Write the answers partners gave to Activity 3 in complete sentences.

Dismissal: Students tell teacher where they will do something later today, e.g.:
   kyooshitsu de ... o benkyoo shimasu,
   toshokan de hon o yomimasu,
   uchi de shukudai o shimasu.

Topic Eight

Lesson Eighty (page 287)

Aims and objectives

- to teach *arimasu*.
- to teach *ni wa*.

Preparation

Photocopy 2 sets of the Dicomm sheets. One set half a class.
Make sure each student gets either the A or the B sheet.

Introduction

(10 minutes)

Tape. Greet, put up date. Show examples of last lesson's homework to class.
Selected students or volunteers read their work aloud to class.
Remind of last lesson. Check particle *de* by asking selected students *sakuban nani o shimashita ka*, then asking *doko de ... o shimashita ka*.

Main theme

(15 minutes)

1 Remind of use of *imasu*. Teach *arimasu* and *ni wa*. (Study pages 287–288)
Draw pictures of the furnished interior of a house and label vocabulary items of this previously known vocabulary.
Make a few sentences together using *ni wa* and *arimasu*.

Anata no heya ni wa nani ga arimasu ka Sheet A

Do not allow your partner to see your sheet.
You have five minutes to find out what items are on your partner's sheet by asking in turn ... *ga arimasu ka*.
If your partner makes an incorrect guess say *chigaimasu/ ... wa arimasen*.
The first one to guess the five items correctly is the winner.

Anata no heya ni wa nani ga arimasu ka Sheet B

Do not allow your partner to see your sheet.
You have five minutes to find out what items are on your partner's sheet by asking in turn ... *ga arimasu ka*.
If your partner makes an incorrect guess say *chigaimasu/ ... wa arimasen*.
The first one to guess the five items correctly is the winner.

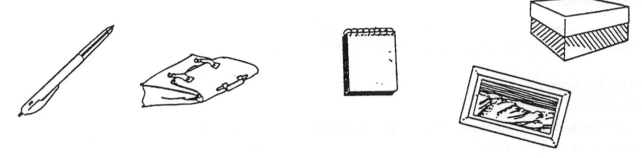

(5 minutes)

2 Each student tells of one item in the classroom. Students listen carefully and add something else (like 'I went to market and I bought ...' game).

   a) *Kyooshitsu ni wa hon ga arimasu ka*

   b) *Kyooshitsu ni wa hon ya enpitsu ga arimasu, etc.*

   When someone forgets the order they are 'out'. Next student continues.

   Aim: How long can the class find new things to add and remember the list?

   When it gets too monotonous, stop!

(5 minutes)

3 Put out a selection of items from students' bags onto a desk.

   One student is sent out of the room, and an item is removed.

   The student returns and tries to identify the item missing: *... wa arimasen*.

   Give two or three students a turn.

   OR

   Variation. While student is out of the room an item is put into a box.

   Student returns, and class ask *hako ni wa nani ga arimasu ka*.

   Student has five chances to guess.

   e.g.: *PEN desu ka ...*   Class respond *chigaimasu*.

(5-10 minutes)

4 Use dicomm sheets,

   OR

   Each student draws a room containing 5 items on one half of a piece of paper and an empty room on the other side. Do not allow papers to be seen by partner.

   Partner tries to guess the items in the room, e.g.: *heya ni wa hana ga arimasu ka*.

   If there are, he/she is allowed to draw them on his/her empty plan.

   They keep going in turn until the first one has found the five items.

   OR

   Read or listen to the dialogue on pages 289–290.

Homework

Read the dialogue on pages 289–290.
Cover *roomaji* except for looking up *katakana* words where necessary.
Check understanding.
Write ten sentences about items in own room.
Do the writing practice.

Lesson Eighty-one (Unit 2, page 291)

Aims and objectives

- to teach *itte mairimasu* and *itte irasshai* lexically.
- to teach *koko, soko, asoko*.
- to teach *doko ni arimasu ka*.

Preparation

Tape.

Introduction

(15 minutes)
Greet, put up date.
Read over new vocabulary. Listen to tape or read pages 291–292. Any problems?
Study (page 292).
Practice making sentences to the patterns suggested, together.

Main theme

(10 minutes)
  1 Activities (page 293). Choose an activity.

(10 minutes)
  2 Check your understanding, page 294. Either oral or written.

(10 minutes)
  3 Choose an activity from pages 295–296.

Homework

Select an activity not yet done from page 296. Writing practice (page 296) Review whole chart.

Lesson Eighty-two (optional lesson)

Aims and objectives

- to give students time to prepare some advertisements for the magazine.
- to make some reports on past activities.
- to consolidate use of *de* and *arimasu*.
- times, days, and dates.

Preparation

Photocopy the genuine Japanese advertisements for possible inclusion for authenticity.

Introduction

Talk about the amount of material accumulating for the magazine. Students need to look at work objectively and choose the best for inclusion. In spare time suggest they look through the material prepared and make a note of what they personally think should appear in the finished product. Read a few more samples that students have not yet heard or show some of the cartoon dialogues.

Main Theme

1 Show the *kanji* for yen, days of the week, year and month. Leave on board for copying.
   Stress the need for students to work within the confines of the vocabulary and grammar learned so that all have equal opportunity to read and enjoy the work produced and so that the material is well consolidated.

2 Students have time to produce material to put on advertisements for (fictional or real) entertainment, which tell place, date, day, time and cost. Leave artwork until material has been checked. Check with a friend to try to eliminate mistakes. Hand in to teacher.

3 Produce a report of some activity which has taken place in the past week.

OR

   Write an advertisement for one of the houses on the photocopy sheets (or draw houses) giving the rooms, and some comment.

OR

   Write advertisements for other things within the students' language experience.
   While students are doing this, teacher may have time to check Activity 2 so that students may continue with the artwork of their advertisement.

Conclusion

Share today's work and display any finished pieces.

Homework

Do a neat copy of today's work.

Dismissal: Tell teacher of some entertainment that is available next week, giving place, date, day, time.

牛丼？ かつ丼？ 親子丼もいいネ！

Lesson Eighty-three (roleplay lesson)

Aims and Objectives
- to give roleplay practice.
- to use new material in own way.

Preparation
Decide on way to group students—free choice or your choice.
Katakana card selection? Put groups of cards out. Students find own card and stay in that group.
Write out tasks for roleplay (or photocopy list below for each group).

Introduction
(10 minutes)
Greet, put up date.
Check *hiragana*. Read out syllables or words for students to write.

Main Theme
(15 minutes)
1 Commend students on the way they have been working.
Today they have the opportunity to show how much they can extend themselves.

Planned RolePlay
Plan to produce a play about five minutes long. In groups of three to five, work out a roleplay situation. It needs to have the opportunity to show as many as possible of the following:

- greet appropriately.
- ask who someone is.
- introduce themselves to friends and strangers.
- ask or tell nationality.
- say what they do at school.
- say what they do out of school.
- comment on the weather.
- mention likes and dislikes.
- make simple requests of each other.
- use numbers (*ichi ni san* list).
- talk about future actions.
- make suggestions.
- say what someone did.
- say what someone didn't do.
- ask why and give a reason.
- arrange to meet someone at a particular place.
- give a time.
- mention activities on particular days.
- talk about own family.
- ask about other's families.

- use general time words like 'always', 'every day', 'last week'.
- describe someone.
- make comments on a house.
- say where things are/or aren't.
- say where you do something.

Work out the framework and then check off the list to see what you will be able to use.

Conclusion
(5 minutes)
Groups report progress without giving their ideas away.
How will they organize the production?
It will be performed next lesson so there is not time to learn 'lines' by heart.
How can they achieve the best possible result?

Homework
Work on Roleplay. Sort out props to bring to school if necessary.

Lesson Eighty-four (roleplay)

Aims and objectives
- to act out the roleplays planned last lesson.

Preparation

Tape.
Arrange for a suitable room for the role plays, or move furniture to give maximum space.
Maybe some reward for best group.

Introduction
(15 minutes)
Tape. Greet.
Give students 10 minutes to practice.
If a student is absent, group must reorganize to manage without him/her.

Main Theme
(30 minutes)
Decide on group order. Watch roleplays.
Students listen and watch attentively, courteously, supportively.
Teacher notes common grammatical errors for gentle general comment later. Note especially participation of less confident students for commendation later.

Conclusion

Ask for students' comments on the group they think fulfilled the tasks best. Commend, and comment on a few common errors.

Homework

Which of the tasks set for the roleplays have students forgotten how to do? Review.

Dismissal: Commendations from the students on one another's performance, e.g.: *joozu deshita ... suki deshita. ... san wa atama ga ii desu ne. ... san no GURUUPU wa joozu deshita.*

Lesson Eighty-five (Unit 3, page 298)

Aims and objectives

- to teach how to talk about daily activities.
- to teach new verbs.
- consolidation of *de* for location of activity.
- to review times and days.

Preparation

Tape. Comments on roleplays.

Introduction

(15 minutes)
Comment on last lesson's roleplays, picking out particularly good moments or aspects. Try to have some special commendations for the less confident members of the class.
Check that students feel confident now with the list of achievements.
Study (page 299), brief review of *de*.
Introduce new vocabulary:
They proved such good actors that today you are choosing volunteers to mime for the class.
Choose students to come and mime the new vocabulary for class to guess which of the new words on pages 298 and 299 they are miming. Class call out the verb as soon as they recognize. Person who guesses first takes next turn.

Main theme

(15 minutes)
1 Pairwork. Listen to tape or read the dialogue on page 298.
   Students ask each other 5 questions each on the passage.
2 Activities (pages 298–299)
   Pairs, groups or whole class.
3 Activity Four lends itself to a group competition, making complete sentences with each verb, using it in as many ways as possible.

Conclusion

(15 minutes)

Line ups. *Nichiyoobi ni nanji ni okimasu ka.*

Students go around room asking the question and slot themselves into a line, starting with the earliest at the front of the line and the latest at the end. Put up the range on the board and the average time. Same thing but with *nemasu.* (*Doyoobi ni nanji ni nemasu ka.*) Again record result.

Homework

Write two sentences using each verb so that all the verb forms known so far are used: *masu, masen, mashita, masen deshita, mashoo,* and with some verbs that have been used in classroom instructions *te kudasai.*

Dismissal: Students tell teacher what time they go to bed on school days.

Lesson Eighty-six (page 300)

Aims and objectives

- to give students the opportunity to tell about own daily activities and put together a good self–introduction.
- to give new verbs further exposure.
- to test response to listening.

Preparation

There are several options offered.
Read through material below to decide which way to use it.
If necessary photocopy mark sheets (one for each student).
If using test as a reading/writing test, photocopy questions for each student.

Introduction

Greet. 'Don't put up date,' as that is one of the questions!

Explain that it's sometimes good to put yourself into an unknown situation to see how you can cope with new experiences. If we didn't have such opportunities we would not be very well equipped to face life. Today's lesson will give students the opportunity to see how well they are able to respond, without being given time to specifically review.

Although it is an 'unknown' situation, there is no need to be nervous as all the material presented has been well practiced through the year. Students should not worry if there are some words they have forgotten but should try to keep aware of tenses used. Listen and challenge themselves to be able to answer every question.

It is an opportunity to find out what they need to review, not a competitive or threatening time, and an opportunity for the teacher to find out where they need help to improve.
Make a recording of the tape script provided, or read from it if you prefer. (See page 269 of this manual.)

Main theme

Listen to the tape and supply an answer in the pause that follows each question. The answers may be given orally, or quickly written in Japanese *roomaji,* or in English depending on the need within your own class and your purpose.

If you decide to use the listening for an oral test some students may be tested while rest of class do work from pages 300–301 and prepare a talk about themselves.

Or all students listen to tape and give answers in writing. (In English or Japanese depending on the skill you choose to test.)

This may be a good preparation to a more formal test using the same material later.

This tape may also be useful for a more formal aural/oral test.

If you use it for face to face orals, choose one question from each bracket of three, fifteen in all excluding the four warm–up questions.

If you have no tape, prerecord the questions onto a tape, leaving twice as long as you take to give an answer, for the students' answers.

One way of conducting an oral (other ideas in introduction chapter of this guide) is to play the tape and ask the student to answer the tape while you sit behind and mark the answers for hesitation, fluency, structural accuracy, and comprehension of the question.

It is possible to test up to five students during the same run through of the tape. Seat five students facing a tape recorder. All students listen and answer at the same time concentrating on their own answer. Sit behind group and tune in to one student at a time, marking a question, turning your attention to the next, etc.

The students' answers may be recorded on a second machine for checking against your 'on the spot' marks, later.

If you need to be with the rest of the class, set up a room the same way. Three students work alongside each other. Each student takes a turn in answering (answers one question in three).

If conducting the test yourself and listening to each group, write the number of the question you heard, as it will be every fifth question for each student to get through a whole class in a reasonable number of lessons or lunchtimes. Later you can diagnose each student's problems from studying the questions missed.

The first four questions are for warm up and it is possible to see if all students have managed to answer without recording specific answers.

Another way to use the test today would be to ask students to listen and write their answers in the pause between the questions

OR

Divide class into groups of three. Give a copy of the questions to each group. Each student takes it in turn to be the question master and asks another student one question out of each bracket of three. The 'spare' student quickly writes down the answer given (in *roomaji*).

Each student in a group is tested by his/her group changing roles using the first question in each bracket for Student One, second for Student Two and third for Student Three.

The test may also be used as a reading/writing exercise instead if used as a listening test now or at another time.

Conclusion

Commend students who have worked well.

Homework

Learn new vocabulary and check *hiragana*.

Think about other information to include in talk about self or family member begun today.

Suggested marking paper for each of three students at one test time

Name of student _____ Class _____

Questions 1–4 answered correctly:

  1 yes/no
  2 yes/no
  2 yes/no
  3 yes/no

Any comment? _____

Write number of question answered, transcript of answers given.

_____

_____

_____

_____

_____

_____

_____

_____

_____

_____

_____

_____

_____

_____

_____

Hesitation

1......2......3......4......5......6......7......8......9......10......11......12......13......14......15......

Slow response

1......2......3......4......5......6......7......8......9......10......11......12......13......14......15......

Quick and fluent response

1......2......3......4......5......6......7......8......9......10......11......12......13......14......15......

Understandable but structurally incorrect

1......2......3......4......5......6......7......8......9......10......11......12......13......14......15......

Misunderstood

1......2......3......4......5......6......7......8......9......10......11......12......13......14......15......

Not understood at all

1......2......3......4......5......6......7......8......9......10......11......12......13......14......15......

Comments

_____

_____

_____

_____

_____

Mark _____

Tape script

(15 minutes)

O namae wa nan desu ka
Nansai desu ka OR Oikutsu desu ka
Doko no kata desu ka OR Nanijin desu ka
Doko ni sunde imasu ka

O genki desu ka
Tadaima
Itte mairimasu

Seito desu ka
Otoko no ko desu ka Onna no ko desu ka

Tanjoobi wa nangatsu nannichi desu ka
Kyoo wa nangatsu nannichi desu ka
Ashita wa nangatsu nannichi desu ka

Kami no ke ga nani iro desu ka
Me ga aoi desu ka
Se ga takai desu ka

SUPOOTSU o renshuu shimasu ka
Ongaku o renshuu shimasu ka
DOITSUgo o hanashimasu ka

Nani ga suki desu ka
Nani ga kirai desu ka
SUPOOTSU ga suki desu ka

Gakkoo wa doko desu ka
Gakkoo wa kootoogakkoo desu ka
Gakkoo de nani o benkyoo shimasu ka

Anata no heya de nani o shimasu ka
Shinshitsu de nani o shimasu ka
Ima de nani o shimasu ka

Mainichi gakkoo ni ikimasu ka
Mainichi TEREBI o mimasu ka
Mainichi hon o yomimasu ka

Gokazoku wa nannin imasu ka
Imootosan ga imasu ka
Okaasan wa se ga takai desu ka

Tomodachi no namae wa nan desu ka
Tomodachi wa se ga hikui desu ka, se ga takai desu ka
Tomodachi wa atama ga ii desu ka, atama ga warui desu ka

Kayoobi ni eiga ni ikimashita ka
Kinoo toshokan ni ikimashita ka
Getsuyoobi ni PUURU ni ikimashita ka

Kyoo wa atsui desu ka
Kinoo wa ii otenki deshita ka
Ashita ame deshoo ka

Doyoobi ni gakkoo ni ikimashita ka
Kyoo eiga ni ikimashita ka
Kyoo TEREBI o mimashita ka

Nanji ni okimasu ka
Nanji ni nemasu ka
Nanji ni uchi ni kaerimasu ka

Lesson Eighty-seven

Aims and Objectives

- to finish oral testing if necessary.
- to give other students time to prepare talk about themselves.

Preparation

Test sheets as last lesson.

Introduction

(2–3 minutes)
Greet.
Comment on last lesson's work.
Ask if anyone has any questions and answer.

Main theme

Give students the opportunity to work on their prepared talks today.
They may be able to check each others' work, suggest extensions to each other, etc.

OR

Work alone silently if testing has to be done in the same room.
While they are working there will be an opportunity to do more oral testing, taking students out of main group in fives.
If they finish they may work on material for the magazine quietly.
Conclusion
Commend those who have worked well. Comment on the oral testing.

Homework

Practice talk. Be prepared to give it or read it (teacher's choice) next lesson, **OR** to tape it for teacher's ears only.

Lesson Eighty-eight (Unit 4, page 302)

Aims and objectives

- to teach students how to talk about a day's activities.
- to use new vocabulary.

Preparation

Tape recorder with record facility if you wish to record students' talks.
Tape.
Hiragana word sheets of songs known.

Introduction

(10 minutes)

Tape. Greet. Sing songs with tape looking at *hiragana* version of words.

Main theme

(20 minutes)

1 *Watashi no ichinichi*. Listen or read about a student's day.
   Each student thinks of a question to ask about the day described. May not repeat a question.

2 Choose activities from page 303.

(5 minutes)

3 Choose three students to give their talks. (Draw *katakana* names from box.)
   Commend particularly for being the first three to try, and elicit commendation in Japanese from other students.
   Reassure that they will not be penalized against others who have more time to practice. It is just not practical timewise to do them all on the same day and also difficult for class to listen to too many at a time, no matter how interesting they are.

Conclusion

(10 minutes)

Play a game in which the first student tells what time he/she woke up today. Each student around class tells of another fictitious activity that was done during the day. Students try to keep it credible. Listen well to avoid repetition.
Last one says what time the student went to bed.

Homework

Practice talks. Be prepared to do them next lesson.

Pictures

Compare the two pictures in each set to find what is missing and report in Japanese.
Pairwork. Give out A pictures to one of each pair, and B pictures to the other. Students keep own picture hidden from partner.
Students ask each other *nani ga arimasu ka. E ga arimasu ka*, etc. (*Hai soo desu/Iie, ... dewa arimasen*) to identify the differences between their two pictures.
First pair to identify the ten differences win.

'Spot the difference' worksheets

Photocopy and cut apart the A and B pictures from the following sheets. Below are some suggestions for use.

1 a) Pair pictures (Use only the vocabulary learned in the course.)
Each pair receives an A and a B picture, but may not look at their partner's picture until the end of the activity.
Student A describes their picture in great detail, saying who is in which room.
Student B listens and looks at their picture to see if the detail is the same as their own picture, and notes differences quickly. Tell partner ... *wa arimasen* if that item does not appear in their picture.
Pairs work quickly to be first to present teacher with a complete list of differences. Then tell the class all the differences they have found.
The full list of differences is given below.
   b) If they were your family, how would you describe them?

2 Use for description of items in room, and activity. Each student gives one sentence until they can think of no more to say.

3 What happened before this picture? Use imagination to tell about person's activities leading up to this point in time.

4 What happened next?

5 Describe the person in as much detail as possible.

6 Use *mo*: *Kono heya ni ... ga arimasu.*

   Kono heya mo ... ga arimasu.

7 Use for *de*—location of activity. *Doko de bangohan o tabemasu ka,* etc.

8 Later, use for *te* form activities.

Differences in 'spot the difference' sheets

1 *Oniisan.*
Chair, flowers, table, rain, flowers on table, watch.

2 *Otoosan.*
Knife, book, tree, table, watch.

3 *Okaasan.*
Big teeth, flower in hand, rubbish bin, watch, no boxes.

4 *Oneesan.*
Glasses, tree, birds, belt, flowers.

A

Oneesan/Ane

Namae: MIRI (18)

B

Oneesan/Ane

Namae: MIRI (18)

A

Okaasan/Haha

Namae: RUBI (46)

B

Okaasan/Haha

Namae: RUBI (46)

A

Oniisan/Ani

Namae: MAIKU (20)

B

Oniisan/Ani

Namae: MAIKU (20)

A

Otoosan/Chichi

Namae: SAMU (47)

B

Otoosan/Chichi

Namae: SAMU (47)

Lesson Eighty-nine (Unit 5, page 304)

Aims and Objectives

- to give students opportunity to give their talks.
- to give students the opportunity to listen to other students' talks.
- to encourage good listening and good pronunciation.
- to encourage support of students, one for another.
- to teach particle *de* for means of transport.
- to give practice in telling times of activities.

Preparation

Tape recorder with record facility if you want to listen to students' talks and evaluate them later. (If you prefer to allow the students to tape record their talks for your ears alone, there is enough work in each lesson without the time taken for talks if you expand the practice of sentences.)

Introduction

(10-15 minutes)
Tape. Greet, put up date.

Main theme

1 Pick out a name from the box to give talk or ask for volunteers.
Give five students the opportunity to speak.
Question lightly between talks, about talks given, to keep class listening properly.

(5 minutes)

2 A break from talks and something new to learn.
Talk about the use of *de* particle to express means of transport.

3 Study 1. Use flash cards of transport to teach vocabulary and elicit sentences from class.
e.g.: Hold up flash card: *Hikooki desu.*
Ask for a sentence that gives an activity and that means of transport e.g.: *Hikooki de AMERIKA ni ikimashita.*
Keep going until all transport means have been introduced.
Using flash cards very quickly elicit names from class. Any they can't remember put into a new pile and try again until all are known well.

(10 minutes)

4 Return to talks. Another five students give talks. Commend and elicit commendation from other students.

(5-10 minutes)

5 Continue with sentence practice page 304, Study 2.

(5-10 minutes)

6 3–5 more talks.

Travel picture cards

Photocopy onto thin card one set per group.

1 Students put cards face-down on a desk. Each student picks up a card in turn and makes a sentence about the means of transport.

2 Students put all cards face-up on a desk. One student secretly chooses one means of transport. Others ask *(BASU) de ikimasu ka*, and are allowed 5 guesses to find the chosen means of transport. The student who guesses correctly takes the next turn. (Answer *Hai, (BASU) de ikimasu*, or *iie chigaimasu, (BASU) de ikimasen.*)

Homework

Practice the sentences on page 305. Learn the new vocabulary

Dismissal: Tell how they did not come to school today, e.g.: *Hikooki de kimasen deshita.*

Lesson Ninety (pages 306–307)

Aims and objectives

- to hear the last of the students' talks.
- to give the students reading practice from *hiragana*.
- to consolidate patterns and vocabulary.

Preparation

Tape recorder with record facility if you want to tape talks.

Introduction

(2-3 minutes)
Greet, elicit date.

Main theme

Continue with the talks, dividing them if necessary into several groups through the lesson depending on numbers.
Intersperse through diverse activities of pages 306, 307:
Reading activity page 306.
Hiragana practice page 307.
Questions and answers page 307.
Translation page 307.
Writing practice and crossword.

OR

Magazine preparation.

Conclusion

Comment on the talks, all of which should now have been given.

Homework

General vocabulary check. *Hiragana* check.

Dismissal: Tell how they will go home after school.

Lesson Ninety-one (optional lesson)

Aims and objectives

- to express comparisons using adjectives and qualitative nouns.
- to give 'real' experience of Japan through film or native speaker contact.

Preparation

Resource magazines of Japan.
Travel film of Japan.
Japanese national to talk about differences he/she has experienced.
Timing this lesson needs to be adjusted according to resources being used.

Introduction

Discuss, in English, the differences students have discovered this year between their own lives and Japanese people's lives.

Main theme

Introduce film or person or books for students to find out more.

Conclusion

(10-15 minutes)

Expand into full lesson if no other resources available.
Groups or pairs make lists of comparisons in Japanese between own families and Japanese families, homes, festivals, using simple pairs of sentences, e.g.:

Nihon no uchi wa semai desu,

AMERIKA no uchi wa hiroi desu.

Read out the pairs and see which pair have the greatest number.
Discuss, in English, what they see as the advantages and disadvantages, comparing what they know of Japan with own lives.
Impress the fact that there are wide differences in Japan as in students' own country but some generalizations may be made.
What are the similarities?
Express them in Japanese.

Homework

Write five pairs of differences or similarities.

Dismissal: Tell teacher a pair of similarities or differences.

Topic Eight Vocabulary cards

gochagocha	oya	POSUTAA	asoko	itte
shinshitsu	taihen	daisuki	ee to	futsuu
hiroi	hirokunai	ima	semai	semakunai
soo shimashoo	yoofuku	de	takusan no mono	daidokoro
omoshiroi	omoshirokunai	reizooko	sara	SHAWAA
heya	honbako	NAIFU	ningyoo	ni wa
arimasu	benri	benri janai desu	chawan	FOOLU

BASU	chikatetsu	densha	fune	hikooki
asagohan	bangohan	hirugohan	ichinichi	tokidoki
SHAWAA o abimasu	tabemasu	tsukimasu	yasumimasu	MAKUDONA-RUDO
niwa	nomimasu	okimasu	ryoori o shimasu	SANDOITCHI
HANBAAGAA	jitensha	JUUSU	kaimasu	nemasu
soko	doko	araimasu	asobimasu	de
itte irasshai	itte mairimasu	koko	mata	mite

SUKEETO BORUDO				
SUKEETO				
TAKUSHII				
kuruma				

TOPIC NINE

Lesson Ninety-two (Introduction and Unit 1, page 309)

Aims and objectives

- to introduce students to Japanese attitudes to health.
- to teach how to express pain.

Preparation

Photocopy family illustration used in Topic Six for each student for listening activity.
Put up on wall the parts of body chart used earlier.

Introduction

(5 minutes)

Greet, using *Ogenki desu ka* for anyone who has been away ill. Put up date.
Discuss the information pages 309–310, and any other personal knowledge of health and illness in Japan.
Point out chart of parts of body on wall.
Play game like Simon Says in which students have to touch part of body called. Last one each time is out, and sits down to watch or is allowed to be the caller. Play fast for maximum fun. Add in the instructions that have been taught previously: *mite kudasai, suwatte kudasai, tatte kudasai,* etc. Keep going until a winner is established.

(10 minutes)

Choose:

On blank piece of paper students draw a body to your instructions. *Atama ga ookii desu.* At the bottom of the sheet write the numbers one to ten. After drawing the appropriate part, write the word and its English equivalent by the side of the number, e.g., '1. *atama*—head'.
Pass paper on to next student who adds the next part called and fills in number two word and translation. Continue until all parts of the body the students should know have been called.
Give each student one sheet to mark and go through list called. Students mark for big and small and for correct part of the body and translation at the bottom of the page.

OR

Pairwork.
Students draw a picture of a body. Do not show to partner.
Students sit back to back. Student One describes his/her 'body', while Student Two draws it.
Student Two finds all the information by questioning. Student One may only give the information directly requested. They find out basic information first, then go on to find out about physical characteristics.

Example question patterns:

> *Otoko no ko desu ka*
> *Onna no ko desu ka*
> *Nansai desu ka*
> *Doko no kata desu ka*
> *Atama ga ookii desu ka. Chiisai desu ka*
> *Kao ga nagai desu ka. Mijikai desu ka, etc.*

When complete, the two pictures are compared for accuracy.

Main Theme

(20 minutes)
Atama ga itai desu.
Teach new vocabulary *byooki, genki, itai desu,* by demonstration.
Dramatize the words, telling the class you feel ill today. Head hurts, sore throat. Have a good moan!
Ask students to find out from the list on page 312 what they could say to show their sympathy:
sore wa ikemasen ne.
Around class each person either moans about some discomfort and class respond with *sore wa ikemasen ne,* or say they are healthy, to elicit response from class: *sore wa ii desu.*

Listening activity

Each student is given a picture of a family and their possible activities. Students identify person who is sick and circle person, part of body that is ailing, and activities done, with a check or those not done, with a cross.
Teacher tells class the following short story (OR use tape)

> *DAMIAN san wa kyoo gakkoo ni ikimasen. Byooki desu.*
> *Atama ga itai desu. Ashi ga itai desu. Nodo ga itai desu.*
> *Onaka ga itai desu. Atama ga itai desu kara hon o yomimasen. TEREBI o mimasen. Nemasu.*
>
> *DAMIAN san no otoosan mo byooki desu. Atama ga itai desu.*
> *Mimi ga itai desu. Hana ga itai desu. Shigoto ni ikimasen. Shinbun o yomimasen. Nemasu.*
>
> *DAMIAN san no okaasan wa genki desu. Kazoku wa byooki desu kara uchi o sooji shimasen.*
> *Mise ni ikimasen. Inu to kooen ni ikimasen.*
>
> *DAMIAN san no oniisan mo byooki desu. Ha ga itai desu.*
> *Shigoto ni ikimasen. Ima de TEREBI o mimasu. Zasshi o yomimasu.*

Mark work by eliciting answers from students. Ask:

> *Dare ga byooki desu ka*
> *... san wa nani ga itai desu ka*
> *... san wa nani o shimasu ka*
> *... san wa (TEREBI) o mimasu ka*
> *Naze desu ka*

Study pages 312–315 (error on page 314, line eleven—better would be *atama wa itakunai desu*).
Pairwork
Students each make a short story off the top of their head that gives the reason for someone's not doing an activity.

Conclusion

(15 minutes)

Groups or pairs roleplay a situation in which someone becomes ill. Give them 5 minutes' verbal preparation time.

Students present roleplays, remembering to listen well, and if the conversation deviates from their initial plan not to worry but try to keep going, following through logically.

Homework

Write a short story similar to the ones worked out in class. Writing practice page 316.

Dismissal: Students think of a reason why they may be ill tomorrow!
(e.g.: *Taihen benkyoo shimashita kara atama ga itai desu. Ashita byooki deshoo!*)

Lesson Ninety-three (Unit 2, page 317)

Aims and objectives

- to teach students how to express ailments more fully.
- to teach how to respond to specific health enquiry.

Preparation

Tape.

Introduction

Ask students how they are as they enter, whether they have headaches, backaches, etc. Greet.
Have a short moan about own imagined or real aches and pains, and elicit response.
Teach new vocabulary, suggesting students make cartoons to show meaning of new words.

Main theme

Listen to the dialogue page 317.
Pairwork. Read the passage with a partner on page 318.
Continue: Work in pairs to explain the situation on page 318.
In groups of six compare notes on the explanations.
Choose an activity from page 318 (Different groups may choose different activities and perform them for each other later.)

Homework

Learn new vocabulary. Do the writing practice. Start reviewing previous Topics.

Dismissal: Tell teacher something about someone who is ill or was ill.

Lesson Ninety-four

Aims and Objectives

- to consolidate health vocabulary
- to practice roleplays

Preparation

Photocopy pictures of doctor's surgery

Introduction

(15 minutes)
Greet. Put up date.
Give out pictures of doctor's waiting room.
Brainstorm all the vocabulary possible out of the picture under headings: people, ailments, adjectives, qualitative nouns, items in room, verbs, phrases, e.g.: *netsu ga arimasu*.

Main theme

(10 minutes)
  1 Each student makes one sentence about someone or something in the picture.

(10 minutes)
  2 Students roleplay the situation in groups.

Conclusion

(10 minutes)
Show roleplays to each other for comparison. Students each find something to commend from each other's roleplays while watching and report at end. Teacher makes notes on competence and confidence for end-of-book evaluation.

Homework

Writing practice page 319. *Hiragana* face competition. Put name on back. Crossword.

Dismissal: Students comment on anything they would like to say to teacher, e.g., *kyoo wa omoshiroi desu, watashi wa ureshii desu, kyoo wa taihen genki desu.*

Lesson Ninety-five

Aims and objectives

- to practice reading and answering questions on passages read.

Preparation

Numbers to put by each hiragana face when displaying for judging.
Drawing pins.

Introduction

Greet. Give out numbers as students arrive to put with *hiragana* faces. Students pin up *hiragana* faces or place on desk for viewing later.

Main theme

Quick *hiragana* test. Each student notes the ones that they do not know well.
Reading practice (passages are also on tape for use as listening comprehension, pronunciation practice, etc.).
Each group takes one passage to read together aloud and to work out meaning.
Each group then reads its passage to the class. Class read along and identify new words. Group asks the class the questions that follow.
Use illustrations A and B of the doctor's waiting room. Student A describes his/her picture to Student B, who listens and finds things that are missing in his/her own picture. Then reverse roles.

Conclusion

View *hiragana* faces and vote secretly on best one. Reward winner. Leave faces on wall for entertainment.

Homework

Learn any *hiragana* that have been forgotten for more formal test soon.

Dismissal: Tell teacher which *hiragana* face was their own, e.g., *juunana desu, suki desu ka.*

Lesson Ninety-six (optional lesson)
Class magazine

Introduction

Greet. Put up date.
Discuss the material prepared for the magazine in Japanese: *Kore o mite kudasai. Ii desu ne.* Choose an editor and staff to make final decisions and start putting the magazine together while rest of class

supply extra artwork and reporting stories based on the roleplays done recently, visits to the doctor by various class personalities, injuries sustained, descriptions of the school with maps to show location of different classrooms, descriptions of *sempai* and *koohai,* of interviews with teachers (done in English, written in Japanese for the magazine).

Make it a really good, interesting magazine by producing enough material from which to choose and by selecting final material carefully.

If possible, arrange for photocopies of the magazine to be available for each student. It should prove to be excellent review of the year's work.

Lesson Ninety-seven (check lesson)

Aims and objectives

• to review Topic Nine structures and vocabulary.

Preparation

Check through exercises below to decide how to use.
Reward for quiz.

Introduction

(10 minutes)
Pairwork or whole class. Play hangman with *hiragana,* using words from Topic Nine.

Main theme

(15-20 minutes)
Do exercises from Topic Nine Check 1 and 2.

Topic Nine, Check 1

A

How would you say the following in English?
1 *SARA san wa byooki desu.*
2 *Atama ga itai desu.*
3 *Guai wa chotto warui desu.*
4 *Ha ga itai desu kara gakkoo ni ikimasen.*
5 *Doo shimashita ka.*
6 *Ima genki desu ga senshuu byooki deshita.*
7 *Me ga itai desu kara watashi no shukudai o shimasen.*
8 *Watashi mo ashi ga itai desu.*
9 *Onaka ga sukimashita.*
10 *Nodo ga kawakimashita.*

B

Expressions you should know.

Describe the situation in which you use the following expressions.

1 *Ohayoo gozaimasu.*
2 *Tadaima.*
3 *Ogenki desu ka.*
4 *Ohisashiburi desu ne.*
5 *Itte mairimasu.*
6 *Arigatoo gozaimasu.*
7 *Itte irasshai.*
8 *Soo desu ne.*
9 *Ee to.*
10 *Doo itashimashite.*

C

Explain the use of the following particles (in English).

1 *wa* As in *Watashi wa juuyonsai desu.*
2 *o* As in *Nihongo o benkyoo shimasu.*
3 *ni* As in *Koko ni arimasu.*
4 *ni* As in *Uchi ni kaerimasu.*
5 *ni* As in *Goji ni aimashoo.*
6 *to* As in *Eigo to nihongo o hanashimasu.*
7 *to* As in *BOBU san to kooen ni ikimasu.*
8 *ga* As in *Ashi ga itai desu.*
9 *ga* As in *Ima genki desu ga senshuu byooki deshita.*
10 *ya* As in *Hon ya zasshi o yomimasu.*
11 *ka* As in *Ogenki desu ka.*
12 *no* As in *Watashi no enpitsu desu.*
13 *mo* As in *Watashi mo gakkoo ga suki desu.* 14 *mo* with a negative As in *Watashi mo FURANSUgo o hanashimasen.*
15 *mo...mo* As in *Watashi mo haha mo hon ga suki desu.*
16 *mo...mo* with a negative. As in *Watashi mo haha mo TEREBI o mimasen.*
17 *de* As in *Shinshitsu de hon o yomimashita.*
18 *de* As in *Densha de Nara ni ikimashita.*

Answers (Topic Nine, Check 1)

A

1 Sarah is sick/ill.
2 I've got a headache.
3 I don't feel very well.
4 Because I've got a headache I won't go to school.
5 What's the matter?/What happened?
6 I'm fine (well) now but I was sick last week.

---

7 Because I've got sore eyes I won't do my homework.
8 My feet/legs are sore too.
9 I'm hungry.
10 I'm thirty

B

1 To say 'Good morning' before around 10.30 am.
2 To say 'I'm home'.
3 To say 'How are you?'
4 To say 'I haven't seen you for ages.'
5 When leaving the house/To say 'I'm going out'.
6 To say 'Thank you'.
7 To say 'Go and welcome home when you return'/To say 'See you later'.
8 An agreement noise.
9 A hesitation noise.
10 To say 'Don't mention it'.

C

1 topic particle/'talking about ...'
2 Object particle, use after object.
3 Position particle (in this place).
4 To show direction/'to'.
5 'at' used with time.
6 'and' used in a defined list.
7 'with'.
8 To focus on a particular aspect of something.
9 'but'.
10 'and the like', 'etc.' used for an undefined list.
11 Marks a question.
12 'Belonging to'.
13 'too/also'.
14 'don't...either'.
15 'both'.
16 'neither...nor'.
17 Location of activity
18 'by means of'. used for transport.

Topic Nine, Check 2

A

Write all the verb that you should know. Draw up five columns and show the *masu/masen/mashita/ masen deshita/mashoo* for of each. You should be able to think of twenty-four verbs.

B

Do a complete check of the vocabulary of each topic and count your score of words you know well, and words you have forgotten.

Prepare for a vocabulary test. (Note: if you can't remember the words the language doesn't make much sense!)

Conclusion

(15 minutes)
Look back through book.
Groups prepare a quick quiz from any material in the book.
Write out ten questions in English or *roomaji*.
Write answers in different colored pen on the back.
Cut up quickly into strips.
Place in box.
Individually or in teams answer questions drawn one by one from the box.
Winner? Winners? Reward them.

OR

Give out and enjoy reading the magazine.
Fill in the second eye of the *daruma!*
Comment to students how rewarding it is that they can do so much! Commend for hard work and participation, encourage for future.

Topic Nine Vocabulary cards

ureshii	zenbu	karada	do	netsu ga arimasu
doo shimashita ka	mizu	SUUPU	tsumaranai desu	tsumaranakunai desu
ude	yubi	AISUKURIIMU	guai wa chotto warui desu	sukimashita
nodo	onaka	senaka	sore wa ikemasen ne	te
itakunai desu	kuchi	me	mimi	mune
byooki	genki	genki janai desu	hana	itai desu
oisha	SARARIIMAN	ashi	ASHIYUBI	atama

うい あ か お え

け く き し さ こ

そ せ す つ ち た

な と て こ ぱ め

ま そ ひ は の ほ

へ ふ む み ま

や も め ら よ

ゆ れ る り を

わ ろ ん